Spain ir

(Volur

Henry D. Inglis

Alpha Editions

This edition published in 2024

ISBN : 9789361479885

Design and Setting By
Alpha Editions
www.alphaedis.com
Email - info@alphaedis.com

Contents

CHAPTER I.

BISCAY.

Departure from Bayonne, the Bidassoa, and entrance into Spain; Precautions against Robbery; Black Mail, and Anecdote; Charming and novel Scenery; Mail travelling in Spain; Vittoria; Spanish Bread; Priests; the Spanish Cloak; Women; Arrival of the Infante Don Francis; a National trait; Spanish Money and expense of Travelling; Journey through Biscay to Bilbao; Chocolate; the Plain of Vittoria; Passage of the Biscayan Mountains; Durango; a Village Misfortune; Biscayan Recreation; the Muleteer's Song; Bilbao; Traits of Spanish Character; Markets; Biscayan Political and Religious Opinions; State of the Inhabitants and mode of Life; Riches of the Corporation of Bilbao; Prices of Provisions; the Campo Santo; the Iglesia de Bigonia and its Superstitions; Trait of Spanish Pride and Generosity; the Convents and their Inmates; the Hospital; curious Customs, and extraordinary scene in a Coffee House; Improvement of Land in Biscay, Climate, Diseases, &c.; peculiar Rights and Privileges of Biscay.

I LEFT England in the early part of the spring of 1830, with the intention of visiting Spain; and taking a circuitous route through the Southern parts of France, to Bayonne, I left that city on the 14th of May, by the Madrid Courier, for Vittoria, and in a few hours we crossed the Bidassoa and entered Spain.

It is impossible to enter any foreign country for the first time, without experiencing some mental excitement; and it seems to me, that among all the countries of Europe, Spain is the most calculated to awaken interest and expectation: for even if it were possible to forget all that links the history of Spain with Carthagenian enterprise, and Roman ambition, and Moorish grandeur, the present condition of the country, and the desire of gratifying curiosity, respecting the manners, character, and condition of the Spanish people, would still be sufficient to justify a strong feeling of excitement.

When I had crossed the Bidassoa, I knew that I was in Spain; and every object immediately acquired a new interest. Three several demands for my passport, within the short space of ten minutes, had not the effect of putting me out of humour; I was prepared for inconveniences greater than this, in journeying through a country so little visited as Spain, and had wisely laid in a stock of philosophy to meet them all.

The frontier town of Spain, Irun, lies within half a league of the Bidassoa: it is an insignificant village, no way calculated to create a favourable impression; but it is improper to form any judgment of a country, from the places that lie along its frontier. At Irun, the mail stops a short time; and before proceeding on its journey, formidable precautions are taken against the possibility of robbery. I saw three carabines, and four cases of pistols, deposited about the coach; and three additional guards, each armed with a long sabre, took their seats behind and in the cabriolet. These preparations naturally create doubts in the mind of the traveller, as to his personal safety: nor are these altogether without foundation: there is undoubtedly some exaggeration on the subject of robbery of the public conveyances in Spain; but it is certain, that the mails are occasionally stopped, especially in the southern parts. It is beneath the dignity of the government, to enter into a treaty with banditti, for the safety of the mails; and as resistance must be made in case of an attack, the traveller by the mail is necessarily placed in a dangerous position; but in the diligence, he runs comparatively little risque. I can state, upon certain information received in Madrid, that every one of the principal Spanish diligences, with the exception of that from Barcelona to Perpignan, pays *Black Mail* to the banditti for their protection. This arrangement was at first attended with some difficulty; and from a gentleman who was present at the interview between the person employed to negotiate on behalf of the diligences, and the representative of the banditti, I learned a few particulars. The diligences in question were those between Madrid and Seville; and the sum offered for their protection was not objected to; but another difficulty was started: "I have nothing to say against the terms you offer," said the negotiator for the banditti, "and I will at once ensure you against being molested by robbers of consequence; but as for the small fry (*Ladrones de ninguna consideracion*), I cannot be responsible; we respect the engagements entered into by each other; but there is nothing like honour among the petty thieves." The proprietors of the diligences, however, were satisfied with the assurance of protection against the great robbers, and the treaty was concluded; but not long afterwards, one of the coaches was stopped and rifled by the petty thieves: this led to an arrangement which has ever since proved effectual; one of the chiefs accompanies the coach on its journey, and overawes by his name and reputation, the robbers of inferior degree.

Nothing can exceed the beauty of the country between the frontier, and *Tolosa*; the road lies through the most enchanting valleys, green and fertile, beyond any that I had seen in the French Pyrenees; and there is one feature in the scenery, peculiar to this part of the Biscayan provinces: the sides of the mountains are not covered with forest trees, as in the Pyrenees, nor with fir, as in the Alps, but with fruit trees: the effect of this was striking, and beautiful; chiefly owing to the variety of colour in the different fruits with which every tree was bowed to the ground. As far as the eye could reach up the mountain side, it rested upon a variegated carpet of the many rich and nameless tints that lie upon the finest and mellowest fruits. The abundance of fruit was sufficiently shewn in the little value that seemed to be attached to it; in place of flowers being thrown into the coach by children, as is customary in many parts of France, the early fruits of the season were tossed in at the windows; and the smallest coin was gladly received as a sufficient compensation.

It will probably create some surprise when I say, that in no part of Europe is it possible to travel with so much comfort, or with so great rapidity, as by the Spanish Courier. The coach is more commodious and roomy than an English private carriage; it is well cushioned and seated; the windows are furnished with Venetian blinds, by which the air may be admitted and the sun excluded; and with silk curtains, by which the sun may be excluded even when the glass windows are closed; and two passengers only are admitted inside: another is admitted into the cabriolet along with the guards. The coach is drawn by four mules, which are kept at a gallop the whole way, up hill and down hill; and the road from Bayonne to Madrid, is generally as smooth as the very best roads in England. I ascertained that the rate of travelling exceeded twelve miles an hour. No time is lost in useless stoppages; the mules are changed with as great expedition as in England; the traveller must be contented with few meals; and against the assaults of thirst, the guards are provided with a well filled wine-skin, to which they never apply, without first offering it to the passengers, who are expected to accept the civility.

At Tolosa, an inconsiderable town, we stopped to sup: it was then nearly dark, so that I was unable to see much of it; and, indeed, no more time was allowed than sufficed for the meal. This was the first meal I had taken in Spain, and the first inn I had entered: of the latter, I was scarcely entitled to form an opinion from seeing only one room; but the exaggerated accounts I had heard of the badness and filthiness of the Spanish *posadas*, were well calculated to put me in good humour with the inn at Tolosa. After the variety and excellence of the French *cuisine*, the supper table seemed a little meagre, but every thing was eatable; the table was cleanly and neatly set out, and the servants were active and attentive. In most of the Spanish posadas in the north of Spain, where Malaga is prized, a glass of it is presented to the traveller after every meal.

When morning dawned, I found myself still travelling through a mountainous country, but less fertile than that which lies nearer the frontier. In ascending the mountains that bound the plain in which Vittoria is situated, the usual rapidity of our travelling was interrupted; here, the mules were changed for oxen, which are used throughout Spain, for every kind of laborious work: we are accustomed to associate with oxen, remarkable slowness of movement; and presuming upon this, and upon the steepness of the ascent, I left the carriage, in the intention of walking to the summit; but contrary to my expectation, I found myself unable to keep pace with the oxen, and had great difficulty in regaining my place.

In approaching Vittoria, the country became less interesting; at the highest part of the ascent, the oxen were again changed for mules, and we descended into the plain at a rapid pace, and soon after entered Vittoria, after passing a number of prisoners, chained together, working on the roads; and several long trains of mules.

I had been warned of the strictness of the custom-house at Vittoria, especially in the search for books; but this, like much of the information I had received before entering Spain, proved an exaggeration. I never passed a custom-house with so slight a scrutiny; not one book was opened, and the whole examination did not occupy five minutes.

I had been recommended to go to the "*Parador*," which has the reputation of being the best hotel in Spain; I found, however, that the whole house was engaged for the reception of the Infante Don Francis, and his suite, who were expected the same morning from Bilbao; but accommodation was provided for me in the house adjoining, where I was immediately presented with the usual Spanish *refresco*, a cup of chocolate, and the most excellent bread in Europe. In this, I found that report had for once spoken the truth: I have no where tasted bread that will compare with that of Spain; and this remark applies to the whole country, and not only to the cities and towns, but even to the villages: in the little village of St. Lorenzo, in the midst of the *Sierra Guadarrama*, I found bread equal to any that can be purchased in Madrid or Seville.

Vittoria being the first Spanish town that I had seen by daylight, I quickly finished my *refresco*, that I might walk into the streets. The first thing that attracted my attention, as being characteristic of Spain, was, the great number of priests, and members of different religious orders; and, at the same time, it was impossible to avoid remarking the difference in the appearance of the Spanish clergy, and the clergy of most of the other Catholic countries, especially of France. I saw no poor looking, half starved priests, in thread-bare garments, and looks of humility; all were well clothed, and seemingly well fed; they were not ashamed to hold up their heads, and appeared, as the French say, *à leur aise*.

The next thing that struck me as being remarkable, was the Spanish cloak. It was about noon, on a summer day, and the sun was out; and yet, every second or third person was muffled up in his ample cloak; these persons were, however, chiefly of the inferior ranks; and I could not help suspecting, that the cloak covered many an infirmity, and perhaps with some, stood in stead of an under garment: even the school-boys had their cloaks thrown over their shoulders; and there appeared something very ludicrous in the spectacle of boys at play, encumbered with these useless appendages. I remarked that brown was the universal colour of the cloak among the lower ranks; blue, or black, among the upper classes.

In the appearance of the women, I noticed nothing very remarkable. The Spanish national dress is scarcely seen so far north—the lower orders wore their hair plaited, and descending behind, to the waist; and but few of the ladies were to be seen with the Spanish mantilla. I am not entitled to say a single word respecting the personal appearance of the Spanish women, from a cursory glance at the streets of Vittoria; upon this subject my expectations were highly excited,—but I reserve my judgment upon so interesting a matter, until I have seen the Capital.

In returning to the hotel, that I might see the arrival of the Infant from my window, I stopped for a moment in the bread market,—the display was tempting and beautiful; loaves of all shapes and dimensions, and as white as unkneaded flour, were piled along the street,—but I was obliged to hasten towards my apartment by a flourish of trumpets, announcing the approach of the Infante,—and in a few minutes more his advanced guard entered the street. I can scarcely expect to be credited, when I say that the Infant, Don Francis, the brother of the King of Spain, arrived in a diligence,—yet such is the fact. He, his consort, and his family, occupied one diligence, and his suite occupied another,—the first drawn by seven mules,—the second, by six. The royal party was received with respect by a considerable concourse of people, and with the military honours usually paid to persons in so exalted a station.

In the afternoon, I made a second tour of the town;—I walked into three or four of the churches, but found no fair devotees before any of the altars; only two or three poor old women were at their devotions. I was particularly amused with a spectacle that presented itself in the *Plaza*—a square, by the by, little inferior to the *Place Vendome* in Paris: between two and three hundred girls, from eight to thirteen or fourteen years of age, were assembled in the middle of the area, dancing with each other, to the music of a fife and a drum, played by a musician whom they had hired to contribute his aid to their favourite pastime: the dances were slow, and conducted with the utmost gravity; every one seemed to consider herself engaged in an important affair, and among the two or three hundred countenances, there was scarcely a smile to be seen.

The neighbourhood of the hotel continued to be the point of attraction to the inhabitants of Vittoria all the evening; an Infante is a rarity in the provincial towns of Spain, and the citizens testified their sense of the honour of a visit, by assembling in the street opposite to the hotel, and by hanging cloths and mattings of various colours from the windows: a mark of respect, which in Spain is always considered due to royal, or religious processions. Deputations of the principal inhabitants also arrived,—among others, one of Capuchin friars; and to my great annoyance, a band of indifferent music continued to entertain the Infante till after midnight.

There was nothing to detain me long in Vittoria, and I hired a cabriolet and two mules, to carry me to Bilbao, the capital of Biscay; the distance is eleven leagues of the country, or something more than fifty English miles, and for this I paid 200 reals; and as I may probably have frequent occasion to mention the expense of travelling, and the value of different articles, the following few explanations will be found of use. Generally speaking, every thing in Spain is calculated by reals, from the price of a ticket to the bull-fight, up to the State expenditure. The value of a real is nearly 2½d.,—so that four reals are equal to a French franc, or 10d. English; all accounts in reals may therefore be easily understood by dividing by four. But in small values, the calculation is made in quartos, eight and a half of which are equal to a real, or 2½d. In stating prices, I shall always make use of these two denominations of money, so that the reader may at once be able to substitute English value.

From Bayonne, into Biscay, the nearest road is not by Vittoria, but along the sea shore by St. Sebastian; but the muleteers considering the coast road unsafe, from the chances of robbery, I was obliged to take the more circuitous line by Vittoria, which I left about five in the morning, after the usual *refresco*. Chocolate in Spain, is very different from chocolate in England: it is served in a very small cup, about the size of the old India china coffee cup; it is about the consistence of thick cream, and is highly spiced with cinnamon: the traveller in Spain who dislikes chocolate, will often find himself exposed to great inconvenience.

Leaving Vittoria, I entered upon the extensive plain in which it is situated, and proceeded along a good road, and at a pleasant pace, towards the mountains. The plain of Vittoria is entirely a corn country, and, at this early season, harvest had already begun: the soil is naturally bad and scanty; but the proverbial industry of the Biscayans forces from it an unwilling crop. From Vittoria to the entrance of the mountains, is about three leagues; I passed through two or three small villages, and at another, somewhat larger, just on the limits of the plain, we stopped to water the mules: it was Sunday morning; there was a fine display of vegetables and fruit in the market-place, and several hundred villagers and peasants were assembled, waiting the summons to go to mass. I walked round the market-place, and observed with pleasure, not unmixed with surprise, that every individual was clean and well dressed. I was not accosted by a single beggar.

Immediately upon leaving this village, I entered the mountains—a delightful change from a wide treeless plain. About a league from the entrance, at the end of a winding valley, and just before beginning a steep ascent, I noticed a house where guards were to be hired; the muleteer asked me whether I chose to have any, but being at that time rather an unbeliever in the frequency of robbery, and liking the expression of the muleteer's countenance, I replied in the negative, and we passed on.

The passage of the Biscayan mountains by this road, affords some very magnificent prospects; the lower parts of the mountains are covered with oak and Spanish chestnut, and the summits rise to the height of at least 5000 feet, in the form of numerous fantastic pinnacles of a reddish colour; the road is constructed upon the most scientific principle, reaching the summit by a zigzag, and very easy ascent, and is as broad and as smooth as the best roads in any other country. The descent towards the north-west is much greater than the ascent from Vittoria, proving the great elevation of the province of *Alava* above that of *Biscay Proper*; the provinces both of *Alava*, and of *Guipuscoa*, are called Biscayan provinces, but Biscay Proper is confined to the country lying to the north of the mountains, and bounded by the sea.

We stopped at *Durango*, the first town after descending the mountains, to dine, and rest the mules during the hottest part of the day. I was equally pleased and surprised with the excellence of the *posada* at Durango; the most scrupulous cleanliness was visible in every thing; the dinner was unobjectionable; and I remarked a refinement to which the best French inns are strangers—the knives and forks were changed with every plate. I learned from the *Señorita* who waited at table, that a sad misfortune had that day befallen the village; the bishop to whose diocese it belonged, had journeyed from Navarre to pay his respects to the Infante at *Bilbao*; on his return he had stopped at *Durango*, as it was improper to travel on Sunday, and after condescending to preach a sermon in the village church, he had reproved the levity of the people, and forbade that there should be any dancing in the village that evening; but the girl added, that she would go to another village, half a league distant, to which the injunction did not extend: this trifling trait, added to another which I shall just now record, first led me to suspect, that the influence of the priesthood was on the decline, in Biscay at least. The landlord, having discovered that I was English, asked me how many priests we might have in England in a town such as Durango? I replied, that we might have one or two; "O Dios," said he, "we have here more than forty!"

After dinner, we continued our journey towards Bilbao. Leaving the town, I remarked on passing the church, that the market was held under the portico, and in the environs I noticed a few specimens of Biscayan enjoyment; groups of men were lying, and sitting under the trees, playing at cards; and women were seen here and there, seated on the grass, singing, and playing the tamborine. The road to Bilbao continued excellent, and lay through a fine fertile valley, bearing luxuriant crops of Indian corn, diversified by meadows, and wood, which also covered the sides of the neighbouring hills. I saw no carriage on the road but my own; carts, and long trains of mules, occasionally passed, and the only travellers I saw, were two gentlemen mounted on mules, accompanied by four guards on foot, each provided with a carabine.

All the way from Vittoria, the muleteer who drove the carriage, sung a remarkably beautiful, but somewhat monotonous air. I was greatly pleased with the muleteer's song, and was anxious that I should not forget it; but I afterwards found that I need not have been apprehensive of this: every where throughout Castile I heard the same air, and in Madrid, nothing else was sung by the lower orders. I was anxious to purchase it, and applied at one of the music-shops, but they told me they dared not sell it; it was forbidden by the government. The air was old Arragonese, but it was revived to new words, in a little comedy that somehow slipped through the censorship a few months before, and related how a certain friar knew too well the road into a certain convent.

As the road approaches Bilbao, the mountains that inclose the valley increase in height, make a curve, and run directly into the Bay of Biscay; and Bilbao is situated in their bosom: it is this that gives to Bilbao its peculiar character. Mountains generally diminish in height as they approach the sea; but here, this rule is reversed, and Bilbao possesses the singularity of being a sea-port, and of yet being all but surrounded by lofty mountains. Owing to this, nothing can be more striking and novel than the view of the city where it is first seen from the bridge that crosses the small river about a mile before entering it. I was obliged to leave the carriage at the entrance to the town, and walk to the posada; for it is the rule that no wheeled carriages of any kind are allowed to drive through the streets of Bilbao. This regulation has arisen from a praiseworthy desire to preserve the purity of the water, which is conveyed in a stone tunnel under the streets; all goods are therefore carried through the town either in panniers, on mules, or in sledges, which are provided with a contrivance by which they constantly moisten their path with water.

Walking through the streets, to the *posada de St. Nicola*, the only good inn in Bilbao, and one of the very best in the Peninsula, I was attracted by two curious exhibitions, one of them very forcibly reminding me that I was in Spain: two well-dressed peasants danced before me the whole length of a long street while another walked behind, playing a sort of trumpet; and in the open space before the principal fountain, some boys were amusing themselves with the representation of a bull-fight; one boy was mounted on another's back, the undermost representing the horse of the *picador*, the other was armed with a long pole, while a third on foot, his head covered with a basket in which he had fixed two horns, imitated the motions and bellowing of the bull; several others with handkerchiefs, represented the *torredores*, throwing them in the bull's face. The bull-fights at Bilbao had newly concluded; the Infante had been treated with eight exhibitions, in which thirty-two bulls were killed. This is the highest mark of respect that Spanish authorities can shew to a visitor, and the greater the number of bulls that are sacrificed, the greater of course is the compliment.

I remained in Bilbao a fortnight, which I found amply sufficient to see all that merited attention, and to inform myself respecting some of the peculiarities of the province of Biscay. I have already spoken of the situation of Bilbao, as striking and beautiful, but the town itself is not remarkable for its beauty or cleanliness; the smells are most offensive; and lying as it does in so deep a basin among the mountains, which even shut it out from the sea, I can scarcely think Bilbao a healthy city. But by the side of the river, there is a fine promenade all the way to the port, which lies about two miles from the city, and here the inhabitants may catch some of the sea breeze which generally comes up with the tide; a part of this promenade is allotted to the fruit and vegetable market, which I strolled through, the morning after my arrival; there was a most abundant display of every sort of which the season admitted, including an extraordinary quantity of *tomata*,—this is known in the south of France by the name of *pomme d'amour*, and is an important ingredient in Spanish cookery. The bread market is held along with the fruit market, and I found the bread of Bilbao quite equal to that of the other parts of Spain.

When I looked from my window in the hotel, I found that I was well situated for observing the inhabitants of all classes: opposite, stood the church of St. Nicholas; at one side was a public fountain, and on the other a brass basin—reminding me of Membrino's helmet—indicated a barber's shop. At all hours therefore I might see some going to mass, and others filling their pitchers at the fountain. The Biscayan deserves the character of strength, that has been given to him; and the contrast between the Biscayan, and the Andalusian peasant, who inhabit the two extremes of Spain, is remarkable: the latter, dark, tall, upright, slim, with something of elegance in his appearance; and the look of pride generally visible in his air and countenance, seeming to have some reference to his personal attractions: the Biscayan, broad, athletic, lounging, with something of peculiar roughness in his look and manner; and his expression of blunt independence, having no reference to himself individually, but arising from the knowledge that he is a Biscayan, and as such, the hereditary possessor of peculiar and exclusive rights. Such seemed to me the Biscayan peasant, whether he filled his pitcher at the fountain, or entered St. Nicholas to mass. As for the women, I do not feel myself obliged to use the same reserve in speaking of them as of the women of Vittoria: because the inhabitants of Biscay being a distinct race, my opinion of them does not compromise the character and claims of Spanish women generally. I saw little beauty in Bilbao, and less elegance; and in the manner of the women I remarked the same bluntness as that which characterizes the men.

But along with Biscayan bluntness, there is much good heartedness and honesty, and a great deal of intelligence; and even the pride of a Biscayan, has given rise to much of the industry and enterprise which in the province of Biscay are so conspicuous in the cultivation of the soil, in the construction of useful works, and in the establishment of praiseworthy institutions. Many of the inhabitants of Biscay in the upper classes have made voyages into other countries, and have returned with diminished prejudices, and increased liberality of sentiment; and the consequence of this has been, that among the educated, and better classes of society, there is little narrowness in political sentiment, and little bigotry in religion. I heard several of the most respectable inhabitants of Bilbao express openly much dissatisfaction at the political debasement of Spain, and breathe ardent wishes for the diffusion of intellectual and religious light; but they added, what my own knowledge has since fully confirmed, that I should not find in any other part of Spain, the same enlightened views as I had found in Biscay. Among the lower orders in Bilbao, and in Biscay generally, there is still much bigotry both in politics and religion, but more especially in the latter; during the existence of the constitution, the prejudices of the lower ranks made it necessary to affix in large letters over the doors of all the churches, and attested by the existing authorities, these important words,— "The Roman Catholic is the only true religion."

In Biscay there are not many poor, nor many rich. Formerly, Bilbao contained many wealthy citizens; but the export trade in wool was then flourishing. At that time the clearances were more than double their present number; but ever since the preference of Saxon wool has begun to be shewn in the foreign markets, the trade of Bilbao has declined, and now, not more than between thirty and forty British vessels visit Bilbao in the course of a year. Some few houses in Bilbao have still considerable returns from the fish trade, and one or two, from the iron export trade; but this has also fallen off, since the demand for Swedish iron has increased. Biscayan iron would still command a preference in the foreign markets, from its superior qualities for finer purposes, if it could enter them at the same price as Swedish iron; but this is impossible, both on account of the expense of fuel for furnaces, and the want of inland navigation. Timber is not scarce in the province of Biscay; but there is an old Biscayan law which tends to keep up its price, enacting that for every tree cut down, six must be planted in its stead; this is often felt to be an inconvenience, and produces scarcity in the midst of plenty. I was informed that two or three houses in Bilbao realize from 2 to 3000*l.* a-year; but I believe I may assert that no one spends 300*l.* It is difficult to spend money in Bilbao: in no part of Spain, least of all in Biscay, is it the custom to live extravagantly or luxuriously. The table of a Biscayan is remarkable for its simplicity and sameness: of whatever rank he may be, he takes his cup of chocolate and bread, followed by a glass of sugar and water, about eight o'clock; he dines about one, and six days out of seven, his dinner consists of broth, and a *puchero*, which is boiled beef, with a small bit of pork, surrounded either by cabbage, or Spanish peas, (*garbanzos*), and varied occasionally with a sausage; a cup of chocolate again in the afternoon, and for supper, boiled lettuce prepared with vinegar, oil and pepper, finish the repasts of the day. The *menage* at home, therefore, costs but a trifling sum; and neither does the Biscayan spend any thing upon entertaining his friends; not that he is unsocial; he is social according to the custom of his country. During the winter, a circle of six, eight, or ten families form themselves into a society, and agree to visit each other; each chooses a week, and during each week the circle assembles every evening at the same house; they take chocolate before going out, and sup when they return; the entertainment is entirely intellectual; music, cards, and dancing fill up the evening. Upon one occasion only, does the circle eat together: all the money lost and won at cards, is made a purse, and is confided to one of the party; and during the summer it is converted into a dinner in the country, of which all the members of the circle partake.

There are no public amusements in Bilbao, excepting occasional bull fights. Two attempts to establish a theatre have failed; a handsome stone theatre erected some years ago, was burnt down not long after it was erected; and there was strong reason to believe, that the conflagration was wilful, and that the friars were at the bottom of it: another theatre constructed of wood, was subsequently opened; but after a very short time it was pulled down by order of the public authorities; and this was also generally believed to have been owing to the interference of the friars.

The town of Bilbao is extremely rich. On the occasion of the king's visit a few years ago, the corporation expended no less than two million of reals (20,000*l.*) in feasts, decorations, bull-fights, &c., and to cover these expenses, it was not necessary to lay on any additional impositions. These funds arise from dues upon the entry of all the necessaries of life, whether by land or by sea: beef is entirely a town monopoly; the meat is farmed to butchers at certain prices, and retailed by them, and by this monopoly the Corporation realizes 1500 reals per day. The duties upon wine, soap, and oil, are also considerable, and the dues of port entry upon all articles of subsistence are 2½d. per cent. But notwithstanding these dues, living is not expensive. The following are the prices of some articles: beef is 10 quartos, or about 3d.; mutton, 3½d., but it is generally of an indifferent quality; a lamb costs from 20d. to 2s.; veal is about 4d. per lb., all of 17 oz. Bread varies in price, according to the quality: the best is 1½d. per lb., but the coarsest kinds, and the bread of Indian corn, is not sold by weight. Many kinds of game are both plentiful and cheap: wood-cocks are frequently to be had at 10d. or 1s. per pair. Groceries are also reasonable, and it is a curious fact, that loaf sugar, coming from England, is cheaper than raw sugar, direct from the Havannah: good wine costs a little less than 3d. per bottle. The Spanish country wines taste unpleasantly to a stranger, for they have almost all contracted, less or more, a peculiar flavour from the skins in which they are carried. There are two reasons why the Spanish wines are carried in skins: in the wine countries there is little wood to make casks; but the principal reason is, that the cross-roads are not suited for carriages, and that mules can more conveniently carry skins than casks. Throughout Biscay, the wages of labour are from 10d. to 1s.; and workmen, such as carpenters, masons, &c. receive from 20d. to 2s. per day.

Among the first days of my residence in Bilbao, I visited the new cemetery, the model of which is worthy of being adopted in other places. This *Campo Santo* has been inclosed in consequence of a quarrel between the Franciscan Convent and the Chapter of Bilbao, respecting the dues of burial, in a place to which both claimed right; and the Corporation completed the new cemetery, at an expense of not less than 30,000*l*. The gateway is beautiful and chaste, with this appropriate inscription over it:

"Cada Paso, que vais dando
Por la senda de la vida
Mas y mas os va acercando
Mortales, á la partida,
Que en vano estais evitando."

The design of the *Campo Santo* is this: a square area of about six acres is surrounded by a covered arcade, supported by doric columns; the back of the arcade is an immense wall of brickwork, in which there are four rows of spaces for coffins, the opening one yard square, and six feet and a half long; into this, the coffin is deposited; the spaces which are not occupied are slightly closed up; and a ring in the centre, shews that they are vacant. When a coffin is deposited, the opening is built up with brick and lime, and a stone or marble slab, fitted into it, records the name of the buried. The cemetery is fitted to receive 3000 dead—a great number for so small a space; and the area beyond the arcade, is tastefully laid out as a garden and shrubbery. Besides the inscription I have noted down, there are several others that struck me as being beautiful and well chosen. The following particularly, over the inner-gate, is striking:—

"Deten sus pasos inciertos
O Caminente! repara,
En que esta Puerta separa
A Los vivos de los muertos."

Which may be freely translated:—"Stop, thoughtless wanderer! and reflect,—this gate separates the dead from the living."

In returning from the cemetery to the town, I made a long circuit, visiting in my way the *Iglesia de Bigoña*, a church which takes its name from a miraculous image of our Lady of Bigoña, deposited in it, and looked upon with extraordinary veneration by the lower orders in Bilbao. It happened to be a feast day, and a great number of persons were collected in the church, because upon all such days, the curtain that screens the miraculous image is withdrawn for a few moments—an opportunity not to be disregarded by any good Biscayan who desires to ensure the kind offices of the sainted Lady of Bigoña. Before the service began, the officiating priest shewed me the sacristy, and a head of John the Baptist in wood; a very clever performance, by a native artist; and I afterwards waited in the church long enough to see the curtain withdrawn, and the prostrations of three or four hundred devotees. There is a small foundation left to this church, for a curious purpose. The curate must go to the gate of the church at the commencement of every thunder storm,—say a certain prayer,—and sprinkle the sky with holy water. It appears, however, that the virtue of the water, as well as the water itself, has been sometimes dissipated before reaching the clouds; for the church tower has been twice struck by lightning.

In the course of my walk, I learned a curious fact, illustrating strongly the mixture of pride and generosity which is often found in the Spanish character. The Corporation being desirous of conducting an aqueduct and a road to Bilbao from a mountain about a league distant, applied to the proprietor (a grandee of Spain) to purchase the land through which these were to be carried. He refused to sell it; but said, that if the Corporation would petition him for a grant of the land, he would make them a present of it: they however wanted no favour, and would not condescend to this; but supposing that the proprietor would be prevailed upon to sell, they commenced, and at length nearly finished the work. The grandee, offended at this insolence, applied to the king for an order to demolish the work, and obtained it; but just in time to prevent this, the Corporation petitioned the grandee, and the order was not only rescinded, but the grant of the land was completed. The water conveyed in this aqueduct forms a reservoir at the entrance of the town for a useful and rather a novel purpose: by opening a sluice, seven of the lowest streets in the town are inundated; this is done every week during the summer heats, and is doubtless very useful in carrying away impurities. I walked through one of the lowest of the streets an hour before, and an hour after the purification; and the difference in smell, freshness, and coolness, was most striking.

Walking either in the streets, or in the neighbourhood of Bilbao, the convents and monasteries are very conspicuous: they are almost all immense piles of building, of little architectural beauty, and are at once distinguished by the strong gratings that cover their windows. In the town there are four monasteries—the Franciscans, the Capuchins, the Augustins, and the Carmelites: the two former of these subsist on charity, which is liberally bestowed, and they in their turn give charity to others. Every day, a great number of poor are fed after the Franciscan friars have dined, and as they are a hundred and ten in number, the refuse of their dinner must be considerable. I visited the Franciscan convent accompanied by an English lady, and although I found the utmost politeness from the Superior, he was deaf to all my entreaties to permit the lady to enter the sacristy, to see a picture said to be by Raphael. This convent was partly destroyed by the French, and it was under its gateway that several of those military executions took place, which so disgraced the conduct of the French during their occupation of the province of Biscay. In the Carmelite convent, there are only five friars, who want for nothing that money can purchase; they are extremely rich, and possess a charming property not far from Bilbao, called "*el Desierto*;" but which might with greater propriety be called "*el Paradaiso.*" Besides these monasteries within the town, there are two at a short distance from it—the Burcena convent of Mercenarios, and the Friars of San Mames, both of the Franciscan order.

The female convents are also numerous; these are, La Conception, a Franciscan order, in which there are 14 nuns; Santa Clara, also Franciscan, in which there are 10 nuns; El Convento de la Encarnacion, where there are 27 nuns; el Convento de la Cruz, containing 12 nuns; Santa Monica, an Augustinian order, with 12 nuns; La Esperanza, containing 12, and La Merced, containing 10. There are altogether about 350 friars and nuns in Bilbao, and about 120 priests. In the province of Biscay, females profess at a very early age; their noviciate generally commences about fifteen, and at the expiration of a year they take the veil. A nun must carry into the convent about 30,000 reals (300*l.*); and to La Merced and Santa Monica, considerably more. I ascertained, from a source of the most authentic kind, that three-fourths of the nuns who take the veil at this early age, die of a decline within four years. The climate, which in Biscay is so prolific in consumption, added to the low and damp situation of some of the convents, may perhaps be admitted to have some influence upon this premature decay; but I should incline to attribute a greater influence to causes more immediately referable to the unhappy and unnatural condition of those who are shut out from the common privileges, hopes, and enjoyments of their kind.

I visited the convent of Santa Monica in company with an old gentleman, an inhabitant of Bilbao, who had known several of the inmates from childhood. We were only permitted to converse through a double grating, which separated the small antechamber where we stood, from the convent burying-ground, where three of the nuns were; two of them seemed to be above thirty, the other was under twenty; my companion, a very jocose old man, jested, and amused them; and they in their turn prated, and laughed immoderately, and appeared to be in excellent spirits; but the sight of an old acquaintance, and the novelty of a visit from an English lady, had probably produced a temporary excitement: while, in the midst of their mirth, they were suddenly sent for by the abbess, who probably thought it wise to turn their thoughts into another channel. It is a pity, I think, that those who have separated themselves from the world, should afterwards be permitted to hold any communication with it; feelings may be stifled, and hopes buried, and time and habit may lead to forgetfulness, and even unconsciousness, of a busier, and it may be, a brighter scene; but recollections are easily awakened, and it is cruel to revive that which must again be buried.

Walking one evening to see the new hospital, which lies on the outskirts of the town, I was surprised at the great number of mules which were entering and leaving Bilbao; the former laden with wine, soap and oil; the latter with dried cod, which forms the staple of the Bilbao trade, and is an article of diet very extensively used throughout the greater part of Spain. There is a curious regulation respecting the trade of Bilbao with the interior,—no muleteer from Castile can carry away a load from any part of Biscay, unless he has brought a load with him; and this load must consist of something that may be eaten, drank, or burnt: this regulation ensures at all times to the Biscayan market an abundant supply, at a reasonable rate, of all the articles that come from the interior; nor is the regulation thought a hard one by the muleteer; because, although owing to the abundant supply, he is frequently a loser by it, he knows that it would be insecure to carry money so far to the market: it is in fact a remnant of the original commerce of all nations— barter.

I found the hospital well worthy of a visit; it is not yet completed, but is calculated to accommodate 250 patients. When I visited it, there were only

50 patients, whose diseases were consumption and old age. One part of the establishment I greatly approve of; a ward of the building is appropriated for the reception of strangers, or persons of a superior rank in life, who may be desirous of good advice at a moderate expense, and without occasioning trouble to friends or relations: these pay half a dollar per day, and have all the best hospital attendance united with the comforts of a private house. I can scarcely conceive a more welcome piece of intelligence to an unfortunate stranger, seized with a severe malady in a foreign place, than the existence of an institution like this.

In walking through the wards, I noticed books in the hands of several of the patients; these were chiefly forms of prayer; but seeing one sick man laughing heartily over his studies, I had the curiosity to approach his bed near enough to ascertain that he was engaged with a comedy of *Lopez de Vega*.

Passing along the streets, I frequently met the boys belonging to a charity school, the only one in Bilbao; they were, with few exceptions, very raggedly dressed, and most of them provided with little bells, with which they produced not an inharmonious music: the cause of their ragged dress is easily explained by the want of funds, which arise solely from the trifling imposition of four reals per ton upon every foreign vessel entering the port. The only explanation I was able to get of the ringing of bells is, that this custom is pleasing to the virgin. There is another sort of music peculiar to Biscay, of the most discordant kind, and which I cannot recollect even now, without unpleasant sensations. This music is produced by the wheels of the carts drawn by oxen: these are solid, without spokes, and a strong wooden screw is made to press upon the axle of the wheel; the consequence of this, is a sound so horribly grating, that the faintest conception of it cannot be conveyed by words. The peasant supposes, that without this noise, the oxen would not go willingly; and if they be once accustomed to it, this may perhaps be true. No carriage being allowed to pass along the streets of Bilbao, they are of course free from this intolerable nuisance: in the town of *Orduña*, also, it is not permitted; but on all the roads of the Basque provinces, and especially in the streets of Vittoria, this noise is so unintermitting, that nothing could tempt me to reside in that town.

Every evening while I remained in Bilbao, I spent half an hour in the Swiss Coffee-house—the only one in the town; and one evening, I was much amused by a very curious scene I witnessed there. Four gentlemen were seated at a card-table when I entered the coffee-house, and at first I paid no particular attention to them; but accidentally resting my eye upon them while sipping my coffee, I was surprised to see one of the players shut one eye, and at the same time thrust his tongue out of his mouth; from him, my eyes wandered to another, who at the same moment squinted with both eyes, and thrust forward his under-lip: I now saw that it was a constant succession of face-making, while all the while the game went on. It is impossible to describe the strange, ludicrous, and hideous faces of the players; I was at first dumb with astonishment, and then convulsed with laughter, and all the while dying with curiosity to know the reason of so grotesque an exhibition. It was a Biscayan game, called *mūs*;—answering to each card there is a particular contortion of the face, which interprets its value; and the point of the game consists in the dexterity with which partners are able to convey to each other by grimaces, the state of each other's hand. This is a favourite game in Biscay, but it is said to require a lifetime to become expert in it: I should think it requires also the natural gift of grimace.

There are many charming walks around Bilbao, up the river, and down the river, and among the neighbouring mountains; and in whatever direction one turns, proofs are at hand, of the enterprising spirit, and great industry of the inhabitants in the improvement of land. Within the last ten years, much waste land has been brought under cultivation: of this waste land, there are two kinds; one, which is the property of the jurisdiction, and which is parcelled out to individuals, the price being fixed by arbitration: the other, which is the property of individuals who possess entailed estates, and cannot dispose of waste land. Some enterprising person offers to cultivate a portion of this land, under the agreement that the produce for a certain period, ten, or twelve years perhaps, is to be the property of the cultivator, and that at the expiration of that term, the cultivator is to rent the land of the proprietor. By these two modes, a great part of the cultivable land of Biscay has been brought under cultivation; and the vine is now extensively grown upon all the surrounding slopes.

The following few particulars respecting the climate, diseases, &c. of Biscay, I obtained from a report drawn up by a few of the principal medical men of the province, at the request of the Royal College of Physicians in London. The medium heat of the thermometer in summer is from 19 to 21 of Reaumur, and in winter from 5 to 7. In summer, the thermometer scarcely ever rises above 26, and in winter, rarely falls below 0: changes in the temperature are sudden and extraordinary; the mercury having been known to rise and fall from 3° to 4° within a few minutes. The most prevalent winds are S. and N. W.; the S. the most constant in autumn, the N. W. in spring. The finest months are August, September, October, and sometimes November; the spring months are the most unsettled, rains being then almost as frequent as in winter. The summer months are the most salubrious; autumn less so; and winter and spring may be said to be unhealthy. The diseases most common in Biscay are cutaneous diseases; and catarrhs, especially pulmonary, which often terminate in pulmon.

phthisis. Inflammations of the pleura, lungs, and bowels,—and rheumatism, are the most numerous after the class of pulmonary diseases; and of all these, the atmospheric changes may be considered the predisposing cause. The province of Biscay abounds in medicinal plants; but excepting a few simples used by the inhabitants, these do not enter into the Spanish pharmacopeia. Amongst these medicinal plants, are laurus nobilis, arbutus unedo, rabnus cartarticus, erica cantabrica, smilax aspera, humulus lupulus, tormentila erecta, poligala amara, digitalis purpurea, daphne laureola, gentiana luthea, anethenus nobilis. The number of deaths in Bilbao, calculated from the parochial register by an average of five years, amounts to one in forty-six yearly.

The Basque provinces enjoy many separate privileges, of which they are extremely jealous; but Biscay Proper enjoys more privileges than either of the other Basque provinces. I shall mention a few of the most remarkable. Biscay acknowledges no king; the king of Spain is not king, but lord of Biscay. This is but a nominal privilege: but the next is more important. The conscription does not extend to Biscay; in case of invasion only, Biscay is bound to furnish troops, but as soon as the demand upon their services is past, they are entitled to disband themselves. The next is a highly honourable privilege, whatever may be thought of its solid advantage: a Biscayan cannot be hanged, but must be strangled, like a Spanish noble; nor can stripes be inflicted as a punishment. The only difference between hanging and strangling consists in this, that the punishment of strangulation is inflicted while the criminal is seated. The next Biscayan privilege is a privilege annexed to his religion; it is, that no foreigner is entitled to establish himself in any trade, unless he profess the Roman Catholic religion. The code of laws by which Biscay is governed, is different not only from those of Spain, but also from those of the other Basque provinces: this is no doubt a right, but whether it be a right conveying any advantage is more questionable. I understood that justice in Biscay was badly administered, and that a code of separate laws in no respect increased the chances of the poor in a contest with the rich. Questions arising in Biscay, although decided by the laws of Biscay, are not decided within the province, but are subject to numerous appeals. They originate with the Court of the Corregidor; from which the first appeal is to the Chancery of Valladolid; from this to the Council of Castile; then to the tribunal *de mil ducados*, so called because that sum must be deposited before the appeal can be received; and lastly to the king, under the name of "*appelar de notoria injusticia.*" It is evident, that with the power of thus prolonging the term of litigation, and the necessity of a large deposit, the richest litigator must enter upon his lawsuit with very reasonable hopes of success.

Biscay is not obliged to pay any government impositions: the king has no certain revenue from Biscay, but when money is wanted, he must ask it, and a part of what is demanded is generally given; but if any demand be made inconsistent with the laws or privileges of Biscay, a thing that has sometimes happened, Biscay returns this contradictory answer; "*Se obedese, y no se cumple.*"

The head of the province, is the Corregidor, who is named by the king of Spain; but an appeal from the corregidor to the deputies, seems to render the precedence of the corregidor merely nominal. The deputies are elected thus: the general election for the nomination of deputies, syndics, and regidores, takes place every three years. Each village within the province sends one or two electors, according to its size; the names of the villages are written upon separate pieces of paper, and all are put into a wheel, and the first four that turn up, have the right of election, or of naming the public functionaries of the province.

The privileges, the civil laws, and the maritime laws of Biscay, are contained in three separate volumes; the latter of these form the basis of the maritime laws of Spanish South America.

CHAPTER II.

JOURNEY FROM BISCAY TO MADRID.

Waggon travelling; Scenery; Bills of Fare, and Expenses; second Visit to Vittoria; Departure for Madrid; the Ebro; Privileges of the Military; Old Castile; Husbandry; Burgos; Beggars; Posadas; Traits of Misery in a Castilian Village; New Castile; Quixotic Adventure; the Somo-sierra and Approach to the Capital; Sketches of the Environs, and Arrival in Madrid; Information for Travellers.

UPON those roads in Spain where there are no diligences, the traveller may generally find an *ordinario*, or *galera*; two kinds of waggons, the former without, the latter commonly, but not always, with springs, in either of which he may be accommodated with a place,—a seat I can scarcely call it,—at a price, moderate in comparison with the enormous expense of hiring a private conveyance. In one of these *ordinarios*, I left Bilbao for Vittoria, by a road different from that by which I had already travelled. Nothing can be more luxurious than travelling by a waggon on springs during hot weather: neither diligence nor private carriage can be compared with it: it is open before and behind, so that there is a fine current of air; it is covered above, so that the sun is excluded, and the traveller may lie all his length upon clean straw. As for the rate of travelling, it is not indeed very rapid; but fifty miles a day is a sufficient distance for one who is desirous of seeing the country he passes through: waggons with springs, however, are much more rarely to be met with, than those without them; and the jolting, of course, neutralizes in part the other advantages I have named.

Leaving Bilbao, the road winds through a narrow valley among hills covered to the summit with oak, and rising to the height of between 2000 and 3000 feet; the valley, varying in breadth from one to two miles, is every where cultivated; the crops, even at this early period, were already partly reaped; and in many places the country people were busy in the fields. Every where around, there was much picturesque beauty and many rural pictures: a little rivulet flowed in capricious turnings through the valley; and as Biscayan industry always carries a road straight forward, whatever obstacles are encountered, the stream was spanned every few hundred yards by a stone bridge, built in the form of an aqueduct, and generally grown over with ivy: fine old Spanish chestnut trees were scattered over the meadows that bordered the stream, and here and there groups of cattle stood, or lay under them. This kind of scenery continued the same for about six leagues, when we stopped at a small town to dine, and refresh the mules. At this village we were destined to fare ill. We were ushered into a room where a priest, and two other persons, had finished what seemed by its wrecks to have been an excellent repast: and the table was immediately cleared to make way for our entertainment: silver spoons and forks, handsome wine decanters, of crystal gilt, and clean napkins, seemed to announce something respectable; but the dinner, when it appeared, consisted of a little cold fish, and the bones—literally the bones, of the chickens which the priest and his friends had picked! I made my way into the kitchen, and discovering a fine fat hen roasting, and almost ready for the table, I began to repent my too hasty condemnation of the entertainment; but upon telling the master that the fowl was sufficiently roasted, I was informed that it was not for me, but for the muleteer, who in Spain always fares better than those whom he conducts. I was forced, therefore, to return to the cold fish and chicken bones, for which the landlord had the effrontery to charge twelve *reals*. I paid him, however, only one half of his demand, and got into the waggon, followed only by a few Biscayan growls.

After leaving this town, we began to ascend the mountains which separate Biscay Proper from the province of Alava. In passing these mountains, a curious illusion is produced by the extreme whiteness of the stone which composes the peaks of some of the Biscayan range. It is scarcely possible to persuade oneself that these are not snow peaks; nothing indeed but a previous knowledge of the elevation of this range, and of the consequent impossibility of snow lying upon it, could dismiss the illusion. A little before dusk we alighted at the parador at Vittoria, where, as the Infante was no longer an inmate, I found comfortable accommodation. At this hotel, and at all the posadas between Bayonne and Madrid, in connexion with the establishment of the royal diligences, there is a tariff of prices, which I shall here transcribe, for the information of those who may wish to know something of the expenses of travelling in this part of Spain.

Desayuno, which means a slight morning's repast, and which may consist either of a cup of chocolate, tea, or coffee, with bread; or of two eggs, with bread and wine, is charged two reals, or five pence.

Almuerzo (Dejeuné a la fourchette), eight *reals*.

Comida (Dinner), twelve *reals*, or 2*s.* 6*d.* This being the most important meal, the tariff specifies the articles of which it must consist, though, for some of these, equivalents are allowed. The following is the bill of fare:—Soup; an *olla*, or *puchero*, which is composed of fowl, bacon, beef, sausage, Spanish peas, and pot-herbs; a fritter, or ham and eggs; two dishes of dressed meat; a pudding; pepper in the pod, dressed with a sauce; small white beans (haricots); a roast; a salad; a dessert of three dishes; a glass of brandy; and bread and wine at discretion. Melon is not included in the dessert of three dishes; this fruit is not eaten in the north of Spain at the dessert, but is introduced after soup. The dinner, it must be admitted, is sufficiently abundant; but, considering the low price of provisions, it is not cheap. The only one of these dishes which a stranger can eat, is the most truly Spanish among them,—the *puchero*,—because it is the only one in which there is neither oil nor garlic. The tariff also provides for the traveller's comfort in bed; this is charged at four *reals* (10*d.*), and the following articles are ordered to be provided: a straw mattress; another of wool; two *clean* sheets; two pillows, and clean pillow-cases; a quilt; and, in winter, a blanket. All that the tariff enjoins, is rigidly complied with; and, whereever there is a tariff, the traveller may always depend upon a sufficient meal, a clean bed, and a just charge.

Vittoria may at present be considered a decayed town. Ever since the war of independence, it has been a falling place; and this may be easily accounted for, from the insecurity of possessions in a town lying so near the French frontier. At the time when Napoleon threatened to annex to France all that part of Spain which lies to the north of the Ebro, many left Vittoria; and several persons exchanged their estates in that neighbourhood, for possessions farther in the interior. At present, there are numerous houses untenanted, and not a few in a state of ruin; and the manufactures of which Vittoria formerly could boast, now scarcely exist,—no one being disposed to sink capital in establishing that which the first commotion upon the frontier might be the means of destroying.

I experienced some difficulties at Vittoria with my passport. I had intended to have entered Spain by Perpignan, but having changed my intention, I was in possession of only a French provisional passport, backed by the Spanish Consul at Bayonne. I was at first told, that I could not be allowed to proceed; but, upon producing a letter of recommendation, from Lord Aberdeen to Mr. Addington, the British Minister at Madrid, the difficulties were overcome, and I was permitted to proceed.

I was detained two days in Vittoria, waiting a vacant place in the Madrid diligence, which I stepped into at three o'clock on the morning of the third day; and, after a few hours' drive through a well-cultivated corn country, we reached *Miranda*, and, crossing the *Ebro*, entered old Castile. The Ebro is here a very insignificant stream, little resembling the majestic river which I afterwards crossed in Catalunia; but the interest with which a river is regarded, is of a borrowed kind; even where the traveller is able to step over it, it is invested with a dignity commensurate with its future destinies. But the Ebro, even if it were possible to deprive it of that charm which is common to every great river when beheld near its source, has claims peculiarly its own; it is full of historic recollections—it gave its name to the whole of ancient Spain—and memory, set sail upon its waters, floats towards the empires of Carthage and of Rome. And the Ebro possesses still another source of interest to all who visit Spain; for it is upon its banks that we are first reminded of the exploits of the valorous Knight of La Mancha, and of the undying genius of Cervantes,—one of whose happiest inventions is the fancy of his hero, that his boat, floating down the Ebro, has crossed the equinoctial; and the proof of this, which he demands of Sancho.

I had been told that on entering old Castile we should be subjected to a rigorous custom-house search; but in Spain, such matters always depend upon circumstances. A Colonel in the Spanish service chanced to occupy a seat in the diligence; and no custom-house officer in Spain, dare to put a person holding a military commission to a moment's inconvenience. The consequence was, that in place of being detained three hours upon the bridge, until every package should be lowered and opened, the Colonel merely thrust his arm out of the window; and the custom-house officers, seeing around his wrist the proofs of his military rank, doffed their caps, and stood back; and the diligence passed on. Superior military rank in the Spanish service is not indicated by more gorgeous trappings: the Colonel discards the epaulets, and is known by two narrow stripes round the wrist, while the General merely invests his loins with a crimson girdle.

Upon first entering Castile, the country affords some promise of interest. We traverse a narrow defile, guarded by precipitous and majestic rocks, and are pleased by the picturesque views which are caught at intervals on both sides; but this defile does not extend more than a league in length, and we then enter upon an open and flat corn country, which stretches all the way to Burgos. The soil in this tract of land appeared to be very unequal. I saw whole fields covered with thistles, among which flocks of sheep were picking a scanty meal; and, although I was unable to judge of the productiveness of other parts by the growing crops, the harvest being in many places already gathered, I observed vast heaps of grain every half league or less; part of it thrashed and winnowed, and part going through these operations. All through both the Castiles, the grain is not housed; large flat spots, one or two hundred yards across, are selected for its reception—here it is thrashed and winnowed; the former operation being performed by passing over it a sledge with a curved bottom, drawn by one mule, which is guided by a woman who stands upon the sledge, and who facilitates the operation by her weight. This custom of keeping the grain in the open air, adds much to the labour of the husbandman: if rain come, there is no remedy but to cover the grain-heaps with cloths,—a very ineffectual protection against the torrents that sometimes descend from

Spanish skies; and when the rain ceases, it is necessary again to spread the grain, and expose it to the influence of the sun.

We reached Burgos early in the afternoon, and the short interval allowed us there, sufficed for a glance at the cathedral. In its exterior, the cathedral of Burgos will yield to no other in Spain: in the number, and elegance of the pinnacles which surmount it, it surpasses them all; but the interior, although remarkable for the beauty of the workmanship with which in some parts it is decorated, and although entitled to rank among the most magnificent temples dedicated to religion, is yet inferior to the cathedrals both of Toledo and of Seville, in grandeur, as well as in richness; and as I purposed seeing both of these cathedrals, I regreted less, the impossibility of examining minutely, the cathedral of Burgos. The little that I saw of Burgos pleased me; and had I not subsequently visited Toledo, I should have set down Burgos as the best specimen I had seen of an old Castilian city: but in this, Toledo stands unrivalled.

Between Burgos and Lerma, I passed through vast tracts of uncultivated, and much of it, uncultivable land, mostly covered with a thick underwood of aromatic and medicinal plants; in some parts, the perfume from these was so strong, that I could scarcely believe myself to be elsewhere than in an apothecary's shop. I found all this part of Old Castile very scantily peopled; and the quantity of cultivated land seemed to be quite equal to the probable demand upon its produce. At night-fall we reached *Lerma*, where a comfortable posada received us. We were beset at the door by a crowd of ragged beggars, who however, urged their claims scarcely more obtrusively than the poor Franciscan monk of Sterne, who crossed his hands upon his breast, and retired. The Spanish beggar is unlike the beggar of every other country, in this—that he is easily repulsed; he seldom urges his claim twice; but indeed, his raggedness, and apparent destitution, often render a second appeal unnecessary. I observed that every one of these beggars wore three or four necklaces, and several rings—baubles, no doubt blessed at the shrine of some saint. In the posada at Lerma, I found iron bedsteads, a most acceptable discovery in a hot climate; and the supper table was both neatly laid out, and well provided. The miseries of an Andalusian Venta were yet in reserve. Between Vittoria and Madrid, the traveller has little cause of complaint; I always found a clean bed, and something upon the table, of which it was possible to make a tolerable meal. There is only one part of the arrangement defective: in place of supping when the diligence arrives, there is generally an interval of two hours, which might be spent in sleep, if the arrangements were better. In all the posadas upon this road, the traveller pays for dinner and supper whether he partakes of them or not: this is what the Spaniards call *indemnificacion*, which is charged at two-thirds of the price of the meal. This indemnification I think perfectly fair; were it otherwise, the traveller could find nothing upon his arrival; for upon a road where there are no travellers, the innkeeper dare not trust to the appetites, or will, of those who arrive by the diligence; because if his meal should be rejected, he could find no other market for it.

The country to the south of Lerma is a desert; indeed it is nothing better than a desert that stretches between the *Ebro* and the *Douro*. I passed this latter river at *Aranda*; a small, wretched place, full of misery and rags; and afterwards traversed extensive woods of chestnut and ilex, which stretch three or four leagues to the foot of a low *sierra*, which is the natural boundary between Old and New Castile. Soon after entering this sierra, I passed through the most miserable village that I have seen in any part of Spain: it is quite impossible for one who has never seen the very lowest of the Spanish poor, to form the smallest conception of the general appearance of the inhabitants of this village. I saw between two and three hundred persons; and among these, there was not one, whose rags half covered his nakedness. Men and women were like bundles of ill-assorted shreds and patches of a hundred hues and sizes; and as for the children, I saw several entirely naked, and many that might as well have been without their tattered coverings. I threw a few biscuits among the children; and the eagerness with which they fought for, and devoured them, reminded me rather of young wolves than of human beings. The badness of the pavement, and the steepness of the street, made it necessary for the diligence to go slowly; and I profited by the delay to look into one or two of the miserable abodes of these unfortunate beings. I found a perfect unison between the dweller and his dwelling: I could not see one article of furniture; no table, no chair: a few large stones supplied the place of the latter; for the former there was no occasion; and something resembling a mattress upon the mud floor, was the bed of the family. Leaving this village, I noticed two stone pillars, and a wooden pole across, indicating that the proprietor possesses the power of life and death within his own domain. I forget the name of the grandee at whose door lies all this misery; but if the power of life and death be his, and if he cannot make the former more tolerable, it would be humanity to inflict the latter.

A short distance beyond this village, we passed into New Castile, and stopped for the night at a small hamlet at the entrance of the *Somo Sierra*. Here, I cannot refrain from relating a somewhat ludicrous incident that took place during the night. The chamber in which I slept, was divided from another smaller chamber merely by a curtain; and this inner room was occupied by a young Spaniard. We retired to our respective beds about the same hour, and I was speedily fast asleep. Some time during the night, I was awoke by loud, and most uncommon noises; and when I was sufficiently awake to be master of my senses, I discovered that the noises proceeded from the adjacent chamber; but the nature of the noise was such, as set at defiance all conjecture as to its cause. I heard the stamping of feet, the clanking of spurs, and the strokes of some heavy instrument; but the combatants, whoever they were, fought in silence, for not a word was uttered. I need scarcely say that sounds so unaccountable in my immediate vicinity, excited my utmost curiosity; and stealing out of bed, I groped my way to the door leading into the passage, that I might obtain a light; this, I soon procured, and returning to the scene of action, I found the noises as loud and as strange as ever. I cautiously drew aside the curtain, and a spectacle was revealed almost worthy of Don Quixote. There stood the Spaniard in his shirt, booted and spurred, his cloak thrown over one arm, and the other, dealing blows right and left with a naked sword. I was about to make a hasty retreat, conceiving the unfortunate gentleman to be in a state of derangement, when he called out to me to give him a light, and at the same time ceased battle. The explanation is this—not being able to get off his boots, my companion had lain down booted and spurred; and as was his usual custom, he had deposited a sword near his bed; he was awoke by the tread of several rats over his face; at least so he asserted; and in a state between sleeping and waking, he had jumped from bed, grasped his sword, seized his cloak as a buckler, and commenced warfare. But for my own part, I believe the action of the Spaniard to have begun in sleep, and to have been the result of a dream. We were afterwards intimately acquainted, and saw each other almost every day while I remained in Madrid; and we often laughed together at the recollection of the Quixotic adventure in the posada.

We left the village where we had slept, some hours before day-break. I never beheld a more refulgent moon than shone that night. I was never before able to distinguish colours by moonlight; but this night, the scene presented almost the distinctness and variety of a sunlit landscape, with the soft and dewy mellowness of a tenderer light. The scenery of the Somo-Sierra is rocky, wild and dreary; robbers are occasionally seen here; and the diligence had taken two additional guards from the last village. Before day-break we had passed the Sierra, and we then entered upon the wide arid desert, in the centre of which stands the capital of Spain. As we approached Madrid, we passed long trains of mules, laden with cut straw for the use of the mules in the metropolis; and we also passed some trains laden with bales of goods, every mule having a carabine slung by its side.

From the Somo-Sierra to the gates of Madrid, a distance of nearly thirty miles, there is not a tree to be seen: not a garden; not one country house; scarcely an isolated farm-house or cottage, and only three or four very inconsiderable villages. Great part of the land is uncultivated, and that part of it which is laboured, and which produces grain, is mostly covered with weeds and stones. In the midst of this desert stands Madrid, which is not visible until you approach within less than two leagues of the gate. Its appearance from this side is not striking: the city seems small; and although we may count upwards of 50 spires and towers, none of these are so elevated or imposing, as to awaken curiosity like that which is felt when we first discover the towers of some of the temples dedicated to religion, in others of the Spanish cities. If the traveller turned his back upon Madrid when within half a mile of the gates, he might still believe himself to be a hundred miles from any habitation: the road stretches away, speckled only by a few mules; there are no carriages; no horsemen; scarcely even a pedestrian: there is, in fact, not one sign of vicinity to a great city.

I entered Madrid about mid-day, and after a very slight examination of luggage at the custom-house, I took up my residence at the *Cruz de Malta*. There are only two hotels in Madrid that are habitable—the *Cruz de Malta*, and the *Fontaña de Oro*,—but both of these are as far as possible from being comfortable. I was charged at the *Cruz de Malta*, the extraordinary sum of 60 reals, 12*s*. 6*d*., for one room, for one day; a charge that immediately suggested to me the propriety of establishing myself in private lodgings as speedily as possible.

Before concluding this chapter, let me say a single word respecting the mode and conveniences, and expenses of travelling from Bayonne to Madrid. There are only a few roads in Spain that are passable for carriages, and these of course connect the great towns. These roads are, from Madrid to Bayonne,—from Madrid to Seville,—from Madrid to Zaragossa and Barcellona,—from Madrid to Valentia,—from Madrid to Salamanca,—and from Madrid to Portugal. There are also a few others from one provincial town to another; such as from Valencia to Barcellona,—from Barcellona to the frontier,—from Burgos to Valladolid, and perhaps two or three others. There are not more than twelve roads in Spain passable for a four-wheeled carriage; and upon all of these, there are now diligences established; of which, the accommodation and conveniences are nearly equal. I confine my remarks at present to *diligence* travelling; I shall by and by, have many opportunities of enlarging upon the very different modes of travelling in Andalusia, Murcia, and Granada. I have no hesitation in affirming, that the Spanish diligences are the best in the world; they are extremely commodious, well cushioned, and well hung, and are admirably contrived for the exclusion of both heat and cold. Like the French diligences, they have a *coupé*, in all respects as good as a postchaise, and generally they have no *rotonde*: they are drawn by seven, eight, or nine mules, according to the nature of the road, and travel at the rate of seven miles an hour. The conductors are remarkably civil; and in punctuality as to the hours of departure and arrival, and in every arrangement that can conduce to the comfort of the passengers, there is no room for improvement. When a passenger secures his seat, he receives a paper from the *bureau*, specifying the precise place he is to occupy; and when he delivers his baggage, he is presented with a receipt for the articles delivered, and for which the proprietors are responsible. The price of places in the Spanish diligences varies greatly. In some roads the fare is as low as in France or England; on others, it is more expensive than travelling post. From Bayonne to Madrid, the fare, including conductor and postilions, is something less than 5*l.*; but from Madrid to Seville, about one-fourth greater distance, the expense is nearly double; and it may be right to mention that each passenger is allowed 25 lb. weight of baggage; for every pound beyond this, he pays one real, 2½*d.* These details may appear to some to be insignificant; but independently of the obligation that lies upon a traveller, to withhold no useful information, I cannot but think that such details may occasionally throw some light upon the state of a country. For my own part, I may say most truly, that the regularity and order, I might almost say, the perfection, visible in every department of the establishment of public conveyances throughout Spain, struck me with astonishment, and may perhaps afford some data by which we may judge of the improvement of which Spain might be susceptible under more favourable circumstances.

CHAPTER III.

MADRID.

Streets and Street Population; Female Dress: the Mantilla, the Fan; aspect of the Streets of Madrid at different hours; the Siesta; Shops; good and bad Smells; State of the lower Orders; Analysis of the Population; Street Sketches; Sunday in Madrid; the Calle de Alcala; Convents; the Street of the Inquisition; private Apartments in Madrid; the Prado and its Attractions; ludicrous Incongruities; Spanish Women, and their Claims; the Fan and its uses; Portraits; inconvenient Exaction of Loyalty; the Philosophy of good walking; the Retiro; Castilian Skies; the Cafe Catalina and its Visitors; other Coffee Rooms, and Political Reflections; the Botanical Garden, strange Regulation on entering; the Theatres; Spanish Play Bills; Teatro del Principe; the Cazuela and Intrigue; Spanish Comedy; the Bolero; the Italian Company; cultivation of Music in Madrid; the Guitar; Vocal Music; Spanish Music.

THE traveller who arrives in Madrid from the north, has greatly the advantage over him who reaches the capital from any other point: every thing is newer to him. If one enter Spain at Cadiz, and travel through Seville and Cordova to Madrid, the edge of curiosity is blunted; much of the novelty of Spanish life is already exhausted; and Madrid possesses comparatively little to interest: but travelling to the capital, through Castile, one arrives in Madrid almost as unlearned in the modes of Spanish life, as if the journey had been performed by sea; nor is the interest with which the traveller afterwards sees Cordova and Seville greatly diminished, by having previously seen Madrid. For, although the aspect of a Spanish town, and the modes of Spanish life are then familiar to him,—Cordova, and Seville, and the other cities of the south, possess an exclusive interest, in the remains of the Moorish empire,—in the peculiarity of the natural productions around them—in the climate, which exercises an important influence upon the habits of the people,—and in the taint of Moorish usages, visible in all those provinces which continued the longest time under the dominion of the Moors. With curiosity therefore on the tiptoe, to see the capital of Spain, and the Spaniards in their capital, I hastened into the streets.

The stranger who walks for the first time through the streets of Madrid, is struck with the sombreness of the prospect that is presented to him: this, he speedily discovers, arises from the costume of the women. It is the varied and many-coloured attire of the female sex, that gives to the streets of other great cities their air of gaiety and liveliness. No pink, and green, and yellow, and blue silk bonnets, nod along the streets of Madrid; for the women wear no bonnets,—no ribbons of more than all the hues of the rainbow, chequer the pavement; for the women of Madrid do not understand the use of ribbons. Only conceive the sombreness of a population without a bonnet or a ribbon, and all, or nearly all, in black! yet such is the population of Madrid. Every woman in Spain wears a *mantilla*, which varies in quality and expense, with the station of the wearer: and, for the benefit of those who, though they may have heard of a mantilla, have an imperfect idea of what it is, I shall describe it. A mantilla, is a scarf thrown over the head and shoulders; behind, and at the sides, it descends nearly to the waist; and falling in front over a very high comb, is gathered, and fastened, generally by something ornamental, just above the forehead, at the lower part of the hair. Of old, there was a veil attached to the fore-part of the mantilla, which was used or thrown back, according to the fancy of the wearer; but veils are now rarely seen in Spain, excepting at mass. Of the rank and means of a Spanish woman, something may be gathered from the mantilla, though this cannot be considered any certain criterion, since Spanish women will make extraordinary sacrifices for the sake of dress. Yet there are three distinct grades of the mantilla: the lady in the upper ranks of life, and most of those in the middle ranks, wear the lace mantilla; some of blond—some of English net, worked in Spain; and these vary in price, from 4*l.* or 5*l.* to 20*l.* The Bourgeoises generally wear the mantilla, part lace and part silk; the lace in front, and the silk behind, with lace trimmings; and the lower orders wear a mantilla wholly of silk, or of silk, trimmed with velvet. Spain is the only country in Europe in which a national dress extends to the upper ranks; but even in Spain this distinction begins to give way. In the streets, no one yet ventures to appear without the mantilla; but French hats are frequently seen in carriages and in the theatre; and the black silk gown, once as indispensible as the mantilla, sometimes gives place to silks of other colours; and even a French or English printed muslin, may occasionally be seen on the Prado.

But although the sombre dress of the women, and the consequent absence of bright colours, seemed at first to give a gloomy cast to the exterior of the population of Madrid, a little closer observance of it disclosed a variety and picturesqueness not to be found in any other of the European countries. The dress of the women, although sombre, bears in the eye of a stranger a character of both novelty and grace. The round turned-up hat and crimson sash of the peasant; the short green jacket and bare legs and sandals of the innumerable water-carriers, who call *aqua fresca*; the sprinkling of the military costume; and above all, the grotesque dresses of the multitudes of friars of different orders, gave to the scene a character of originality exclusively its own. No feature in the scene before me appeared more novel than the universality of the fan; a Spanish woman would be quite as likely to go out of doors without her shoes, as without her fan. I saw not one female in the streets without this indispensible appendage. The portly dame, and her stately daughter; the latter six paces in advance, as is the universal custom throughout Spain, walked fanning themselves; the child of six years old, held mamma with one hand, and fanned herself with the other; the woman sitting at her stall selling figs, sat fanning herself; and the servant coming from market, carried her basket with one arm, and fanned herself with the other. To me, who had never before seen a fan but in the hands of a lady, this seemed ridiculous enough.

The streets of Madrid present a totally different aspect, at different hours of the day: before one o'clock, all is nearly as I have described it; bustling and busy, and thronged with people of all ranks, of whom the largest proportion are always females; for the women of Madrid spend much of their time in the streets, going and coming from mass, shopping (a never failing resource,) and going and coming from the Prado. But from one o'clock till four, the aspect of every thing is changed: the shops are either shut, or a curtain is drawn before the door; the shutters of every window are closed; scarcely a respectable person is seen in the street; the stall-keepers spread cloths over their wares, and go to sleep; groups of the poor and idle are seen stretched in the shade; and the water-carriers, throwing their jackets over their faces, make pillows of their water casks. But the *siesta* over, all is again life and bustle; the curtains are withdrawn, the balconies are filled with ladies, the sleepers shake off their drowsiness, and the water-carriers resume their vocation, and deafen us with the cry of aqua fresca. These water-carriers are a curious race, and are as necessary to the Spanish peasant as the vender of beer is to the English labourer: with a basket and glass in the right-hand, and a water jar on the left shoulder, they make incessant appeals to the appetite for cold water, and during the summer, drive a lucrative trade; and so habituated is the Spaniard to the use of cold water, that I have observed little diminution in the demand for it, when the morning temperature of the air was such as would have made even an Englishman shrink from so comfortless a beverage.

Frequently, while in Madrid, I walked out early in the morning, that I might hear the delightful music that accompanies the morning service in the *Convento de las Salesas*; and then the streets wore a different appearance,— flocks of goats were bevouacked here and there to supply milk to those who cannot afford to buy cows' milk. Porters, water-carriers, stall-keepers, and market people, were making a breakfast of grapes and bread; and here and there a friar might be seen, with his sack slung over his back, begging supplies for his convent. One morning, I had the curiosity to follow a young friar of the Franciscan order the whole length of the *Calle de Montera*;

he asked upwards of forty persons for alms, and entered every shop, and only two persons listened to his petition,—one of these was an old lame beggar, sitting at a door, who put half a quarto into his hand; the other was an old gentleman with a cocked hat, and certain other insignia of holding some government employment.

In my first perambulation of the streets of Madrid, I remarked, with astonishment, the extraordinary number of shops appropriated to the sale of combs. Throughout Spain, but especially in Madrid, the comb is an indispensible and important part of every woman's dress, and a never failing accompaniment of the mantilla. A fashionable Spanish comb is not less than a foot long, and eight or nine inches broad; and no woman considers from nine to fifteen dollars (from 2*l.* to 3*l.*) too much to give for this appendage; accordingly, every tenth shop, at least, is a comb shop. Another very numerous class of shops appeared to belong to booksellers; and a third—shops filled with remnants and shreds of cloth of all kinds and colours, which partly accounts for the patched appearance of the garments of the lowest orders, who doubtless find in these repositories the means of repairing their worn-out clothes. I had one day the curiosity to walk leisurely through two of the principal commercial streets, and to take a note of the different shops they contained. In the *Calle de Carretas*, I found sixteen booksellers, ten venders of combs, three jewellers, two hardware shops, two gold and silver embroiderers, two chocolate shops, two fan shops, six drapers and silk mercers, one woollen draper, one hatter, one perfumer, one fruiterer, one print shop, one wine shop, and one stocking shop. In the *Calle de Montera*, I found eight drapers and silk-mercers, eight jewellers, five hardware shops, four watch-makers, three china and crystal shops, three grocers, five embroiderers, three booksellers, three perfumers, three pawnbrokers, three chocolate shops, two fan shops, four comb shops, four provision shops, two money changers, two venders of ornaments for churches, two glove shops, two shoemakers, two gunsmiths, three venders of cocks and hens, and two of singing birds.

Walking through the streets of Madrid, you are one moment arrested by a pleasant smell, and the next stunned by a bad one; among the former, is the fragrant perfume from the cinnamon to be mixed with the chocolate: at the door of every chocolate shop, a person is to be seen beating cinnamon in a large mortar. Another pleasant smell arises from the heaps of melons that lie on the streets. This custom, by-the-by, of heaping fruit on the street, requires that one unaccustomed to the streets of Madrid should look well to his feet,—melons, oranges, apples, and many other kinds of fruit, lie every where in the way of the passenger, who is in constant danger of being toppled over. Among the bad smells that assail one, the most common, and to me the most offensive, is the smell of oil in preparation for cooking. The

Spanish oil is unpleasant both to the taste and smell; but I have heard well-informed persons say that the fault does not lie in the oil, but in the manner of expressing it; this may probably be true,—the oil of Catalunia is as unpleasant as that of Andalusia, and yet the olives of Catalunia grow in a latitude little different from the most southerly parts of France, from which the most excellent oil is produced. As I have mentioned offensive smells, let me not omit one offensive sight,—I allude to the constant practice of combing and cleaning the hair in the street: in most of the less frequented streets, persons are seen at every second or third door intent upon this employment; and sometimes the occupation includes a scrutiny, at the nature of which the reader must be contented to guess; and even in the most frequented streets, if two women be seated at fruit-stalls near each other, one is generally engaged in combing, assorting, and occasionally scrutinizing the hair of the other. Sights like these neutralize, in some degree, the enjoyment which a stranger might otherwise find in the delicious flavour of Muscatel grapes.

I was prepared to find much more wretchedness and poverty among the lower orders in Madrid, than is apparent—I might perhaps say, than exists there. There is much misery in Madrid, but it lies among a different class, of whom I shall have occasion to speak afterwards: at present, I speak merely of the lowest class of the inhabitants, among whom, in every great city, there is always a certain proportion of miserably poor. I purposely walked several times into the lowest quarters of the city, but I never encountered any such pictures of poverty and wretchedness as are to be found abundantly in Paris, London, Dublin, Manchester, and other great towns of France and England. When the king arrived in Madrid from *La Granja*, there were at least 10,000 persons present at his *entrée*; and upon the occasion of the queen's accouchement, there were three times that number in the court of the palace; and yet I did not see a single person in rags—scarcely even a beggar. It is possible, however, that a cloak may conceal much wretchedness; and of this I had one day an example. Sauntering one morning in the retired part of the Prado, in front of the botanical garden, I sat down upon the low wall that supports the iron railing: a man, with a decent cloak wrapped around him, sat a few paces distant, seemingly in a reverie; he happened to have taken his seat upon some prohibited place, and one of the guards, unperceived by him, walked forward, and tapped him on the shoulder with his musket: whether the sudden start which this intrusion occasioned had unfastened the cloak, or whether he had accidentally let go his hold of it, is of no consequence; but the cloak dropped half off his body, and I discovered that it was his *only* garment, excepting his neckcloth: the man was no beggar; he hastily replaced the cloak, and walked away. He was probably one of that class who, in Madrid, sacrifice all to the exterior; or, possibly, one of those very few Castilians, who yet inherit old Castilian pride, and who would die rather than ask an alms.

But it is not difficult to assign plausible reasons for the fact, that the utterly destitute form but a very trifling proportion of the inhabitants of Madrid. Madrid lives by the court; it is said that the *employées*, including all grades, and the military, form one fourth part of the whole inhabitants. The professional persons, especially those connected with the law, form a large body; the friars and priests, a still larger. In Madrid, too, are assembled the greater number of the nobles and rich proprietors; so that more than one half of the inhabitants live upon their salaries and rents. We have then to consider the great number of tradespeople, artificers, and shopkeepers required to supply the wants of the former classes; add to these, the common labourers, servants, market people, itinerant venders, porters, water carriers, fruiterers, and the seminaries, hospitals, and prisons; and if, as is said to be the case, the employées, the military, the professional men, and all their families, together with priests and friars, amount to 80,000 persons, we may easily account for the other 80,000, without the necessity of filling up a blank with the utterly destitute. Indeed, the lowest orders in Madrid, are the water-carriers and fruiterers; and these are not a fixed population; many belong to the neighbouring villages, and to the fruit countries bordering on the Tagus; and in the winter months, these leave the capital. There is always a resource for the most destitute in Madrid, in the trade of a water-carrier: he weaves a little basket of rushes; pays a couple of reals for a couple of glasses, and he is at once equipped as a vender of aqua fresca. Madrid has no manufacture, so that labour is not attracted to the capital, to be afterwards subject to the vicissitudes of trade; nor is there any spirit of enterprise, whose caprices demand a constant supply of superabundant labour. These may, or may not, be deemed sufficient reasons for the fact I have wished to account for,—the reader may probably be able to add others. The fact, however, is certain, that in no city of Europe ranking with Madrid, is there so little apparent wretchedness.

There is less appearance of business in the streets of Madrid, than in any city I have ever seen: the population seem to have turned out to enjoy themselves. Two things contribute mainly to give that air of ease and pleasure to the pursuits of the inhabitants of Madrid; the great proportion of women of whom the street-population is composed,—and the extreme slowness of movement. The women of Madrid have nothing to detain them at home; the ladies have no home occupations as in London; nor have the majority of the bourgeoises any shop duties to perform as in Paris,—the street is, therefore, their only resource from *ennui*. And there is something in extreme slowness of motion, that is entirely opposed to business and duties,—a quick step, and a necessary one, are closely allied; but the street population of Madrid, with few exceptions, merely saunter; and wherever you reach an open space, especially the *Puerta del Sol*,—a small square in the centre of the city,—hundreds of gentlemen are seen standing, with no other occupation than shaking the dust from their segars. The great numbers of military too, strolling arm in arm, and, above all, the innumerable priests and monks, with whom we at once connect idleness and ease, give to the street population of Madrid an appearance of pleasure seeking, which is peculiar to itself, and is perhaps little removed from truth.

On Sunday, Madrid presents the same aspect as on other days, with this difference, that the shops and the streets are more crowded; and that the lower classes, and the bourgeoises, are better attired. On Sunday evening, the houses are deserted; the whole population of Madrid pours down the *Calle de Alcala*, to the Prado. Every Sunday afternoon, from four o'clock until six or seven, this street, nearly a mile in length, and, at least, twice as broad as Portland Place, is crowded from end to end, and from wall to wall, so that a carriage finds some difficulty in making its way. Among this crowd, I have often looked in vain, to find an ill-dressed person; but this exterior is no real index to the condition of those who throng the Prado. I have reason to know, that hundreds, who by their dress might pass for courtiers, have dined upon bread and a bunch of grapes, and go from the *Paseo* to hide themselves in a garret; and females have been pointed out to me, whose mantilla, comb, and fan could not have cost less than 10*l.*, who were starving upon a pension of 2,500 reals (25*l.*).

As I have mentioned the Calle de Alcala, let me speak of this street as it deserves to be spoken of. I know of no finer entry to any city; I might perhaps say, no one so fine, as that to Madrid by the Calle de Alcala. Standing at the foot of this street, you have on the right and left the long, wide Prado, with its quadruple row of trees stretching in fine perspective to the gates that terminate it; behind is the magnificent gate of Alcala, a fine model of architectural beauty; and before lies the Calle de Alcala, reaching into the heart of the city,—long, of superb width, and flanked by a splendid range of unequal buildings,—among others the hotels of many of the ambassadors; the two fine convents of *Las Calatravas*, and *Las Ballecas*, and the Custom-house. But the Calle de Alcala is the only really fine street in Madrid; many of the other streets are good, and very many respectable, of tolerable width, and the houses lofty and well built; but there is no magnificent street, excepting the Calle de Alcala. Like all the other cities in Spain, the streets, abstracted from the population, have a sombre aspect, owing to the number of convents, whose long reach of wall, grated windows, and lack of doors, throw a chill over the mind of the passer by. There are no fewer than sixty-two convents for men and women in Madrid; and it frequently happens that one side of a whole street is occupied by a convent: in the *Calle de Atocha* there are no fewer than eight convents; and some of the streets on the outskirts, contain scarcely any houses, but those dedicated to religion.

Walking one day in company with a priest,—a very intelligent and learned man, of whose society I was always glad,—I chanced to observe the inscription upon the corner of one of the streets, and read *Calle de la Inquisicion*; my curiosity was immediately awakened; I had intended before leaving Madrid, to have sought out the spot memorable from the atrocities with which it is connected; and this accidental *rencontre* saved me the trouble of a search. I immediately expressed my anxiety to see the building, and to enter it if possible; and requested my companion to have the goodness to be my *Cicerone*; but I found that the terrors of the Inquisition had outlived its power; my companion assured me there was nothing to see; the building he believed was shut up, and no one could enter; indeed he doubted if he perfectly knew where the building was situated. I saw the difficulty of the priest; there might be danger in guiding a heretic to the precincts of the holy office; and so, requesting him to wait for me, I went in search of the building. I had no difficulty in finding it, but there was little to reward my search; it was the building in which prisoners were confined, but not that in which they were judged and tortured. This was in an immediately adjoining street, formerly called the street of the Grand Inquisitor, whose house, including all the offices of the court, fills almost one side of the street. It seems at first sight surprising, that the Inquisition, like the Bastile, was not torn down during the time of the Constitution; but the prime movers, and even the instruments in that revolution, were of the upper ranks; and it is a certain fact, that many among the *Pueblo Bajo* look even now without any horror, some with veneration, upon the building once dedicated to the maintenance of the Roman Catholic faith. The building used as the prison of the Inquisition, was constructed above immense vaults, originally formed by the Moors; and afterwards converted into dungeons. I requested permission to visit them, but I was told that the air in the dungeons was such as to render a visit to them unsafe.

From the prisons I went to the other branch of the Inquisition in the adjoining street. A part of the house of the Grand Inquisitor is in a dilapidated state, but other parts are inhabited by private individuals. The porter, notwithstanding a liberal bribe, made much difficulty in allowing me to enter, but I at last prevailed with him, and he conducted me to the room formerly used as the hall of justice, or rather of judgment; and although I saw nothing but a long gloomy room without one article of furniture, it required but little exercise of imagination to see, in fancy, the Inquisitors and their satellites, the trembling accused, and the instruments of torture. It appears incredible, that any others than those to whom its existence would bring power or wealth, should desire the re-establishment of the Inquisition; and yet, I feel myself justified in believing, that many would look upon its restoration with complacency; and that the great majority of the lower orders would behold this with perfect indifference. If so, they deserve to be cursed with it.

The dirtiness and want of comfort in the *Cruz de Malta*, would have driven me into private lodgings, even if the charges in the hotel had been supportable; I hastened therefore to deliver my letters, that I might be aided in my search by those to whom I carried recommendations; and by the kind assistance of Sr. Mozo, one of the *Conséjeros del Rey*, I was soon established in comfortable apartments in the *Calle de la Madalena*. It may be interesting to some, to know the nature and price of private accommodation in Madrid. My apartments were on the second floor, (in Madrid every floor is a separate house, excepting among the very highest ranks) and consisted of one very large room, 40 feet long, by 22 broad, with two very large windows facing the street; a small bed-room, separated from this large room by a glass door; and another small room, beyond the bed-room, to be employed as an eating room. These rooms were brick-floored, as every room is, in the northern and central parts of Spain; and the walls white-washed. The apartments were furnished with basket-chairs and sofas, a bed, and two or three tables; and for this accommodation, including service and cooking, I paid 20 reals per day, or 1*l.* 9*s.* 2*d.* per week. This was certainly not remarkably cheap; but the situation was good, and the rooms were clean and airy.

Being thus established in lodgings, my first duty was to find the hotel of the British minister, and to present to him my letter of introduction from Lord Aberdeen; and I gladly avail myself of this opportunity to express my obligations to Henry Unwin Addington, Esq.; not only for his uniform kindness and attention while we remained in Madrid, and for the often repeated hospitalities of his house; but for his readiness to assist me in whatever way the representative of the British Government could make his interest available in forwarding my objects. For some lesser favours, I am also Mr. Addington's debtor; among others, the privilege of perusing the English newspapers, no small privilege in a country where the only journal is the *Gaceta de Madrid*. Walking one day towards my lodgings, with a file of *Couriers* in my hand, I noticed that I was followed, and narrowly scrutinized by some persons in authority; but they, no doubt, became informed where I procured this forbidden fruit, and I never suffered any farther interruption.

The day after my arrival in Madrid was Sunday, and having finished my puchero, and drank a reasonable quantity of *Val de Peñas*, I prepared to join the tide that was slowly rolling towards the Prado.

Every Spaniard is proud of the Prado at Madrid; and but for the Prado, the inhabitants of Madrid would look upon life as a thing of very little value; every body goes every night to the Prado; every body—man, woman, and child—looks forward to the evening promenade with pleasure and impatience; every body asks every body the same question, shall you be on the Paseo to night? how did you like the Paseo last night? every night, at the same hour, the dragoons take their place along the Prado, to regulate the order and line of carriages: and the only difference between Sunday night and any other night on the Prado is, that on Sunday it is frequented by those who can afford to dress only once a week, as well as by those who can dress every day. It was impossible that I could permit the first Sunday to pass away without seeing the Prado; accordingly, accompanied by a colonel in the Spanish service, whose name, for certain reasons, I refrain from mentioning, I took the road to the Prado.

The Prado, divested of its living attraction, is certainly not entitled to the extravagant praises bestowed upon it by the Spaniards: it is a fine spacious *paseo*, at least two miles long, and from 200 to 300 yards broad, adorned with rows of trees, and with several fountains; the frequented part, however, is not more than half a mile in length, and has scarcely any shade. But the Prado, although in itself not possessing the natural attractions of that of Vienna, or perhaps of some others, is an admirable resort for a stranger who is desirous of seeing the population of Madrid. When I reached it, it seemed already crowded, though a dense stream of population was still pouring into it from the *Calle de Alcala*. On the part appropriated to carriages, there was already a double row of vehicles, bespeaking, by their slow motion, the stateliness of character said to belong to the Spanish aristocracy. The turn-out of carriages presented a strange *melange* of elegance and shabbiness; some few were as handsome as can be seen in Hyde Park; some—truly Spanish,—were entirely covered over with gilding and painting; many were like worn-out post chaises; and several like the old family pieces that are yet sometimes to be seen at the church door on Sunday, in some remote parishes in England, I observed the most ludicrous incongruity between the carriages and the servants; many a respectable, and even handsome carriage might be seen with a servant behind, like some street vagabond who, seeing a vacant place, had mounted for the sake of a drive. I actually saw a tolerably neat carriage driven by a coachman *without stockings*; and another with a rheumatic lacquey behind, whose head was enveloped in flannel. But let me turn to the pedestrians.

The Paseo was crowded from end to end, and from side to side; so crowded, indeed, that by mixing with the tide, it was impossible to see more than one's next neighbour; and that I might better observe the elements of the crowd, I contrived, with some difficulty, to extricate myself from the stream, and get into the carriage drive. Before visiting Spain, I had heard much of the beauty of Spanish women,—their graceful figures,—their bewitching eyes,—their fascinating expression,—in short, their personal attractions. Whether owing to the representations of travellers, or the unreal descriptions of poets, or the romance with which, in the minds of many, every thing in Spain is invested,—it is certain, that a belief in the witchery of Spanish women obtains very general credence in England. With curiosity, therefore, considerably excited, I took up a station to decide upon the claims of the ladies of Spain. In my expectations of beauty I was miserably disappointed; beauty of features I saw none. Neither at that time, nor at any subsequent visit to the Prado, did I ever see one strikingly lovely countenance; and the class so well known in England, because so numerous, denominated "pretty girls," has no existence in Spain. The women were, without exception, dark,—but the darkness of the clear brunette, is darkness of a very different kind from that of the Castilian. I saw no fine skin, no glossy hair: dark expressive eyes I certainly did see, but they were generally too ill supported to produce much effect. But let me do justice to the grace of the Spanish women. No other woman knows how to walk,—the elegant, light, and yet firm step of the small and well attired foot and ancle,—the graceful bearing of the head and neck,—the elegant disposition of the arms, never to be seen hanging downward, but one hand holding the folds of the mantilla, just below the waist; the other inclining upward, wielding, with an effect the most miraculous, that mysterious instrument, the fan,—these are the charms of the Spanish women. As for the fan, its powers are no where seen displayed to such advantage as on the Prado. I believe I shall never be able to look at a fan in the hands of any other than a Spanish woman,—certainly no other woman understands the management of it. In her hands it is never one moment at rest,—she throws it open, fans herself, furls it to the right,—opens it again, again fans herself, and furls it to the left, and all with three fingers of one hand. This is absolutely marvellous to one who has been accustomed to see a fan opened with both hands, and furled only on one side. But that I may at once exhaust the subject of fans, let me add, that in the hands of its true mistress, the fan becomes a substitute for language, and an interpreter of etiquette. If a lady perceives that she is an object of attention to some inquisitive and admiring *caballero*, she has immediate recourse to her fan, that she may convey to him one most important piece of information. If she be married, she fans herself slowly; if still señorita, rapidly. The caballero, therefore, at once ascertains his chances and his risks. This fact I obtained from a Spanish lady of rank in Madrid, the wife of a gentleman in a high official situation. The motion of the fan too, marks distinctly, and with the utmost nicety, the degree of intimacy that subsists between one lady and another. The shake of the fan is the universal acknowledgment of acquaintance; and according as the fan is open or shut, the intimacy is great or small. These are trifling things, yet they are worth telling. But let me return to the Prado, where, having decided upon the claims of the Castilian ladies, I had leisure to observe its other novelties. Here I saw little of the sombreness I had remarked on the streets, for many of the ladies wore white mantillas; and in the evening, coloured rather than black gowns are the *mode*. The very great number, too, of officers of the guards, with their high cocked hats, and coats entirely covered with silver lace, gave additional animation to the scene. Other pictures of a different kind the eye occasionally caught,—here and there a portly priest, with his ample gown and great slouched hat, mingling in the throng, and evidently enjoying the scene and its gaiety,— aloof from the crowd, and in the most retired walks, with hurried step and downcast head, a friar, in his grey, brown or white cassock,—now and then a tall Andalusian peasant, with his tapering hat, his velvet and silver embroidered jacket and crimson sash, his unbuttoned gaiters and white stockings,—the Asturian nurse, with her short brown jerkin, petticoat of blue and yellow, trimmed with gold, and bare head. It is always a mark of a woman's consequence in Madrid to hire an Asturian nurse; they are supposed to be models of health and strength, and certainly if breadth of figure be the criterion of these, the ladies of Madrid make a prudent choice: I never saw such women as the women of the Asturias. In France, where the women are generally *mince*, one of them might be exhibited as a curiosity.

There is one very unpleasant thing connected with a promenade on the Prado, whether in a carriage or on foot; this is the necessity of paying honour to every branch of the royal family, however frequently they may pass along. Every carriage must stop, and those within must take off their hats, or if the carriage be open stand up also; and every person on foot is expected to suspend his walk, face-about, and bow, with his head uncovered. When the king passes, no one perhaps feels this to be a grievance; because, however little respect the king may in reality be entitled to from his subjects, it is felt to be nothing more than an act of common good breeding to take off one's hat to a king; but I have fifty times seen all this homage paid to a royal carriage with a nurse and an infant—not an *infanta*—in it; and one evening I was absolutely driven from the Prado by the unceasing trouble of being obliged to acknowledge the royal presence every few minutes, the spouse of the Infante Don Francis having found amusement in cantering backward and forward during an hour at least. From the expected homage, no one is exempt: even the foreign ambassadors must draw up, rise, and uncover themselves, if but a sprig of royalty in the remotest degree, and of the tenderest age, happens to drive past. Both the British and the American Minister told me, that for that reason they never went to the Prado.

The promenade continues long after dark; and on fine moonlight nights in the month of September, I have seen it continued without any diminution in the crowd until after ten o'clock; generally, however, when dusk begins to usher in darkness, and when the great object of going to the Prado is accomplished,—seeing and being seen—the crowd thins, and there is soon no remnant of it visible, excepting pairs, or single individuals, here and there, who have their reasons for remaining. In Madrid,—indeed throughout all Spain, nobody walks for pleasure; at all events no woman: and this fact is I think sufficient to account for the superiority of the Spanish women in the art of walking, without making it necessary for us to suppose any deficiency in elegance of limb or symmetry of form among the women of other countries. An Englishwoman walks for health; she puts on her bonnet, and a pair of strong shoes, and a shawl, and walks into the country; and the nature of the climate creates a necessity for walking fast; there is no one to look at her, and she thinks of nothing so little as her manner of walking: but a Spanish woman never walks for health or exercise; she never goes out but to go to the Paseo, and never without having paid the most scrupulous attention to her toilette. On the Paseo, she studies every step, because the object of going there is to be seen and admired, and the nature of the climate, obliges her to walk slow.

My evening walk in Madrid was more frequently to the *Retiro* than to the Prado; this is a vast and ill-laid out garden and shrubbery, three or four miles in circumference, situated upon an elevation behind the Prado, the entrance to which is by the court of the old palace, which was destroyed daring the war. The Retiro possesses no particular attraction, excepting its fresh air, and freedom from dust. There are some elevations in this garden, from which an extensive prospect is enjoyed; but it embraces little that is interesting, excepting the city, and the skies—an object of no small interest to one accustomed to the dense atmosphere and cloudy heavens of a northern latitude. During the several months that I remained in Madrid, I scarcely ever saw a cloud; and I frequently walked to the Retiro for the sole purpose of looking at the glorious sky, and the gorgeous sun-set: such skies are glorious, even when they canopy a desert. From the Retiro, the eye ranges over nothing but a desert, bounded on one side by the *Siérra Guadarama*, on the other by the Toledo mountains; and Madrid, standing alone in the midst of this treeless and lifeless plain, seemed, when the setting sun flamed upon its domes and spires, to have been placed there by enchantment.

Returning from the Prado, or the Retiro, I frequently stepped into the Café de *Santa Catalina*, the most brilliant place of the kind in Madrid, and generally resorted to after the promenade, by many of the most distinguished persons. I greatly prefer this *café* to any in Paris; to any, indeed, that I have seen elsewhere. You pass through a magnificent and brilliantly illuminated room, where those who love the light are assembled, into an open court,—open to the skies above, but surrounded by the backs of lofty buildings; a covered arcade runs round the court, dimly lighted by suspended lamps, to meet the taste of those who desire a certain quantity of light and no more. But this light scarcely reaches the centre of the court, which is illuminated only by the stars; and here, as well as under the arcade, tables and chairs are placed for those who are indifferent about light. All sorts of refreshments suited to a warm climate, are to be found in this café; and rows of sweet smelling flowers in pots, add to the luxury of the place. It may easily be believed, that the Café Catalina is celebrated on other accounts than for the excellence of the refreshments which it furnishes. In the illuminated room, all is mirth and gaiety: the ladies, escaped from the monotony, and proprieties, and etiquette of the Prado, give way to their natural liveliness and wit; and accept, with smiling looks of conscious merit, and with quick flutterings of the fan, the proffered courtesies and gallantry of the caballeros who escort them. In the court, the scene is different: within the arcade, quieter parties are seated, enjoying a sort of half-seclusion; while, throughout the centre, are scattered, pairs in conversation; and the light of a lamp, as it occasionally flashes upon their privacy,—revealing a sparkling eye, and the flutter of a fan,—interprets its nature. The use of the *toledo* or the *bravo*, to avenge private wrongs among the upper ranks, is now comparatively unknown in Spain; else I should often have run some risk, by strolling leisurely through the centre of the Café Catalina, that I might get some insight into the state of Castilian morals.

There is a great paucity of cafés in Madrid; excepting the Café de Santa Catalina, and another, the name of which I forget, in the neighbourhood of the Prado, there is only the *Fontaña de Oro* in the *Calle de San Geronimo*. But it is not likely that there should be many coffee-houses in a country where there are no newspapers. Both in France and in England, the majority of persons who frequent coffee-houses, go to read the newspapers; but in Spain, no one enters a coffee-room except to sip iced water. During the forenoon, indeed, the doors of the cafés, excepting the Fontaña de Oro, are generally shut, and nobody is within. An Englishman, or a Frenchman, who is accustomed to connect with a coffee-room,—half-a-dozen public journals,—organs of intelligence and public opinion, upon subjects connected with his political rights, and with the state of his country,—is instantly reminded on entering a Spanish coffee-room, of the degraded political condition of the country he is in: and the difference between the enjoyment and the want of political rights, is forcibly thrust upon him. He takes up the *Gaceta de Madrid*, and finds there a royal ordinance, breathing vengeance against those who desire to be restored to their homes and their country; and whose prayers are for its happiness. He turns over the leaf, and he finds another ordinance, declaring that the universities shall be closed, and education suspended, during his Majesty's pleasure; and he then looks for the comment upon these facts: but he looks in vain. He sees that his Majesty and the royal family enjoy good health; that the king has appointed a bishop to one cathedral; and that the bishop has named a canon to another; and that the procession of *St. Rosalio* will issue from the convent of St. Thomas, precisely at four o'clock next day; but he sees not a syllable about the ordinances that deal out injustice, or strangle improvement; and he says within himself, this is the most wonderful country under the sun; for here, intellect wields no power.

Before dismissing the Paseos of Madrid, I must notice the Botanical Garden; not much used as a Paseo, but certainly the most charming of them all. While I remained in Madrid, waiting until the heats had so far subsided as to allow me to journey into Andalusia, I generally walked there during an hour or two after breakfast, having access to it at all times, through the interest of a friend. The garden is very extensive; the trees are full-grown; and there is a charming variety of rare and beautiful plants. The garden, although not by any means neglected, is not in such perfect order, or under such excellent management as it was during the time of the constitution: it was then under the direction of *S^r. La Gasca*, Professor of Botany, and a Member of the *Cortes*; now a resident in England, where I believe his learning is appreciated as it deserves. There is a curious and very unmeaning regulation, connected with the *entrée* of this garden. Every lady, on entering, must throw aside her mantilla, and walk with the head uncovered; she is not even allowed to drop it upon her neck; it must be carried upon the arm. This regulation is almost an order of exclusion to a Spanish woman, who considers the proper arrangement of the mantilla no trifling or easy matter, and not to be accomplished without the aid of a mirror; it is rarely, therefore, that a Spanish woman subjects herself to a regulation by which she runs the risk of afterwards appearing on the Paseo with her mantilla awry.

The only occasion upon which a Spaniard absents himself from the Paseo, is when he goes to the theatre. The inhabitants of Madrid are a theatre-going population; but their propensities that way are sadly cramped for want of room; if, however, the theatre now erecting in the neighbourhood of the palace be ever finished—a point certainly doubtful, since the palace itself makes no progress towards completion—half Madrid will find accommodation in it, and have the honour of being seated in the largest theatre in Europe. I should probably not have visited the theatre so soon, if the road from my lodgings to the Calle de Alcala had not led me daily past the theatre, where I generally stopped a moment to read "the bills of the play." These, as in the olden times in England, set forth the merits of the play,—narrate a few of the principal events,—tell how, in one act, there is a most witty dialogue,—and how, in another, there is a scene which must delight every body; and conclude with some eulogy upon the genius of the writer. The first visit I made to the theatre was to witness the representation of a comedy by *Solis*, to be acted in the *Teatro del Principe*. I walked in and took my seat without any one asking for my ticket, which is not demanded until the play is nearly concluded; so that a lover of the theatre, who might be scarce of money, might gratify his appetite for nothing.

The Teatro del Principe is miserably small for a metropolitan theatre: it will contain no more than 1500 persons; but it is light and pretty, painted in white and gold, and round the ceiling are the busts of the principal Spanish poets, dramatists and novelists, their names being inscribed under each. The six in front are no doubt intended to occupy the most honourable places: they are Calderon, Lopez de Vega, Cervantes, Garcilaso, Ercillo, and Tirso. Calderon and Lopez are placed in the front, where I think Cervantes ought to have been. The house was well filled; the ladies generally wore mantillas, but some were in full dress; and a few had ventured upon French hats. There is one peculiarity in the Spanish theatres, which seems at first sight, inconsistent with the state of society and manners. Excepting the private boxes, there is scarcely any place to which a lady and a gentleman can go in company. In Madrid the only places of this description will not contain thirty persons; but, on the other hand, an ample provision is made for ladies. The greater part of the space occupied by the first tier of boxes in the English theatres, is thrown into one space, called the *cazuela*; and here, ladies, and only ladies, have the right of entrée. The most respectable women go to the cazuela, and sit there unattended; nor is this arrangement unfavourable to intrigue. The entrée to the cazuela secures the entrée of the whole house; and between the acts the cazuela is almost deserted, some having gone to visit persons in the boxes, but the greater number getting no farther than the lobby, where it is not unusual to meet a friend; and when the comedy ends, every lady finds an escort ready. It is a fact too, that if the cazuela be crowded during the first act, there is generally room enough during the second, and more than enough during the third. This needs no explanation.

I saw only one really beautiful countenance in the theatre; but there were some expressive faces, and inexpressibly fine eyes, almost worthy of a serenade. Here, the fan seemed a most indispensible companion; for besides its common uses, it exercised the powers of a critic, expressing approbation or dislike; and between the acts, it proved itself a powerful auxiliary to the language of the eyes.

The play, like most of the Spanish comedies, was a piece of intrigue, plot within plot, and abounding in strange situations, and innumerable perplexities and difficulties, scarcely to be comprehended by a spectator unless possessing a previous knowledge of the piece; and to be thoroughly enjoyed by a Spaniard only. The acting was spirited, the dresses characteristic, and the orchestra not contemptible; and the satisfaction of the audience was shewn in immoderate bursts of laughter.

The play being ended, the next part of the entertainment consisted in the *Bolero*. This is danced by two persons; the man, in the dress of an Andalusian peasant—for to Andalusia the dance properly belongs—with dark embroidered jacket, short white embroidered waistcoat, crimson sash, white tight small clothes, white stockings, and the hair in a black silk knot; his partner in a gaudy dress of red, embroidered with gold. These are nothing more than the usual holiday-dresses of the Andalusian peasantry. The dance itself, is a quick minuet; advancing, retiring, and turning; the feet all the time performing a step, and the hands occupied with the castanets. I had heard much of the indelicacy of the Bolero, but I could find nothing in it in the slightest degree indecorous. The dance is long, at least it is often repeated; three or four times the dancing ceases, the music continuing, and the dancers standing opposite to each other; and after a short interval, the entertainment is resumed.

At this theatre, and at the *Teatro de la Cruz*, Italian operas are performed twice a week; sometimes at the one theatre, and sometimes at the other; a very bad arrangement, because it forces the lover of Italian music to have a box in both houses; and after all, one is apt to make a mistake as to the house in which the opera is performed. The Italian opera is a losing concern in Madrid; the prices are too low, and the house is not large enough to ensure a return. The star, when I was in Madrid, was a *Signora Tossi*, who received no less than 1,200*l.* sterling to perform three nights a week for five months. This Signora Tossi was a remarkable favourite in Madrid; she performed in an opera which had been written expressly for her; and when this opera was announced, the house would have been filled even if it had been three times larger. Nothing could gain admittance but bribery; if one inquired for a ticket, the answer invariably was, that all were sold: but if one chose to add, "I would give a handsome gratuity for a ticket," a ticket was produced, and an additional dollar given for it. Upon this occasion the corregidor of Madrid pocketed as many as 40 or 50 dollars a day by trafficking in tickets; he bought 40 or 50 tickets before the theatre opened, and sold them during the day at different prices, according to the demand. So great was the rage for the opera, and so great the dearth of tickets, that the most disgraceful means were resorted to in order to gain admittance: one evening I myself saw two persons detected with forged tickets. The excellence of the Opera of Madrid last season, almost excused the madness,—not the meanness of the public. Tossi, I thought a great singer: she resembles Catalini more nearly than any one I have ever heard; but she possesses more sweetness and melody of tone; and is a better actress, and a finer woman than Catalini ever was. The other vocal parts were well supported, and the orchestra, with a hint and a rebuke now and then from Tossi, acquitted itself well. The prices of the theatres in Madrid are as moderate as the poorest amateur could desire; the best places in the house are to be had for 2*s.* 6*d.*, and very excellent seats cost but 1*s.* 3*d.*; the public benches in the pit are only 10*d.*

The existence of a good Italian opera in Madrid, and the easy access to it, have no doubt had some effect in fostering a taste for music, especially Italian music. Spain, with all its sins, has not to answer for the sin of neglecting the fine arts. There are at this moment four Italian operas in Spain: in Madrid,—in Malaga, in Granada, and in Barcellona; and this is fewer than usual; for Cadiz and Seville can also generally boast of an Italian company; and wherever there is an operatic company, there is also a company of comedians. I shall have occasion afterwards, to notice the operas of Malaga, Granada, and Barcellona; at present I confine myself to Madrid. There, music is universally cultivated; and it is rare to find a Spanish woman, even in the middle ranks, who is not a good pianist. The music of Rossini, set to the piano, is the most in vogue; but the German masters also are known to many,—and justice is done to them. That instrument so interwoven with our ideas of Spain—the guitar, is now little cultivated in Castile by the higher or middle ranks; it is in the southern provinces, and in some of the more retired Spanish towns, such as Toledo, that the guitar still maintains its power, and exercises its witcheries. In Madrid too, in the evening, the lower orders are frequently seen sitting at their doors thrumming their guitars; and I have more than once observed a soldier sitting before the guard-house with his guitar, while his comrades sat on the ground listening, and joining in the chorus. If the ladies of Madrid know how to play the guitar, they refrain from displaying their knowledge. The piano is their instrument, and they do it justice. In vocal music, the ladies of Madrid are not proficients; there is a want of melody in their voices which forbids excellence. This roughness in the voices of the Spanish women, forcibly strikes a stranger upon his first entrance into Spanish society, and is felt to be disagreeable even in conversation: of its effect in vocal performance, one has rarely an opportunity of judging.

In Madrid, Spanish music is not much cultivated,—this is a pity; for although it knows neither operatic performances, nor any compositions of a sustained character, it owns many beautiful and original airs, well worthy of being preserved. A collection of these has lately, I believe, been published in England, accompanied with some charming poetry, from the pens of Mrs. Hemans and Dr. Bowring.—These are to be heard in the theatres, and occasionally in the mouths of the lower orders. If a lady be requested to play a Spanish air, she will comply; but otherwise, she will always prefer Italian music.

CHAPTER IV.

MADRID.

The King, Queen, and Royal Family; Personal Appearance of Ferdinand; a Royal *Jeu d'esprit*; the King's Confidence in the People, and Examples; Character of the King; a Carlist's Opinion of the King; Favourites,—Calomarde,—Alegon,—Salsedo,—the Duque d'Higar; rising Influence of the Queen; Habits of the Royal Family; Court Diversions; Rivalry of Don Carlos; the Queen's Accouchement, and Views of Parties; Detection of a Carlist Plot; the Salic Law; Court Society; Persons of Distinction, and Ministerial Tertulias; Habits and Manner of Life of the Middle Classes; a Spanish House, and its singular Defences; Abstemiousness of the Spaniards; Evening and Morning Visits; Balls and Spanish Dancing; Character of Spanish Hospitality; Spanish Generosity and its origin; Examples of Ostentation; Morals; Gallantry and Intrigue; the Morals of the Lower Orders; Religious Opinions in the Capital, and decline of Priestly Influence; Jesuitical Education; the Influence of the Friars; Causes of the decline of Priestly influence, and the continuance of that of the Friars; Convent Secrets; curious Exposé at Cadiz; Devotion in Madrid.

THERE is perhaps no European Court about which so little is known, as the Court of Madrid,—nor any European sovereign whose character and habits are so little familiar to us, as those of Ferdinand VII. The first time I saw the king, was on the day of my arrival in Madrid: he was expected to return from *St. Ildefonso*, and I mixed with the crowd in the palace-yard about an hour before he appeared. There were several thousand persons present, of all ranks, and his Majesty was received with respect, but with no audible demonstrations of welcome. Upon this occasion, I was not sufficiently near to observe the countenance and demeanour of the king.

The next time I saw his majesty, was on the Prado, the Sunday following, when he appeared in his state equipage, followed by the equipages of the two Infantes. The display was regal: his majesty's carriage was worthy of a more powerful monarch: it was drawn by eight handsome horses, elegantly caparisoned, and was followed by the two carriages of Don Carlos and Don Francis, and by that of the Princess of Portugal, each drawn by six horses; and the cavalcade was attended by a numerous party of huzzars. There were no other persons than their Majesties in the royal carriage. The king was dressed in military uniform, and his royal consort wore a pink French crape hat, and printed muslin gown. When the royal cavalcade passed, the king was received with the usual silent tokens of respect; but when the carriage of the infante Don Carlos appeared, I could distinguish a few *vivas*. The king took scarcely any notice of the obeisances of his subjects; but the queen seemed anxious to conciliate their favour by many sweet smiles and affable bendings of the head. As for Don Carlos, none of the *vivas* were lost upon him: he had a bow and a grim smile for every one. It is said, and I believe with truth, that the king does not like this public competition with his brother for popular favour; but it has long been the invariable custom for all the branches of the royal family of Spain, to attend prayers every Sunday evening in the royal chapel in the convent of *San Geronimo*, and afterwards to drive along the Prado.

A few days afterwards I met the king and queen in the Retiro, on foot; they had been viewing the menagerie, and were returning to their carriage. Ferdinand VII. king of Spain, is like a lusty country gentleman, not the meagre figure he appears in Madame Tassaud's exhibition; he is large, almost to the extent of corpulency; his countenance is fat and heavy; but good natured, with nothing of *hauteur*, still less of ferocity in it: it betrays, in fact, a total want of character of any kind. The queen is a remarkably pleasing, and, indeed, a remarkable pretty woman; and the charm of affability, which is universally granted to her by those who have had the honour to approach her person, shines conspicuously in her countenance: she looks like 28 years of age, but I believe she is some years younger. The king took little notice of the people who stood by, and who acknowledged the royal presence; but the queen bestowed upon them her usual smiles and curtesies. She was then an object of much interest with the public, for she was expected shortly to give birth to an heir to the Spanish throne; and to this event, most thinking persons looked forward, as one that must produce an important influence upon the future condition of Spain. His majesty stepped into the carriage first, leaving the queen to the gallantry of an old general, who was their only attendant,—perhaps this is Spanish court etiquette: but that I may not be the means of fixing upon his majesty the character of an ungallant monarch, I must relate a circumstance that will certainly make amends for this seemingly ungracious act.

I happened to be walking one day in the Calle de Alcala, when the royal carriage drove up to the door of the Cabinet of Natural History, and being close by, I stopped to see the king and queen. The king stepped from the carriage first; he then lifted from the carriage, a very large poodle dog, and then the queen followed, whom, contrary no doubt to royal etiquette, his majesty did not hand, but lifted, and placed on the pavement; and then turning to the crowd who surrounded the carriage, he said to them "*Pesa menos el matrimonio*," which means, Matrimony is a lighter burden than the dog,—a very tolerable *jeu d'esprit* to have come from Ferdinand VII.

It is a general belief in England, that the king of Spain seldom trusts himself out of his palace; at all events, not without a formidable guard: but this idea is quite erroneous; no monarch in Europe is oftener seen without guards than the king of Spain. I could give numerous instances of this, which have fallen under my own observation; but I shall content myself with one. A few days before leaving Madrid, while walking in the Retiro about six in the evening, in one of the most private walks, I observed a lusty gentleman, in blue coat and drab trowsers, with one companion, about twenty paces in advance; and, as my pace was rather quicker than their's, I caught a side look of the lusty gentleman's face: it was the king, accompanied by a new valet, who had just succeeded Meris, who died a week or two before, of apoplexy. I had frequently seen the king without guards; but never before, at so great a distance from attendants, or in so retired a place; and that I might be quite certain that this was indeed the redoubtable Ferdinand, I followed, in place of passing. He walked the whole length of the Retiro, parts of which are more than a mile from any guard or gate; the garden is open to every body; some of the walks are extremely secluded; so that he was the whole of the time, entirely in the power of any individual who might have harboured a design against him; and all this struck me the more forcibly since, upon that very day, it had been announced for the first time in the *Gaceta de Madrid*, that the refugees had passed the frontier; and in the same paper the ordinance had appeared, for closing the universities. The king walked like a man who had nothing to fear; and never once looked behind him, though his companion occasionally did. Before making the circuit of the Retiro, he reached the frequented walks, which were then crowded, and where he was of course recognized, and received as usual. This exposure of himself seemed to me extraordinary, and scarcely to be accounted for: the best of kings have occasionally suffered by their temerity; and surely Ferdinand can have no right to suppose himself without an enemy: his conduct shewed either a very good, or a very hardened conscience.

But, in truth, the king has not many enemies; many despise him, but few would injure him. I have heard men of all parties,—the warmest Carlists, the most decided liberals, speak of him without reserve; and all speak of him as a man whose greatest fault is want of character; as a man not naturally bad; good tempered; and who might do better, were he better advised. An honest adviser, a lover of his monarch, and a lover of his country, Ferdinand has never had the good fortune to possess; but, counselled always by men who desire only to enrich themselves, and to maintain their power, he is constantly led to commit acts both of injustice and despotism, which have earned for him the character of tyrant. A despicable king might often make a respectable private gentleman. That capital failing in the character of an absolute king, which may be called want of character,—leading him to listen to every tale that is told,—is the fruitful source of injustice in every department of the Spanish government. And the same fault that in a king, leads to the advancement of knaves, and the neglect of deserving men—to robbery of the nation, and the ill-serving of the state, would, in a private sphere, only lead to the dismissal of a footman, or the change of a fruiterer. I am acquainted with a Colonel in the Spanish service, who, after serving his country fifteen years, and receiving seventeen wounds, was rewarded with the government of an important fortress; two months after being appointed to this employment he lost it; and a distant connexion of the mistress of one of the ministers, was put in his place. The colonel demanded, and obtained an audience of the king; shewed his wounds, and asked what crime he had committed: the king said he must inquire of *Salmon*, who had told something to his disadvantage; and this was all the satisfaction he ever obtained. This man, a brave officer, and a loyal subject, was converted into a disaffected person; and yet even he, although then leagued with the Carlists, spoke of the king as a man who would act better if he were better advised: "Leave him," said he, "the name of king; let him perceive no difference in the externals of royalty; leave him his secretaries and valets; give him his segar; and let him have his wife's apartments at hand; and he would consent to any change that might be proposed to him by an honest and able minister." A bad education has produced its worst effects upon a naturally irresolute and rather weak mind. Ferdinand was badly brought up, by his mother; at an early age he was shamefully kidnapped by Napoleon, and long kept a prisoner, where he could learn nothing of the art of good government. He afterwards fell into the hands of a bigot, his late wife: and constantly assured by those around him of the precariousness of his throne, with the liberals on one side, and the apostolicals on the other, he has felt the impossibility of acting for himself; and has confided all, to those who have undertaken to keep the state vessel afloat.

The man who has most the ear of the king, is Don Francisco Tudeo Calomarde, minister of justice, as he is called in Spain. The private opinions of Calomarde, are decidedly apostolical; but the opinions of his colleagues being more moderate, he is obliged to conceal his sentiments, and to pretend an accordance with theirs. The ministers who are reputed to be moderate in sentiment are Don Luis Ballasteros, minister of finance; Don Luis Maria Salagar, minister of marine, and generally considered the most able in the cabinet; and Don Manuel Gonsalez Salmon, secretary of state, and nominally prime minister. This minister, for several years, held only the office of *interim* secretary of state; because, as was generally believed, etiquette forcing the king to take the prime minister along with him to his country palace, the advancement of Salmon would have deprived Calomarde of this privilege: lately, however, Salmon has been named secretary of state without reserve, probably because he would not serve upon other conditions; or, according to another version, because he threatened Calomarde with some *exposé* if he opposed his advancement.

Calomarde, unquestionably no fool, is understood to keep all together; the minister of the marine is the only other man of talent, and he is a new man, possessing little influence, and who could not, for a moment, support himself against Calomarde; he was only a few months ago presented with the rank of general, that etiquette might enable him to hold some office with which the king wished to reward his services.

But Calomarde had not the king's undivided ear; and, if report speak truly, he has tale-telling and cabal to encounter, as well as those in inferior stations. There are two other individuals who, without high state offices, possess great private influence, and are generally looked upon in the light of favourites. These are the Duque de Alegon and Salsedo. The former was appointed last autumn to the office of captain-general of the guard; an office that keeps him much about the king's person. This Alegon is a dissipated old man, long known to the king, and who used, in former days, to pander to his pleasures; the king has never forgotten the convenient friend of his younger days, and has now thought of rewarding him. The services of the Duque de Alegon refer to many years back. Before the king wedded his bigot wife, not affection, but religious fear kept him faithful during that connexion; and now, the love he bestows upon the young queen, entirely supersedes any call upon the services of Alegon.

The other individual, who is justly considered the royal favourite, *par excellence*, is Salsedo, who holds the office of private secretary. A dishonourable link formerly bound him to his sovereign, and he still retains his influence. It is generally known, that previous to the marriage of the king with his present wife, the wife of Salsedo was in royal favour. Salsedo is decidedly a man of good tact, if not of talent; his having retained his post fourteen years is some proof of both. His principles are understood to be moderate; at all events his advice is so, for he has sense to perceive that an opposite policy would probably accelerate the ruin of both his master and himself. Salsedo possesses more influence in the closet than Calomarde,— the king likes him better, and confides in him more. The influence of Calomarde is not favouritism; the king looks to his opinion, because he trusts to his knowledge. There are still one or two others who have something to say at court, particularly the Duque d'Higar, the best man of the *Camarilla*, and a man both of talent and information: but the influence of the Duque d'Higar is not great. The favourite *valet de chambre*, who died of apoplexy some months ago, was also fast creeping on towards high favour; and his death has thrown more influence into the hands of Salsedo.

But it is now generally supposed, that the rising influence of the queen will in due time discard every other influence about court. No king and queen ever lived more happily together, than the present king and queen of Spain. The king is passionately attached to her; and it is said she is perfectly satisfied with her lot. He spends the greater part of the day in her apartments; and when engaged in council, leaves it half a dozen times in the course of an hour or two, to visit his queen. The habits of the court are extremely simple: the king rises at six, and breakfasts at seven; he spends the morning chiefly with the queen, but receives his ministers and secretary at any time before two; at half-past two he dines, always in company with the queen. Dinner occupies not more than an hour; and shortly after, he and the queen drive out together: he sups at half-past eight, and retires early. The queen does not rise so early as the king; she breakfasts at nine; and the king always sits by her. There is scarcely any gaiety at court. The queen is fond of retirement; and excepting now and then a private concert, there are no court diversions.

While I was in Madrid, the favourite pastime of the king and queen was of rather an extraordinary kind; especially as the queen was on the eve of her accouchement. It consisted in looking at the wild beasts, which are kept in the Retiro. Almost every evening about five o'clock, the royal carriage might be seen crossing the Prado, on its way towards the menagerie; and as the Retiro was generally my afternoon lounge, I had frequent opportunities of seeing this royal diversion. There is a large square court about 200 yards across, inclosed with iron railings, and round the interior of this court, are the cages of the wild animals; and in this court, sat the king and queen upon a bench, while the animals were turned out for their amusement,—such of them at least as were peaceable,—camels, elephants, zebras, &c. &c. The keepers mounted upon the backs of the animals, and made them trot round the area; and when this had been done often enough to please their majesties, the beasts were led in front of their royal visitors, and made to kneel,—which act of homage however they sometimes refused to perform. Upon one occasion, the man who rode the camel, not being able to keep his seat, turned his face towards the tail, sitting upon the neck of the animal; their majesties were in ecstasies at this exhibition; the king, I thought, would have died with laughing.

I was witness, another time, to a strange scene of rivalry between the king and Don Carlos. When the king's carriage drove up to the gate of the court, Don Carlos and his wife and family were seated in the area, and his carriage was in waiting: upon this occasion, the king arrived in state; a party of dragoons attended him, and his coachmen were in court dresses. The carriage of Don Carlos was in strange contrast with that of the king; it was drawn by six mules, harnessed with ropes; in place of postilions in court dresses, his servants were in the dress of Spanish peasants in their holiday clothes,—one on the coach-box,—the other employed as a runner by the head of the mules. Don Carlos affects all this appearance of simplicity and Spanish usage, to please the people; and for the same reason, his wife generally appears in a mantilla. The moment the king's carriage appeared, Don Carlos left the court with his wife, and continued to walk in the most crowded part of the garden while the king and queen remained, dividing the attention which their majesties would otherwise have received, and indeed engrossing the larger share of it. I could not avoid remarking the greater popularity of Don Carlos among the lower orders: while they only took off their hats as the king passed, they bowed almost to the ground at the presence of the Infante. The appearance of the queen, however, always produced a favourable impression, especially when contrasted with that of her aspiring rival. One cannot look at the spouse of Don Carlos, without perceiving that she covets a crown; while in the countenance of the queen, we read indifference to it.

Upon frequent other occasions while in Madrid, I had proofs of the anxiety of Don Carlos to recommend himself to the people. The most marked of these, was upon the evening when the queen gave birth to a princess: not an hour after this was known, the Infante drove through the streets and along the Prado, in an open carriage, along with his three sons, who, by the repeal of the Salic law, were that day cut out of their inheritance.

The event to which I have alluded,—the accouchement of the queen—was a matter of deep interest in Madrid; and before its accomplishment there was the utmost anxiety among all ranks. Each party had its own views. The moderate, or government party, and many belonging to the other parties, who desired peace and tranquillity, anxiously looked to the birth of a prince, as an event that would at once extinguish the claims of those who, but for the repeal of the Salic law, would have had a right to the throne, in case of the birth of a princess. The Carlists secretly wished that the event might be precisely the opposite; and the liberal party, seeing some possible advantage in whatever should tend to unsettle the existing government, united their wishes with those of the Carlists: but, the great majority of the respectable inhabitants, perceiving in the birth of a prince, a guarantee for the tranquillity of the kingdom, and the security of property, devoutly wished that such might be the event.

The anxiety that filled the public mind, was fully partaken by the government; for it was well known to the heads of the state, that conspiracies were on foot; and that, in the event of the birth of a princess, the Carlists would have a pretext for an open manifestation of their views. They, however, had resolved not to wait this event, but to anticipate it; and a plot, which might possibly have proved successful, and which, at all events, must have led to scenes of blood, perhaps to revolution, was fortunately discovered on the day before that appointed for its execution; and the most prompt measures were immediately taken for crushing it. On the fifth of October, about midnight, carriages, accompanied by sufficient escorts, were taken to the houses of Padre Cirilo, the chief of the Franciscan order of friars; of Don Rufino Gonsalez; of Don Man. Herro, both Counsellors of State, and of thirteen others; the conspirators were put into the carriages, and driven off,—Cirilo to Seville; Rufino to La Mancha, and the others to different places distant from the metropolis. The conspirators intended that some of the heads should have repaired to the inner court of the palace while the king was engaged in his evening drive; that about a thousand of the royalist volunteers—who are for the most part Carlists—should assemble at the palace yard; that the entrance to the palace should be taken possession of; the king seized upon his return, and forced to change his ministers, and to restore the Salic law. I feel little doubt, that if this plot had not been discovered, it would have led to more than a change of ministers. Among the military, and even among the guards, there are many discontented men, who fancy they see in the elevation of Don Carlos, a guarantee for a more impartial system of promotion; and the royalist volunteers of Madrid, 6000 strong, and all provided with arms, and accustomed to manœuvre them, are, with few exceptions of the lowest classes, and chiefly Carlists.

I walked to the palace yard the evening when it was expected the event would be known: it presented a dense mass of persons, chiefly of bourgeois and of the middle classes, all waiting with anxiety the announcement of the event, upon which the tranquillity of the country so greatly depended. At length the white flag—the announcement of a princess—was slowly hoisted. There was a universal and audible expression of disappointment: *"Que lastima! que lastima!"* and the crowd slowly dispersed.

The repeal of the Salic law was not in itself an unpopular measure; and had there been no claimants to the crown under the old law, or no party to take advantage of disunion, and support these claims, it would have been a matter of indifference to the people, whether the queen gave birth to a son or a daughter: the repeal of the Salic law was only the revival of the ancient law of Castile, and *per se*, gave no dissatisfaction. It was the peculiar circumstances in which the country was placed, and the state of parties, that rendered the birth of a prince or a princess a matter of importance: the event created much disappointment to the government party, but no discontent: it is well known that the Constitutionalists on the frontier had trusted to the latter, and hoped to profit by it: but the effect was rather against than favourable to that party; because the Carlists, seeing their own ultimate chances increased, were therefore more interested in assisting government to suppress the Constitutionalists, whose ascendancy would leave them no hope.—But to return to the court.

There is nothing of court society at Madrid: the secluded habits of the king and queen, I have spoken of already; and there is scarcely any visiting among the courtiers. The persons of distinction in Madrid lead a most monotonous life: one lady only, the Duchess of Benevente, opens her house once a week,—this is on Sunday evening, and she receives, among others, those of the foreign ministers who choose to visit her. Her parties, however, are far from being agreeable: the Spaniards of distinction who frequent her *tertulia*, generally withdraw when the foreign ministers are announced. This disinclination on the part of the Spanish grandees, and others holding high court preferment, to associate with the foreign ambassadors, is notorious in Madrid. At the tertulia, of the wife of Don Manuel Gonsalez Salmon, the foreign ministers used formerly to be present, but they discovered that they were regarded in a light little different from that of spies; and they are now never seen at these tertulias. In Madrid there are no ministerial, no diplomatic dinners; and among the persons of most distinction, entertainments are extremely rare. There is, in fact, nothing like gaiety among the upper ranks in the Spanish metropolis. And yet, if you remark to a Spanish lady that there is little society among the higher classes in Madrid, she will express the utmost astonishment that you should have imbibed so false a notion of Madrid and its society; but her idea of society and yours differ widely. If a dozen houses are open, into which a Spanish lady may go when she pleases, sit down on the sofa with her friend, fan herself, and talk till she is tired; this she considers society,— and this is the only form of society to be found among the highest classes in Madrid,—gaiety there is none.

Previous to travelling into Spain, I had heard much of the difficulty, if not impossibility, of obtaining access to Spanish society; and before I had the means of judging for myself, I received frequent corroboration of this opinion. One of his majesty's consuls, whom I accidentally met in the Pyrenees, and whose appointment lies in the largest city of Spain, next to Madrid; a man too, who, both by his rank, for he is the nephew of a peer, and by the affability of his manners, would be likely to be every where well received, told me that I should probably leave Spain with no greater knowledge of Spanish society than when I entered it; that it was more than probable I should never see the inside of a Spanish house: and he concluded by saying, that he had been four years in Spain, and actually *did not know if the Spaniards dined off a table cloth.* This was rather disheartening: and when I waited upon the British minister upon my arrival in Madrid, I received from him no greater encouragement. He told me that Spanish houses were closed against foreigners; and that, for his own part, he knew nobody, and visited no where.

I am not able to reconcile these opinions, and the experience of others, with my own; my advantages, considerable as they certainly were, could not be compared with those of the accredited representatives of government, who had resided many years in the country. It is a fact, however, that I had not been many days in Madrid, before I had the entrée of several Spanish houses, both in the higher and in the middle classes of society: this good fortune I may partly attribute to my intimacy with an *attaché* of the Spanish embassy in London, who, grateful for the attentions he had received from my countrymen, repaid them in the manner most acceptable to me,— namely, by making me acquainted with a numerous circle of friends and relatives. His father, a member of the council of state, may easily be supposed to have possessed the power of assisting the inquiries of a traveller; and to him, and to my young friend, now secretary to one of the legations in Italy, I have to return my best thanks for a hundred civilities.

It is the habits of the middle classes, that best interpret the condition and character of a people; and to these I mean at present to confine myself. I shall begin by giving the reader some idea of the interior of a Spanish house; but let me premise, that the houses in the different cities of Spain, bear scarcely any resemblance to each other: the houses of Madrid differ in almost every thing from those of Seville,—which, again, are in many respects different from the houses in Malaga and Valencia. These distinctions are sufficient to excuse a detail so apparently trifling, as the description of a house; because they arise from a distinction in the manners and habits of the people inhabiting the different provinces of Spain.

In Madrid, the whole of the middle classes, and, indeed, all excepting the very highest ranks, live in stories, or flats, as they are called in Scotland,— each story being a distinct house. The outer door of every house in Madrid is of an enormous strength, more like the door of a prison, or of a convent, than of a private dwelling house; and in the centre, there is a small window, about six inches long by two broad, grated with iron, and with a sliding shutter. When one rings at the door of a Spanish house, the answer to the bell is a voice, which calls out *"Quien es?"*—who is it? or who comes? and the person wishing to be admitted, must answer *"Gente de paz,"*—literally, People peace. But this assertion does not content the person within, who then shoves aside the shutter and peeps through; and the usual colloquy is carried on through the grating, before the door be thrown open, unless the person without, be known to the servant within. One cannot help endeavouring to account for the origin of so singular a custom; and perhaps the truest guess that can be made, is, to refer it to the suspicion, and feeling of personal insecurity, which are the offspring of bad government, of political persecution, and religious inquisition. The window shutters of the houses are as massive as the doors; and the glass of the windows is purposely so bad, that it is impossible to see into a house from the opposite side of a street: three panes, however, are always of good glass, so that one may be able to see out.

The house which I select for a description of its interior, as a fair sample of the dwelling-houses of the middle classes in Madrid, belonged to a gentleman holding a government appointment of 50,000 reals (500*l.*) per annum; which may be equal to about 700*l.* a-year in London: and, with very few variations, this house may be taken as an average specimen of the houses of professional men, *employées*, and independent persons, of from 500*l.* to 1,000*l.* per annum. The principal room, answering to the English drawing-room, is large, and well-lighted; a handsome straw matting, worked in a pattern of coloured flowers, and which looks quite as pretty as a carpet, entirely covers the floor, which is generally of brick. There is no fire-place in the room; the walls and roof are both what is called stained, and this is as well executed as I have ever seen it in England; and the furniture of the room consists of a large mahogany sofa, with hair cushion, covered with flowered black satin; mahogany chairs, with green and straw-coloured basket-seats; four small mahogany tables, of good material, and prettily carved, and a large round table in the centre of the room—just an English loo-table—upon which stands a handsome service of china; a mirror, and two marble slabs between the windows, and a few pictures—copies from Spanish masters,—complete the furniture: but let me not omit five or six low stools, scattered here and there; for every lady has her footstool.

At one end of this room, opening from the side, is a recess, twelve or thirteen feet square, and not concealed by any curtain. This is a bed-room,—a bed-room too in constant use. The bedstead is of steel or brass wire; the bed is covered with a counterpane, trimmed with broad lace; the furniture is all of mahogany, and the wash-hand basin and ewer are of brass.

A wide archway opening at the other end of the drawing-room, leads to an ante-room, covered with the same matting as the drawing-room, and furnished with a couch, chairs, and footstools, covered with blue satin. At the side of this ante-room is another recess, open like the other, containing two beds, between them a small marble slab, with a vessel of holy-water, and at the head of each a small image of Christ in ivory. This is the matrimonial chamber. The rest of the house consists of a long, tortuous, and rather dark passage, from which the other rooms enter: these are, a small parlour, or study, always poorly fitted up; a boudoir, with a low couch covered with black satin, a couple of footstools, a table, and very handsome looking-glass; this important room is either matted, or floored with

Valencia tiles; and the walls are generally covered with a French paper, and adorned or disfigured as the case may happen, with a few pictures, religious, or of an opposite character, or both, according to the taste of the señora.

The worst room in almost every Spanish house, is the dining-room, or rather eating-room, for every meal is taken in the same room: the floor has generally no matting,—the walls are unadorned,—the furniture is of the commonest description,—and the room itself so small, that the table, which nearly fills the room, is rarely large enough for more than six persons. This at once lets a stranger into an important secret in the economy of Madrid society; that there is no probability of receiving an invitation to dinner. I say Madrid society, because in the southern provinces, the dining-room and its uses are different. But although a stranger must not expect many invitations to dinner in Madrid, yet, if he be once received into a family upon a familiar footing, and should pay a visit while the family are at dinner, or just sitting down to dinner, he will not be denied admittance, but will be requested to walk into the eating-room, and a chair will be immediately placed for him at table. This civility, however, must be accepted with discretion; because the civil speech, which is invariably addressed to a stranger, when he concludes his first visit,—*Esta casa es a la disposition de V^{d.}*,—"This house is at your disposal,"—is a form of words not to be always interpreted literally. I have omitted to mention the Spanish kitchen, which is provided with a stone table, in which there are six or eight circular holes for charcoal, and numerous earthen vessels to fit these holes. Generally speaking, respectable Spanish houses, whether in Madrid, Seville, or Valencia, are scrupulously clean. I have never in any country, seen kitchens and bed-rooms so clean as they are in Spain. The description I have given may serve to convey to the reader a tolerably accurate idea of the houses of Madrid: some may contain a greater number of apartments, and others fewer; and some may be a little better, others a little worse furnished; but in the material points, they are all the same; they have all an elegant drawing-room, bed-rooms in recesses, a wretched dining-room, and a luxuriously fitted-up boudoir.

In a former chapter, I spoke of the manner of living among the middle classes in the northern provinces. In Madrid, and generally in Castile, there is somewhat more luxury in the table, though the Spaniards as a nation, may justly be characterized as abstemious, and little addicted to the pleasures of the table. The *olla* or *puchero*, is not the sole dish that graces the tables of the middle and upper classes in Madrid: there is generally a stew of some kind added, and dinner is always followed by cakes, sweetmeats, and fruit; but this is after all but an indifferent dinner for one with an income of 700*l.* or 800*l.* a-year. And there are still very many in Madrid, even in the upper ranks, who are contented with the puchero; and I was myself acquainted with one or two families in good circumstances, who yet lived in a way which we should call *piggishly* in England, sending to the cook-shop for a puchero, and to the wine-shop, for the daily portion required at dinner.

The inhabitants of Madrid, excepting the trades people, rise late, and breakfast between ten and eleven, upon a cup of chocolate, with scarcely any bread, and a glass of cold water. Going to mass, dressing, paying and receiving visits, and walking the streets, occupy the ladies till the dinner hour; and this, following the example of the court, and in order that it may not interfere with the claims of the Prado, is early, even among the highest ranks. Then follows the siesta; and the interval between the siesta and dressing for the Prado, is usually passed upon the balcony. After the Prado, is the tertulia, which may be said to be the only form of Spanish society. When you have the entrée of a house in Madrid, and pay your visit in the evening, you find the family assembled near the windows, with two or three strangers, chatting and laughing; the ladies of the house without mantillas, and the visitors generally wearing them. The young ladies, or señoritas, are in one part of the room, with one or two caballeros; and the Senora de Casa in another, probably conversing with a priest or friar; unless she be young, in which case there is no division in the society. The room is usually badly lighted, most commonly with a semi-luna at the farthest corner,—and the master of the house is rarely one of the party. He is a member of another tertulia. The conversation is always lively, and somewhat piquante, and the visitors stay late, and are not presented with any refreshment.

If the visit be made in the morning, the lady, if not walking the streets, or gossiping, is found in her boudoir, seated upon a low couch, in a black silk dress; her feet upon a footstool; and beside her, a large basket, such as Murillo has so often painted. She is always engaged in some kind of embroidery,—and her fan, which she resumes the moment you enter, lies on the table before her.

The only kind of party to which a stranger is invited in Madrid, is a ball; but there is no necessity for an invitation, if one has the entrée of the house. At these parties, the ladies are rarely dressed in the Spanish fashion, but generally *à la Française*, with white or coloured dresses,—the only distinguishing, and never to be mistaken mark of a Spanish woman, being the fan. The Spanish ladies invariably dance well; and yet their mode of dancing is as opposite as possible from the French style: it is the management of the head and shoulders; and the *manner*, not the power of motion in the limbs, that distinguish the Spanish woman. There is another remarkable difference between the Spanish, and the French or English dance: the gravity of countenance,—and generally, the silence that prevails among quadrillers, both in France and England, is remarkable, and even ludicrous; but the Spanish ladies talk and laugh while they dance,—seeing no reason why one pleasure should suspend another. At these parties there is rarely any refreshment offered; a glass of water may be had, but nothing more.

Are the Spaniards a hospitable people?—This is a question that cannot be answered by a simple monosyllable: it seems difficult to separate hospitality from generosity; and yet this distinction must be made in speaking of the conduct of Spaniards towards strangers. A Spaniard considers himself to be remarkable for his hospitality, because he is at all times happy to see a stranger within his doors: he says, speaking to an Englishman, "in your country you invite a foreigner to your house, and there the civility ends; he cannot return without another invitation. But here, if a stranger be once received within our houses, they are ever afterwards at his disposal; he needs no farther invitation." This is true enough, but it scarcely amounts to hospitality. This word, from the days of Abraham, who fed the angels, has signified setting meat before one; but a stranger might live years in a Spanish city, and be on terms of intimacy with many wealthy Spaniards, and might yet never break bread within a Spanish house,—certainly never by invitation. I speak at present of Madrid, and the cities of the interior. In Cadiz, Malaga, Valencia, and Barcellona, dinner parties are occasionally given. But, with this seeming want of hospitality towards strangers, there is much, and very uncalled-for generosity. Wherever a stranger goes in company with a Spaniard,—if to a coffee-house, to the theatre, to a bull-fight,—even to shops where fancy articles are sold, the Spaniard insists upon paying: any remonstrance offends him; nor will he ever, at any after time, permit you to repay the obligation in a similar way. He is at all times ready with his purse; and draws its strings with the alacrity of a man who is eager to give away his money. It is difficult to refer to any common principle, the different ways in which a Spaniard and an Englishman shew kindness to a stranger. The Spaniard lays out his money upon him cheerfully; but gives him nothing to eat: the Englishman, on the other hand, would dislike paying a crown for a foreigner, but would ask him to dinner again and again, and thus lay out ten times its amount.

I fear this apparent disregard of money, may have some connexion with that great and unfortunate failing in the character of the middle classes in Spain, particularly in Castile—love of display, or ostentation. This failing belongs to the middle and upper classes in an extraordinary degree; while inconsiderateness, and carelessness of to-morrow, are conspicuous in the characters both of the middle and lower classes. Almost every one in Spain lives up to his income. Even the employées, who hold their posts by a very uncertain tenure, seldom lay by any thing; they generally die pennyless: and it is a certain fact, that the families of employées who have died beggars, have swelled the Spanish pension list to a most formidable length. A Spaniard will dine without a table-cloth, to save the expense of washing; but this, not that he may lay by his money,—but that he may have the eclât, not the *pleasure*, of frequenting the opera; the *pride*, not the *gratification*, of eating ice in the *Café Catalina*. I have known some extraordinary instances of this love of display: a Spanish officer, with whom we had some acquaintance, invited us to accompany him and his wife to the Prado. A handsome carriage drove up to the door, attended by two servants in gay liveries: will it be believed, that the carriage and servants were hired for the occasion; and that this officer was married, had a family, and possessed only his pay, amounting to about 140*l*. a-year? What sacrifices must have been made for the indulgence of this piece of vanity! I knew the family of a judge, consisting of a widow, and four daughters, all of whom appeared every Sunday on the Prado with new satin shoes and clean white gloves: the pension of a judge's widow is 8000 reals, (80*l*. sterling). There is nothing remarkable in these instances; and the same love of display is visible among the lower orders in Madrid, as far as this can be shewn in their rank of life. Persons in very humble circumstances are seen in most expensive dresses; and it is not at all unusual to meet a female servant with a comb, fan, and mantilla, whose united expense would amount to 4*l*. or 5*l*.

In the upper and middle classes of society in Madrid, morals are at the lowest ebb: though veils are almost thrown aside, and serenades are rare, Spain is still the country of gallantry and intrigue. Want of education among the women, and the absence of moral and religious principle among the men, are the fruitful sources of this universal demoralization. In the education of a Spanish woman, all has reference to display; knowledge forms no part of it. The business of her life, is dress and show; and its object, admiration: this leads to gallantry, and all its train of consequences. It is impossible to walk into the street, or along the Prado, without perceiving even among children, that the rudiments of Spanish indiscretion are already laid. Little girls of the tenderest age shew by their gait and manner, that they are already initiated in the business of life. I have heard others, scarcely escaped from childhood, talk in a manner that would have made an English married woman blush,—and, to gather something even from infancy, I have heard a child five or six years old, ask its companion, how it could disregard appearance so much as to venture out without a proper *ceinture*.

In married life, I have reason to think that infidelity is more universal than in Italy; but the origin of it is different, and the thing is differently managed in the two countries. It is a great error to imagine—as some old writers upon Spain, and accurate writers in other respects, have asserted—that there is any connivance in Spain on the part of the husband: Spanish husbands, with few exceptions, are too proud to bargain for their own dishonour. While I was in Madrid, two instances occurred, in which husbands murdered their wives in fits of jealousy: in neither of these cases was the thing sifted to the bottom; because it was known that in doing this the villany of two priests would have been brought to light. The *Cortejo* of Spain is by no means the *Cisesbeo* of Italy. The *liaison* in Spain is a secret one; it has not originated in interest or vanity, but in passion; and the greatest pains are taken to conceal it from the husband, and even (intimates excepted) from the world. There are not in Madrid the same opportunities for the formation and prosecution of intrigue, as in Seville and the cities of the south. In these, the gardens and summer houses,—the walls of both forming a part of the street,—are particularly favourable to the serenade, the billet-doux, and their recompense. In Madrid, opportunities are more precarious: the mass, the street, the balcony, are the only places of rendezvous; and of these, the latter is the most prized. Walking the streets, while all the world enjoys the siesta, wakeful señoras and señoritas are here and there seen behind the curtains that fall over the balconies, and which are supposed to shade the light from the eyes of the sleeper; and now and then some medium of intelligence is seen fluttering downward, to be picked up by a cloaked *cabalero*. There is another important difference between the gallantries of Spain, and of Italy or France: in Spain, they are not confined to married women: improper *liaisons* are not unfrequently formed by unmarried ladies; and those whom one sees on the balconies, are much more frequently señoritas than señoras.

Intrigue is not confined in Madrid to the upper, or even the middle classes of society; but is found also among the trades people. Sometimes during the hours of sleep and silence, I have ventured, in passing along the street, to draw aside the curtain that is meant to secure an uninterrupted siesta to the inmates of the embroiderers, perfumers, or dress-makers' shops; and I have more than once interrupted a *tête-à-tête*. It is fair to add, however, that I oftener found the señorita fast asleep. It is well understood in Madrid, that during the time of siesta, no one enters a shop where a curtain is drawn; but a stranger may sometimes do unpermitted things, under pretence of ignorance.

The lower orders in Madrid cannot be characterized as grossly immoral: they are not drunken and brutal, like the mob of London; nor ferocious and insolent, like the *canaille* of Paris. In walking the streets of Madrid, it is rarely that one sees either quarrelling or gambling; and I believe it might be possible to walk through any part of the city with the corner of a handkerchief hanging out of the pocket, and to return with it in its place: petty larceny, a Castilian thinks beneath him. Between the character of the Castilian and the Andalusian, there is as marked a distinction as that which exists in the characters of any two people inhabiting different kingdoms; but I will not anticipate.

I suspect that among the upper and middle ranks in Madrid, religion is as low as morals: among them, priestcraft exercises very little influence; and, indeed, ridicule and dislike of all orders of religion, form a very common seasoning to conversation. There can be no doubt that the occupation of the Peninsula by the French army, has gone far towards diminishing the respect in which the priesthood was formerly held by the great majority of all classes in Spain. In Madrid, I have never heard one individual above the rank of a small tradesman, speak with respect, of religion,—or with affection, of the priesthood. There cannot be the smallest doubt that, in the capital at least, both the clergy and the friars are sensible of a great diminution in the power which they formerly enjoyed; and their tone and bearing are altered accordingly. At present, they, at all events the regular clergy, yield a little to the tide that has set in against them. I have been surprised to hear the freedom with which some of the priests have spoken of the state of Spain. I have heard them particularly lament the difficulties that stand in the way of publishing books, and admit the oppressive nature of the enactments that regard education. The clergy have not the same interest as the friars, in supporting the present system, because they have not the same fears. A revolution that might possibly chase every monk from the soil, and which would, at all events, despoil them of their possessions and terminate their dominion, would probably but slightly affect the clergy of the church; and I have observed that since the French revolution, their fears have diminished. The example of France, in the respect it has shewn for the rights of the church, they look upon as a guarantee of their own security; and perhaps justly. Government still seeks for support in the influence of the church, and endeavours, by every means, to keep up this influence. This, it may easily be supposed, is attempted through the medium of education, which, throughout Spain, may be said to be a government concern. The schools in Madrid are all conducted by Jesuits; and the education received in them, is such as might be expected from their heads. This surveillance commenced when the king returned to the head of the government, in 1824. The colleges were then remodelled; and all the public seminaries, even those destined for military education, were placed under Jesuit heads. I have frequently met in the streets of Madrid, long lines of students of the *Colegio Imperial*, and of the *Semmario de Nobles*, some in military uniform, and each company headed by a priest. And no choice is left to the people, as to the education of their children: the only choice is, the government school, or no school; for obstacles, almost insurmountable, are thrown in the way of private tuition. Before a family dare employ a tutor, the permission of government must be obtained; and the tutor must provide himself with a license: this implies minute inquiries into character, political and religious opinions, &c.; so that, in fact, no tutor is ever licensed, unless there is a perfect security that the system of education to be pursued by him,—intellectual, political, and religious,—shall be precisely the same as that taught in the public seminaries: there is nothing therefore gained by private tuition. Whether the priesthood may possibly regain any part of its lost influence, owing to the present system of education, may admit of a question. If Spain should remain in its present condition, without revolution or change, it is probable that the growth of liberal opinions may be retarded; the thousands now educated on jesuitical principles, and denied the means of real knowledge, were not old enough during the existence of the constitution, to have caught a glimpse of the light which at that time dawned upon the darkness of Spain; nor have they had opportunities of being influenced by French principles, during the time of the occupation of the Peninsula. The policy of the Spanish government, therefore, with respect to its surveillance of education, is not unworthy of a government that desires to maintain itself by the blindness of the people.

The influence of the friars is much greater than that of the priests; though this also diminishes daily. I speak of Madrid only. In many of the other cities of Spain, of which I shall afterwards speak more in detail—particularly in Toledo, Seville, Granada, Lorca, and Murcia, and in most of the smaller towns, I think it almost impossible that the influence of the friars could ever have been much greater than it is. In Madrid, less attention is paid to religious ceremonials and processions, than in any other city of Spain: and one sees fewer external proofs of the veneration of the people for the character of friar. A Franciscan may pass from one end of Madrid to the other, without having one claim made upon his paternal blessing by a grown-up person. I have seen the Virgin of St. Rosalio, and an image of St. Thomas, carried through the streets, with some hundreds of friars accompanying them, without any one being excited to a greater act of devotion than raising the hat from the head: and during my morning walk, when I invariably looked into the churches belonging to whichever of the convents that happened to lie in my way, I seldom saw more than half a dozen persons at their devotions. All this is very different at Toledo and Seville; and judging by the difference I have observed in the proofs of bigotry apparent in the different Spanish cities, I feel myself justified in believing that the influence of the friars, as well as that of the priests, has sensibly diminished in Madrid. But it is far from being small: it still exists, with less or more force, among all ranks: and the breast of a friar is still the favourite depository of family secrets. From my house, I could see the regular visits made by friars to several houses within the range of my window; and little children may at all times be seen in the street, running after the monk of any order, to kiss his hand and beg his blessing.

There are many reasons why the influence of the friars should decline more slowly than that of the priesthood: as the first of these may be mentioned, the greater immorality of the lives of the latter. This immorality is notorious throughout Spain; and, indeed, they take little pains to conceal,—I will not say their pecadillos,—but the opportunities and temptations to commit them, which they create for themselves; and they obtain full credit for yielding to these temptations. Perhaps it is doing wrong to the clergy to assign to the friars greater purity of life than to them; but whatever may be the immoralities of the monks, they have more the art, and they possess better opportunities too of concealing them. Priests live in the world, and have worse opportunities of concealment than other men, because their profession lays them open to scrutiny; but friars live in a world of their own, fenced round, not only by walls of stone, but by a more impenetrable wall of prescriptive veneration,—and they are very daring eyes that pry into the secrets of the cloister. But strange, and even dreadful events, occasionally occur, to lay open the hidden scenes that are transacted within a convent's walls. One such occurred last September, while I was in Madrid. One morning, the Superior of the monastery of San Basilio was found in bed murdered,—his throat cut, his hands tied, and several stabs in his body. There could be no doubt that the murder had been committed by the friars; and as no pretence could be found against instituting an inquiry, a commission was accordingly appointed to investigate, and sat during several days. Strange disclosures were made: it appeared that the superior had been a good man, and remarkably strict in the observances enjoined upon the order,—too much so for the inclination of the friars, who had been accustomed to commit every kind of excess, and to transgress in the most essential points, the rules of the convent; particularly in being absent during the night. The superior used to reprove this laxity, and exerted his authority to restrain it; and dislike towards him was naturally produced. In these circumstances, no doubt, rested in the mind of any one, that the murder was committed by the monks; but it had been resolved, that in some way or other the affair should be got rid of. The porter of the convent, who, previous to the appointment of the commission, had declared that no one had entered, so qualified his words before the commissioners, that through his evidence, they found a loop-hole by which justice might ooze out:—he said, that he had some recollection, when half asleep, of having seen a person enter; but besides the impossibility of any one entering, unless the porter had been so much awake as to open the gate, the murder could not have been committed by one person. The result was, that the commission broke up without coming to any decision; but as a sacrifice to public opinion, three of the friars were committed to prison on suspicion. It was well understood that the affair would never go further; and I was assured by the wife of a person holding a high official employment, that in a few months the imprisoned monks would be found again in their convent. When the king returned to Spain in 1823, he hanged a friar for a murder; but this was done at that particular juncture to please the Constitutionalists; and while the investigation I have mentioned was proceeding, every one knew that his majesty dared not venture upon a repetition of this.

A few years ago, a curious exposé was made at Cadiz, which, as I am upon the subject of friars, I shall mention in this place. There was, and still is, a banker named Gargallo, one of the richest men in Cadiz, whose magnificent dwelling-house is separated from the wall of the Franciscan monastery only by one small house; and this house also belonged to Sr. Gargallo, although it was not inhabited. The master of the house, who though a rich man, looked closely into his affairs, perceived that his cook's bill greatly exceeded the sum necessary for the subsistence of the family; and after bearing this during a considerable time, he at length discharged his cook. The cook applied for service elsewhere; and upon his new master applying to Gargallo for a character, he refused to give one, alleging as a reason, the dishonesty of his servant: the cook enraged at this injustice, and more solicitous to preserve his own good character than that of the friars, returned to Gargallo's house, taking witnesses along with him; and aloud in the court-yard told this story: that every day he had carried a hot dinner into the house adjoining, where Gargallo's wife and daughter entertained a select party of Franciscan friars; and what was worse still, his late master's money had been expended in the support of three children and a nurse, who all lived in the adjoining house. The truth of this story was easily put to the test; the three children and a nurse were found in the house, and the whole affair was brought to light. The especial favour of the ladies was reserved for only two of the friars: the very reverend father Antonio Sanches de la Camissa, Sacristan Mayor, was the favourite of the wife; and another, whose name I forget, but who was next in rank to the prior, and had formerly been confessor in Gargallo's house, was the selection of his daughter. These had the entrée of Gargallo's house at all hours; and in order to keep quiet a few others, who were supposed to be in the secret, a savoury dinner was provided every day for the self-denying Franciscans. Gargallo married his daughter to an old apothecary, at Chiclana, where she now lives a widow; and he confined his wife during two years in an upper room in his own house; but she now lives again with her husband. At the first disclosure of the affair, he wished to send both offenders to the Penitentiary; but the captain-general of the province interfered, to prevent so much publicity in an affair compromising the character of the Franciscans. No notice whatever of this disgraceful transaction was taken in the convent. Both reverend fathers continued to bear the character of good Franciscans; and doubtless returned for a time, to the austerities of the order,—and when I was in Cadiz, one of them every day accompanied

Manuel Munoz, the superior, and Cerillo, who had been banished to Seville, in an evening walk.

But these immoralities of the friars, although some such are occasionally brought to light, and although much that exists is hidden, are yet far more rare than the immoralities of the priests; and, it is without doubt, the greater immorality of the clergy, and the greater belief in that immorality, that are the primary reasons why the influence of the friars diminishes more slowly than that of the priesthood.

Several other reasons might be given, why the influence of the friars maintains itself better than that of the clergy, in the minds of the people,— especially the lower orders: one may be stated to be, the known austerities practised by some of the orders, particularly by the Franciscans, the Capuchins, and the Carthusians; another, the greater alms given by the convents than by the church; another, the mystery that involves the lives and habits of the friars,—for mystery recommends any thing to the ignorant; and a fourth, which addresses itself to all classes, is, the direct tax which the support of the clergy imposes. The friars, whether poor or not, have the semblance of poverty; at all events, the sources of their revenues are not seen to flow into their treasury; and, although the nation at large groans under the weight, individuals feel no part of it. Such are a few of the causes which, in my opinion, operate in supporting the influence of the friars; and in diminishing that of the clergy.

Comparatively with the rest of Spain, there is little attention paid to the ceremonials of religion in Madrid. I often strolled into the churches at all hours; and, excepting at time of mass, few were to be seen at prayer. One morning I walked into the collegiate church of St. Isodro, and found the pulpit occupied by a priest, who was exclaiming, apparently extempore, and with great vehemence, against the sin of religious infidelity. St. Isodro is the principal church of Madrid, and yet I do not believe there were 300 listeners to the discourse; and of these at least five-sixths were women. It is a curious spectacle to see the women all sitting upon the ground *à la Turque*, on little round mats, and every fan in quick motion. The entrance of a stranger into a church during mass, always creates a sensation: a hundred eyes may at any time be withdrawn from the contemplation of either a preacher or an image, by the slightest possible cause.

CHAPTER V.

MADRID.

The Profession of a Nun; Reflections; Description of the Interior of a Convent; the Monastic Life; Description of a Bull-Fight; Sketches of Spanish Character; a Horse Race.

NO one ever visited a Roman Catholic country, without feeling some curiosity upon the subject of nuns and convents, monks and monasteries; and there is certainly no country in the world that affords so many incitements to this curiosity, or so many facilities for gratifying it, as Spain. Among all the ceremonies belonging to the church of Rome, none perhaps possesses so much interest in the eyes of a stranger, as that which is denominated "taking the veil;" chiefly, because it is the only one of them all, that addresses the heart more than the eye. I had always felt great curiosity to witness this extraordinary sacrifice of reason and nature, at the altar of bigotry and ignorance; but I found the gratification of this curiosity more difficult than I had imagined. Heretics are no welcome guests at such times; and during the first month of my residence in Madrid, I made two unsuccessful attempts to witness the ceremony of taking the veil! It fortunately happened, however, that the priest whom I had engaged at my arrival in Madrid, to speak Spanish, and read Don Quixotte with me, and with whom I passed much of my time, was the officiating priest in the convent of *Comendadoras de Calatrava*; and as I had often expressed a strong desire to see a profession, he came one day with the welcome intelligence, that in that convent, a profession would take place on the Sunday morning following; and as it was his duty to officiate on the occasion, and to administer the sacrament to the new sister, he had it in his power to gratify my wishes, and to admit me at an early hour: and he also all but promised, that after the ceremony, I should be permitted to see the interior of the convent—a privilege even greater than the other.

The chapel of the convent is separated from the apartments by a wide iron grating—so wide, that every thing which takes place on the other side, is seen as distinctly as if there was no separation whatever. I placed myself close to this grating some little time before the ceremony commenced.

How many strange, wild, and romantic associations are connected with "taking the veil!" The romances of our earlier days,—the tales, that professed to reveal the mysteries of the cloister, crowd upon our memory: we see standing before us the creatures of our imagination—the inflexible lady abbess—the trembling nun—we hear the authoritative question, and the timid reply—we see the midnight procession, and hear the anthem of sweet and holy voices—and a crowd of mysterious and half-forgotten dreams and visions float before us. Some of these early visions I had learned to doubt the reality of,—I had already caught occasional glimpses of those mysterious creatures who inhabit convent walls, without finding any realization of my vision of charms more than mortal. I had learned to know that nuns grow old, and that the veil does not always shadow loveliness; but having understood that the victim about to sacrifice herself was scarcely seventeen, I dismissed from my mind all the realities that warred with my romantic illusions, and recurred to the dream of my earlier days.

At the hour appointed, the abbess entered the room on the other side of the grating, accompanied by all the nuns, and by several ladies, friends and relatives of the novice. She entered a moment after; and immediately knelt down, with her face towards the grating, so that I had a near and distinct view of her. She was attired in the novice's robe of pure white, and wore a crown of flowers upon her head. She seemed scarcely more than sixteen. Her countenance was gentle, sweet, and interesting;—there was an expression of seriousness, but not of sadness, in her face; and a skin, fairer than usually falls to the lot of Spanish women, was sensibly coloured with a fine carnation,—the glow of youth, and health, and happiness, yet lingering on her cheek; and connecting her with the world of light, and life, and freedom, about to close upon her for ever.

The administrator now entered by the chapel, and placed himself in a chair close to where I was stationed, and at the side of an opening in the grating of about a foot square. The novice then rose, and walking forward to the grating, presented him with a paper, which he read aloud: this was the act of renunciation of all property, then and for ever; and during this ceremony the novice retired and knelt as before, holding in her hand a long lighted taper, with which the abbess presented her. The preparatory service then commenced by reading and chanting; and this, although monotonous, was pleasing and impressive, according well with the solemnity of the scene that had introduced it; and in this service the novice joined, with a clear sweet voice, in which nothing of emotion could be distinguished. When this was concluded, the novice again rose, and advanced to the grating, and pronounced slowly and distinctly the three vows that separate her from the world,—chastity, poverty, and obedience. Her voice never faltered; nor could I perceive the slightest change of countenance; the colour only, seemed to be gradually forsaking her. The lady abbess, who stood close by her side, wept all the while. Ah! if each tear could have told why it flowed, what a history might have been unfolded. Indignation was the feeling produced in my mind. I wished for the cannon of the Constitutionalists, to throw down these most odious of prisons; and even to the priest, who stood by me in his crimson and gilded surplice, I could not restrain myself from saying, half audibly, "*Que infamia!*"

When the vows that could never be recalled had been pronounced by this misguided child, she stepped back, and threw herself prostrate upon the ground,—this is the act confirmatory of her vows,—symbolical of death, and signifying that she is dead to the world. The service was then resumed,—a bell continued slowly to toll; and the priest read; while the nuns who stood around their new-made sister, responded,—"dead to the world—separated from kindred—bride of heaven!" and the nun who lies prostrate is supposed, at the same time, to repeat to God in secret, the vows she has already pronounced aloud. When this was concluded, a slow organ peel, and a solemn swell of voices rose, and died away; and the abbess then raised the nun from the ground, and embraced her; and all the other nuns and her relations also embraced her. I saw no tear upon any cheek, excepting upon the cheek of the abbess, whose face was so full of benignity, that it half reconciled me to the fate of the young initiated who had vowed obedience to her. When she had embraced every one, she again knelt for a few moments, and then approached the grating along with the abbess; and the priest handed to the abbess through the opening, the vestments of a nun. Then came the last act of the drama:—the crown was lifted from her head; the black vestment was put on, and the girdle and the rosary; and the black hood was drawn over her head;—she was now a nun, and she again embraced the abbess and all the sisters. Still I could not discover a single tear, excepting on the cheek of the abbess, who continued to weep almost without ceasing to the very end: the countenance of the young nun remained unmoved. The crown was again replaced upon her head, to be worn all that day; the sacrament was administered, and one last embrace by friends and relations terminated the scene.

I had thus seen what I had long felt so much anxiety to see,—"taking the veil;" and I found it, at the same time, a stirring and a melancholy spectacle: stirring, because it filled the mind with indignation against those whose cruel and insidious counsel had misled an innocent girl; and melancholy, because it pointed to a life uncheered by life's sweetest charities,—unblest by its holiest ties,—life without interest, without change, without hope; its sources of enjoyment dried up; and its wells of affection frozen over.

It is not difficult to account for such sacrifices as this. A young person enters a convent as a novice at fifteen or sixteen: this requires little persuasion,—the scene is new, and therefore not without its attraction. Mothers, sisters, and friends are occasionally seen; and no vow prevents a return to the world. During the noviciate, she forms attachments among the nuns, who exert themselves to the uttermost to please her. The attractions of the world are not presented to her, and they are, therefore, not felt to be attractions; and all the while, the priests and confessors have been labouring to impress her with a notion of the excellence of a religious life,—its pure enjoyment in this world, and its certain and great reward in another; and these arguments are enforced by strictures upon the vexations and evils of the world without, and the lack of enjoyment to be found in it. Such reasoning cannot fail to produce its effect upon the mind of a young person who has never known the world, and who is daily assured by the sisters in the convent that they are happy: add to this, a certain eclât in taking the veil,—extremely captivating to a youthful mind,—and it will scarcely seem surprising, that when the noviciate expires, there should be nothing terrible, or even very affecting in the ceremonial that fixes the destiny of the novice. She feels that she is vowing a continuance of the same life that she has already led, and for which habit may even have taught her an inclination; and her days are to be spent with those whom she probably loves more than any others without the convent walls. And what are the vows, to a child who has entered a convent at fifteen? She vows obedience to one whom she feels pleasure in obeying. She renounces property she never enjoyed, and whose uses are not understood; and in vowing chastity, she knows only that she is dedicating herself to heaven. The profession of a girl of sixteen or seventeen, is an abomination; and admitted so to be, even by the priests. A canon at Seville—nay, more, a Dominican friar near Alicante, agreed with me in opinion, that no woman ought to be permitted to take the veil at an earlier age than twenty-four. If a woman who has tried the world, and knows its enjoyments and its dangers, chooses to renounce it, and retire into a convent, she can only accuse herself of folly, or bigotry; but it is altogether a piece of villany when a child leaves the nursery to begin her noviciate.

The priest, who had led me to hope that I might be permitted to visit the interior of the convent, did not disappoint me. This convent is one of the most complete, and the best fitted up of any in Madrid. No one enters it who cannot bring to its treasury a considerable fortune; and its accommodations are accordingly upon a scale of corresponding comfort. In company with the priest and the porteress, an old nun, I went over the greater part of the building. The accommodations of each nun consist of a small parlour and a dormitory adjoining, and a small kitchen. The nuns do not eat in company. The dinners are separately cooked, and the whole is then carried to a public room, where it is blessed; and again carried back to the separate apartments, where each nun eats alone. The little parlours of the nuns are plain and clean; the walls white-washed, and the floors generally matted; but the room is without any fire-place, and contains a table and two chairs. The beds are extremely small, and extremely hard; and upon the table, in every dormitory, there is a crucifix. Among other parts, I was conducted to the chamber of the new-made nun. The bed was strewn with flowers—marigolds and dahlias,—and a crown of jilly-flowers lay upon the pillow. Here every thing was new; yet all would grow old along with the inmate. A new bright lamp stood upon the table; and as I looked at it, I could not avoid the picture that presented itself in fancy,—the dull light falling upon the white wall; and the silent inmate of the chamber with her book and rosary, through the long chill evenings of winter;—what a contrast from the picture of a cheerful home!

The rooms of the nuns all look into the garden. Those in front are occupied by ladies who have not taken the veil, but who have retired from the world, and who live there in tranquillity and seclusion. Many of these rooms are prettily fitted up, and contain small libraries, altogether of religious books, and a few pictures of the same character. In going through the convent, I saw two of the nuns,—old, disagreeable, ill-favoured women,—the younger sisters were not visible, excepting the new-made nun, who seemed that day to be allowed the range of the convent; for I saw her, with her crown still upon her head, in her own chamber, in one of the corridors, and in the garden: she looked quite happy. After having been conducted through almost every part of the convent, I was introduced into the refectory, and presented with wine and cake. I shall never forget the taste of that cake; it seemed to me, to taste of the tomb; and crumbled in one's hand like something touched by the finger of decay.

The order to which this convent belongs, is not so strict as many others. The chief difference in strictness between one order and another, consists in the more rigid observance of fasts, the number of meagre days, the obligation to night prayers, and the rules as to solitude and society. In some of the orders, dispensation from the vows of poverty and obedience may be obtained; and such dispensations occasionally *are* obtained,—if, for example, the labour or service of a nun should be required for the support or comfort of a destitute or aged mother. Dispensation from the vow of chastity is scarcely to be obtained; yet even this has sometimes been known. Last year, a lady of high family who had taken the vows in Barcellona, obtained a general dispensation, and married,—it is said that she was never happy; and she died a few months afterwards. It may easily be supposed, that long accustomed prejudices, and a superstitious bias, acting upon the imagination, might produce disastrous effects both upon mind and body. In the case of the late Countess Ofalia, a dispensation was also obtained. She was five years a nun. She entered the convent at the age of fourteen; and the dispensation was granted upon the ground of her youth, and also because her consent was supposed to have been extorted. This lady had, fortunately, less superstition than the other. She left the convent at nineteen; and married the Count Ofalia, with whom she lived happily.

During the French government in Spain, under Joseph Buonaparte, and also during the time of the constitution, the doors of the convents were open to whosoever might choose to go again into the world: it is said, that not more than two in Madrid, and four or five throughout the rest of Spain, availed themselves of this privilege. This is scarcely to be wondered at; superstitious fears, and conscientious scruples, interfered no doubt with the wishes of many; others had grown grey within their convent walls, and to whom could they return? Some, who might yet have found enjoyment in the world, had no means of living in it, having renounced their inheritance; and many, no doubt, had contracted a partiality for a religious life, and were actuated by pious motives.

Next to the curiosity I had felt to witness the profession of a nun, was my curiosity to witness an exhibition of a very different kind: the spectacle of a bull-fight. This is one of the many things that are to be seen in Spain, and in no other country in the world; and, however barbarous the spectacle must seem to every one but a Spaniard, it is, nevertheless, one of so stirring and so extraordinary a kind, that I think it would almost repay a journey to Madrid, even if the traveller set off next morning upon his return.

The bull-fight is the national game of Spain; and the love of the Spaniards for this spectacle, is almost beyond belief. Monday, in Madrid, is always, during the season of the bull-fights, a kind of holiday; every body looks forward to the enjoyments of the afternoon; and all the conversation is about *los toros*. Frequency of repetition makes no difference to the true amateur of the bull-fight; he is never weary of it; at all times he finds leisure and money to dedicate to his favourite pastime. The spectacle is generally announced, in the name of his majesty, to begin at four o'clock; and, before three, all the avenues leading towards the gate of Alcala, are in commotion; the Calle de Alcala, in particular, throughout its whole immense extent, is filled with a dense crowd, of all ranks and conditions, pouring towards the gate: a considerable number of carriages are also seen—even the royal carriages; but these arrive later: and there are also many hack cabriolets, their usual burden being a peasant, and two girls, dressed in their holiday clothes; for there is no way of shewing gallantry so much approved among the lower orders, as *treating* to a bull-fight; and when this is carried so far as to include a drive in a red and gilded cabriolet, the peasant need sigh no longer.

I had been able to secure a place in one of the best boxes, through the kindness of one of my friends; and, some little time before the fight begun, I was comfortably seated in the front row, with quite enough to occupy my attention, until the commencement. The spectacle was most imposing. The whole amphitheatre, said to contain 17,000 persons, was filled in every part, round and round, and from the ground to the ceiling; carrying the imagination back to antiquity, and to "the butcheries of a Roman holiday." The arena is about 230 feet in diameter; this is surrounded by a strong wooden fence, about six feet in height, the upper half retiring about a foot, so as to leave, in the middle of the fence, a stepping-place, by which the men may be able, in time of danger, to throw themselves out of the arena. Behind this fence, there is an open space about nine feet wide, extending all the way round, meant as a retreat; and where also the men in reserve are in waiting, in case their companions should be killed, or disabled. Behind this space, is another higher and stronger fence bounding the amphitheatre, for the spectators; from this fence the seats decline backward, rising to the outer wall; and above these are the boxes, which are all roofed, and are, of course, open in front. Those on the east side, which are exposed to the sun, (for the spectacle always takes place in the evening), have awnings; but these are insufficient to screen the spectators from the heat; and accordingly, the price of the places on the west side, is considerably more than the price of those exposed to the sun. Below, in what may be called the pit, the difference in price, according to sun or shade, is still greater, because there are there neither coverings nor awnings: so important, indeed, is this distinction considered, that there is not only one price for places in the sun, and another for places in the shade, but there is an intermediate price for places partly in the sun and partly in the shade,— exposed to the sun during the first part of the evening, but left in shade the latter part of it. The best places in the boxes cost about 4s.; the best in the amphitheatre below, about 2s. 6d.; the commonest place, next to the arena, costs four reals. In the centre of the west side, is the king's box; and scattered here and there, are the private boxes of the grandees and amateurs, distinguished by coloured silk drapery hanging over the front. In the boxes, I saw as many women as men,—and in the lower parts, the female spectators were also sufficiently numerous; all wore mantillas: and in the lower parts of the amphitheatre which were exposed to the sun, every spectator, whether man or woman, carried a large circular paper fan, made for the occasion, and sold by men who walk round the arena before the fight begins, raising among the spectators their long poles, with fans suspended, and a little bag fixed here and there, into which the purchaser drops his four quartos (1¼d.).

The people now began to shew their impatience, and shouts of *el toro* were heard in a hundred quarters; and soon after, a flourish of trumpets and drums announced that the spectacle was about to commence. This created total silence,—one of the results of intense interest,—and the motion of the fans was for a moment suspended:—First entered the chief magistrate of the city, on horseback, preceded by two alguacils, or constables, and followed by a troop of cavalry, who immediately cleared the arena of every one who had no business there; next, an official entered on foot, who read an ordonnance of the king, commanding the fight, and requiring order to be kept; and these preliminaries having been gone through, the magistrates and cavalry retired, leaving the arena to the two picadores, who entered at the same moment. These are mounted on horseback,—each holding a long lance or pike, and are the first antagonists the bull has to encounter; they stationed themselves on different sides of the arena, about twenty yards from the door at which the bull enters; and at a new flourish of trumpets, the gate flew open, and the bull rushed into the arena: this produced a deafening shout, and then total silence. The bulls differ very widely in courage and character: some are rash,—some cool and intrepid,—some wary and cautious,—some cowardly. Some, immediately upon perceiving the horse and his rider, rush upon them; others run bellowing round the arena,—some make towards one or other of the Chulos, who at the same moment that the bull appears, leap into the arena with coloured cloaks upon their arms; others stop, after having advanced a little way into the arena, look on every side, and seem uncertain what to do. The blood of the bull is generally first spilt: he almost invariably makes the first attack, advancing at a quick trot upon the picador, who generally receives him upon his pike, wounding him somewhere about the shoulder. Sometimes the bull, feeling himself wounded, retires, to meditate a different plan of attack; but a good bull is not turned back by a wound,—he presses on upon his enemy, even if in doing so, the lance be buried deeper in his flesh. Attached to the mane of the bull is a crimson ribbon, which it is the great object of the picador to seize, that he may present to his mistress this important trophy of his prowess. I have frequently seen this ribbon torn off at the moment that the bull closed upon the picador.

The first bull that entered the arena, was a bad bull: he was deficient both in courage and cunning: the second, was a fierce bull of Navarre, from which province the best bulls are understood to come; he paused only for a moment after entering the arena, and then instantly rushed upon the nearest picador, who wounded him in the neck; but the bull disregarding this, thrust his head under the horse's belly, and threw both him and his rider upon the ground: the horse ran a little way; but encumbered with trappings, he fell,—and the bull, disregarding for a moment the fallen picador, pursued the horse, and pushing at him, broke the girths and disengaged the animal, which finding itself at liberty, galloped round the arena—a dreadful spectacle, covered with gore, and its entrails trailing upon the ground. The bull now engaged the chulos: these young men shew great dexterity and sometimes considerable courage, in the running fight, or rather play, in which they engage the bull,—flapping their cloaks in his face,—running zig-zag when pressed, and throwing down the garments to arrest his progress a moment, and then vaulting over the fence,—an example which is sometimes followed by the disappointed animal. But this kind of warfare, the bull of Navarre seemed to consider child's play,—and leaving these cloaked antagonists, he made furiously at the other picador, dexterously evading the lance, and burying his horns in the horse's breast: the horse and his rider extricated themselves, and galloped away; but suddenly the horse dropped down, the wound having proved mortal. The bull, victorious over both enemies, stood in the centre of the arena, ready to engage another; but the spectators, anxious to see the prowess of the bull directed against another set of antagonists, expressed their desire by a monotonous clapping of hands, and beating of sticks, a demonstration of their will perfectly understood, and always attended to.

The *banderilleros* then entered: their business is to throw darts into the neck of the bull; and in order to do this, they are obliged to approach with great caution, and to be ready for a precipitate retreat; because it sometimes happens that the bull, irritated by the dart, disregards the cloak which the banderillero throws down to cover his retreat, and closely pursues the aggressor. I saw one banderillero so closely pursued, that he saved himself only by leaping over the bull's neck. The danger, however, is scarcely so great as it appears to the spectator to be; because the bull makes the charge with his eyes shut. The danger of the picador who is thrown upon the ground, is much greater; because, having made the charge, the bull then opens his eyes, and the life of the picador is only saved by the address of the chulos, who divert the attention of the victor. Generally, the banderilleros do not make their appearance until the bull appears by his movements, to decline the combat with the picadors; which he shews by scraping the ground with his feet, and retiring. If the bull shew little spirit, and the spectators wish that he should be goaded into courage, the cry is "*fuego*," and then the banderilleros are armed with darts, containing a kind of squib, which explodes while it sticks in the animal's neck.

When the people are tired of the banderilleros, and wish to have a fresh bull, they signify their impatience in the usual way, and the signal is then given for the *matador*, whose duty it is to kill the bull. The matador is in full court dress, and carries a scarlet cloak over his arm, and a sword in his hand: the former he presents to the bull; and when the bull rushes forward, he steps aside and plunges his sword in the animal's neck; at least so he ought to do, but the service is a dangerous one, and the matador is frequently killed. Sometimes it is impossible for the matador to engage upon equal terms a very wary bull, which is not much exhausted. This was the case with the sixth bull which I saw turned out: it was an Andalusian bull, and was both wary and powerful. Many times the matador attempted to engage him, but without success; he was constantly upon the watch, always disregarding the cloak, and turning quick round upon the matador, who was frequently in imminent danger. At length the people were tired of this lengthened combat, and seeing no prospect of it ending, called for the *semi-luna*, an instrument with which a person skulks behind, and cuts the ham-strings of the animal: this the bull avoided a long while, always turning quickly round; and even after this cruel operation was performed, he was still a dangerous antagonist, fighting upon his knees, and even pursuing the matador. The moment the bull falls, he is struck with a small stiletto, which pierces the *cerebellum*; folding doors, opposite to those by which the bull enters, are thrown open, and three mules, richly caparisoned and adorned with flags, gallop in; the dead bull is attached by a hook to a chain, and the mules gallop out, trailing the bull behind them: this is the work of a moment,—the doors close,—there is a new flourish of trumpets; and another bull rushes upon the arena.

And how do the Spaniards conduct themselves during all these scenes?—The intense interest which they feel in this game is visible throughout, and often loudly expressed; an astounding shout always accompanies a critical moment:—whether it be the bull or the man who is in danger, their joy is excessive; but their greatest sympathy is given to the feats of the bull. If the picador receives the bull gallantly, and forces him to retreat; or if the matador courageously faces, and wounds the bull, they applaud these acts of science and valour: but if the bull overthrow the horse and his rider; or if the matador miss his aim, and the bull seems ready to gore him, their delight knows no bounds. And it is certainly a fine spectacle to see the thousands of spectators rise simultaneously, as they always do when the interest is intense: the greatest and most crowded theatre in Europe presents nothing half so imposing as this. But how barbarous, how brutal is the whole exhibition! Could an English audience witness the scenes that are repeated every week in Madrid?—a universal burst of "shame!" would follow the spectacle of a horse, gored and bleeding, and actually treading upon his own entrails, while he gallops round the arena: even the appearance of the goaded bull could not be borne,—panting, covered with wounds and blood, lacerated by darts, and yet brave and resolute to the end.

The spectacle continued two hours and a half; and during that time, there were seven bulls killed, and six horses. When the last bull was dispatched, the people immediately rushed into the arena, and the carcass was dragged out amid the most deafening shouts.

The expenses of the bull-fights are great; but the receipts far exceed them, leaving a very handsome sum for the benefit of the hospital, which, it is said, draws a revenue from these entertainments of 300,000 reals, (3000*l.*

sterling). Some persons begin to affect a dislike of the bull-fight, but they go to it notwithstanding; and I think I may venture to say, from my own observation, that this national entertainment is not yet on the decline. The king occasionally goes; Don Carlos rarely; but Don Francis and his wife are generally to be seen there; and I noticed, that the private boxes of the nobility were as well filled as any other part of the house. On leaving the amphitheatre, I counted forty-five private carriages in waiting.

A few weeks afterwards, I was present at another bull-fight. I have no intention of describing this also; but I gathered some information from it that had escaped me upon the former occasion. This time, I paid more attention to the demeanour of the people, than to the fight; and instead of securing a place in the boxes, I took my seat in the commonest division, that I might the better observe the character of the lower orders. It is not at all unusual for those of the nobility who are amateurs of the bull-fight, to place themselves among the lowest classes; a true lover of the bull-fight likes to be under no restrictions, but to express his delight as loudly as a peasant. In that place he is at his ease; he gives himself up to the full enjoyment of his passion; he applauds, he condemns, and gives vent to his joy like the people that surround him. This is true happiness to him. It is said that Don Francis occasionally disguises himself; and enjoys, even though Infante, the pleasure of a water-carrier.

At this fight, all the bulls were indifferent excepting one; but he proved himself a perfect master of the science. He rushed first at one picador and then at the other, and overthrew both the horses and their riders; killing both horses, and wounding one of the picadores. Two fresh picadores immediately appeared; and these, he served in a precisely similar way: but the overthrow was more tragical—one of the horses and his rider were raised fairly into the air; and the horse falling so as to crush the rider between its body and the fence, he was killed upon the spot. The bull was now master of the arena; he had cleared it of men—three horses lay dead— and he stood in the midst, lashing his tail, and looking round for another enemy. This was a time to observe the character of the people. When the unfortunate picador was killed, in place of a general exclamation of horror, and loud expressions of pity, the universal cry was *"Que es bravo ese toro!"* Ah, the admirable bull!—the whole scene produced the most unbounded delight; the greater horror, the greater was the shouting, and the more vehement the expressions of satisfaction—I did not perceive a single female avert her head, or betray the slightest symptom of wounded feeling. Accidents do not occur so frequently as a spectator would be apt to imagine: danger is in fact more apparent than real, because those who engage the bull are well trained to the combat. There is, both in Madrid and at Seville, a regular school of instruction, where those destined for Las

Corridas, practise the art with young animals; and excepting the matadores, who are occasionally killed, no other of the combatants runs great risk from the bull. When the picador is killed, the catastrophe is always occasioned by the horse falling upon his rider, or crushing him against the inclosure.

Every time I attended a bull-fight, I was more and more impressed with a conviction of its cruelty and brutality. It is improperly termed a fight, because the bull has never a chance of victory and escape; it is merely a massacre,—and the series of abominable cruelties exhibited in the treatment of the horses, stamps the whole with a character of brutality and barbarism, sufficient, in my opinion, to separate Spain from the list of civilized nations. It is not merely the atrocities that an interested contractor for the bull-fights may permit,—not merely that the picador continues to ride upon an animal bathed in blood, and whose entrails trail upon the ground,—but that the Spanish people can witness and tolerate such barbarity. I do not wish to seem prejudiced; but I cannot believe that there are many among the very lowest ranks in this country who would not, at such a spectacle, cry out "kill him!" It was proposed by the present queen to envelope the horses in a net, by which the most disgusting part of the exhibition would have been concealed; but this was a refinement which it was thought would not be relished by the mob, and I believe it was never attempted. By the horses having no power of defence, and by their being deprived of the means of consciousness of their condition, the cruelty of the spectacle is increased. Townshend, that very respectable and accurate writer, is in error when he speaks of the courage shewn by the horses in facing their enemies: this, if true, would give a character of greater nobility to the entertainment; but the horses know neither their enemies nor their danger; their eyes are blinded, and their ears are tied up. If the horses were netted round the body, and if they were led off the arena when wounded; if their eyes were uncovered, that when the rider was unhorsed, they might have a chance of escape, in place of standing to be gored, unconscious of the vicinity of the enemy,—if the semi-luna were discontinued;—and, above all, if a valiant bull, which could unhorse two picadores without being wounded, and parry two or three thrusts of the matador, were allowed the reward of its victory—life: then the bull-fight would be divested of much of its barbarism, without losing, but, on the contrary, greatly adding to the interest which it at present possesses.

It is impossible to witness a spectacle like this, without being impressed with a conviction that such exhibitions must produce some influence upon the character of a people. One would naturally argue that there must be an affinity between the character of a people and their amusements, especially since we actually find this affinity among several savage nations; and yet I should be doing gross injustice to the Spanish character, if I said that any such affinity existed in Spain. There is nothing of deliberate cruelty in the character of a Spaniard,—less hard-heartedness than I have found among most other nations:—he invariably treats his mule with the utmost kindness, he is mindful even of his dog and his cat. The murders which are so frequent in the south of Spain, are the result of an irascible temper, brandy, and a hot climate; but are never deliberate: and the robberies, which originate in poverty, and which bad laws encourage, are rarely attended by violence. All this is a riddle,—nor is it less a riddle, that the females who can look unmoved, and even with pleasure, upon scenes from which a woman of any other nation turns away disgusted, do not possess less refinement than the females of other countries. Generally speaking, the character of the Spanish woman is kind and compassionate; and even among the lower ranks, I have heard sentiments that would do honour to the women of those countries that are esteemed the foremost in refinement.

The first attempt at a horse race in Madrid, was made last autumn; and as I am upon the subject of diversions, I shall give a slight sketch of the Spanish mode of conducting these things. The ground chosen for the race, was a sandy road, extending from the bridge of Toledo along the canal. The road is a common cart road, covered with stones, and full of ruts; and the distance was about two miles. A large concourse of persons was attracted to the spot by the novelty of the entertainment. There were between two and three hundred horsemen, and upwards of twenty carriages on the ground; among others, the handsome equipage of the Duke of San Carlos, the owner of one of the horses, an English mare, called Pensive. Her only opponent was a Spanish horse. Pensive was ridden by a jockey, dressed in the English fashion; the horse, by a Spanish groom, in the dress of a peasant. Pensive was a very indifferent animal, but had seen better days, and would have been distanced at a sixth-rate English race. Before starting, the horses were held by a man at the head of each, and at a signal, they were let go. The greatest possible anxiety was shewn by the spectators, that the English mare might be beaten; but it came in two or three lengths before its opponent. This created extraordinary disappointment; but the crowd resolved that the next heats should be different; and they carried their resolution into effect. They formed an avenue just wide enough for the horses; and as the Spanish horse passed, every one struck it with a stick, a whip, a stone, or whatever was at hand, and so urged it on; and partly owing to this, and partly owing to some carts intercepting the road, the Spanish horse gained both heats. This triumph was followed by loud acclamations; and so intemperate was the mob in its joy, that the grossest insults were offered to the carriage of the Duke of San Carlos as he left the ground. I heard it reported, that the Duke intended to take the field again with better horses, and upon better ground; and that horse races in Madrid would re-commence at a future time, under the patronage of one of the Infantes.

CHAPTER VI.

MEMOIR OF MURILLO.

A SLIGHT sketch of the life of Murillo, will not be considered an inappropriate introduction to some notice of his principal works, yet to be found in the Picture Gallery of Madrid; and in the churches, convents, and hospitals of Seville.

ESTABAN MURILLO, the prince of painters, was born at Seville, on the 1st of January, 1618. The small town of *Pilas*, in Andalusia, has disputed this honour with Seville; but the claim of Pilas to this distinction has probably arisen from the fact, that his mother was from Pilas, and that he inherited, through her, some property in that neighbourhood. But it is of little importance whether the courtly Seville, or the lowly Pilas, gave birth to Murillo; they may feel equally honoured in his name, for the name of Murillo belongs to his country. How he acquired the name of *Estaban*, has also been matter of dispute: some say he derived it from his father, who, it is said, was called Gaspar Estaban Murillo; and others are of opinion, that he took the name of his maternal uncle; but this dispute is of even less importance than that respecting the place of his nativity. Neither of the Estabans are now alive, to claim the honour of such a name-son; and Murillo's honours are independent of his kindred.

Great painters, more than any other class of eminent men, have given intimation, during childhood, of the distinction to which they have afterwards attained; and if the chronicles and traditions of Murillo record truly, his infancy did not form an exception. This fact is not difficult to account for; because, at the earliest age, the genius of the painter finds facilities for displaying itself. The infant musician to whom nature has denied a vocal talent, cannot, without an acquaintance with some instrument, convey a knowledge of his powers; still less can the infant poet embody poetic conceptions, without an acquaintance with language: but the painter finds, every where around, the means of giving expression to his thoughts: a dark and a light substance are all he requires; and in Spain, where the walls of the rooms are almost universally white-washed, the infant Murillo could find no obstacle to the indulgence of his genius.

The parents of Murillo saw no good likely to arise from an inclination for daubing the walls, and scratching the brick floors; and did all that lay in their power to discourage it; but the boy knew his calling, and still continued to disappoint the hopes of his father, who had destined him for the church; and to exhaust the patience of his mother, who, as it is said, returning one day from mass, found that her only picture, which she prized highly—an infant Christ and a lamb—had suffered an extraordinary transformation. Murillo had taken the glory from the head of the Christ, and substituted his own little hat, intending to represent himself; and the lamb he had converted into a dog—an animal in which he took great delight. Murillo was then too young to be conscious of any impiety in this transformation; the bent of his mind through life, was wholly averse from this: but his parents, despairing of a cure, thought it advisable to let him have his own way, and sent him to the house of his kinsman, *Juan de Castillo*, who undertook to teach the youthful Murillo the first principles of design and colouring.

This Castillo was no despicable hand; especially in the art of colouring, for a knowledge of which, he was partly indebted to Luis de Varjas, who had sometime before returned to Seville from Italy, bringing along with him the knowledge which he had acquired in Florence. Besides the youthful Murillo, Castillo could boast of several other disciples in his school; particularly Pedro de Moya,—of whom, more hereafter,—and Alonzo Cano, whose freedom of touch, natural design, and charming colouring, afterwards secured for him a high rank among Spanish painters. But Murillo, whose genius was of still a loftier kind, soon supplanted his companions in the favour of his master, by the yet more rapid progress which he made in the art; but he continued, notwithstanding, to discharge the menial offices of grinding the colours, cleaning the brushes, and preparing the canvas,—such being the original conditions upon which he had been admitted into his relation's workshop.

There was at this time much rivalry among the masters in Seville, each of whom had a school in his own house,—and this rivalry was fully partaken by their pupils; for the reputation of the schools necessarily depended, in a great measure, upon the proficiency of the pupils. Murillo felt deeply interested in the honour of his kinsman's school; and he, probably perceiving in his young disciple, a promise of excellence that might afterwards reflect honour upon himself, was the more assiduous in his instructions; so that, after a few years, Murillo had well nigh exhausted the information which his master was able to communicate.

But at this time Castillo suddenly quitted Seville to reside in Cadiz; his school was broken up, and Murillo was left without a master. It is probable that the most important moment of his life,—that upon which has hinged his future character,—was, when feeling the helplessness of his condition, he meditated upon his future prospects, and present necessities; and asked himself that plain question, which must be put and answered by all who are situated like him, "What shall I do?" How much depended upon this resolve! for often has genius been extinguished because no friendly hand was by, to fan the flame yet struggling for existence,—often discouraged, by being left to grope its way in darkness. Some in Murillo's condition, might have abandoned a profession that held out no solid advantages; and others, would have sought a new master. But Murillo, whether from a confidence in his own powers, or from an unwillingness to enter any of those other schools which had been rivals to Castillo's, came to a resolution more fortunate for himself and for the world: he determined to throw himself upon his own resources, and to trust in his genius.

It happened, at this time, to be the fair at Seville, at which season there was always a demand for devotional pictures, both for the uses of the pious at home, and for exportation to America. But these pictures were always of the most wretched description, and painted by the lowest artists; and with so much haste, that it not unusually happened that some favourite saint was painted during the time that the devout purchaser bargained for the price; nor was it a rare occurrence that the painter should be required to change a Magdalen into a Madonna; a Virgin into St. Anthony of Padua; or a group of cherubs into the souls in purgatory. Murillo took his place in the fair, and painted whatever was required, at whatever price was offered; and there can be little doubt that this varied and rapid practice gave a freedom to the pencil, and a facility in the expression of ideas, which years of study under a master might have failed to produce.

Murillo had now attained his twenty-third year; and at this time a circumstance occurred, which had an important influence upon his future career; this was, the arrival in Seville of Pedro de Moya. It will be recollected, that Pedro de Moya was a co-disciple with Murillo, in the school of Castillo; but he had, some years before, and while Murillo was still a pupil, left it and Seville; and had subsequently gone to Flanders as a soldier, with a greater disposition to see the world than to paint. But his natural propensities had only been suspended by the desire of novelty, so natural to youth: for meeting in Flanders with the works of Van Dyk, and other eminent Flemish masters, he returned to his profession, and became a disciple of that great painter, under whom he acquired those graces, with which he returned to Seville, to excite the admiration and the hopes of Murillo.

Murillo, struck with the improvement of his former companion, set himself to imitate his style; but fortunately for Murillo, who might otherwise have degenerated into a copyist, Moya soon quitted Seville, and he was left to his aspirations and his difficulties. Conscious of his own great imperfections, he had obtained a glimpse of what might be the reward of courage and perseverance; and his desires suggested many projects for their gratification. It is a trying, and yet a happy moment for genius, that in which humility and pride arise together, bringing with them the discovery, that the past has been a blank leaf in existence; but begetting a desire to turn over another, and to fill it with things that shall never be blotted out. Such was, doubtless, the state of the young painter's mind, when he resolved upon quitting his native city, and seeking in Flanders, or Italy, the opportunities by which he might hope to realise his dream of fame.

But Murillo was without money, and without friends; and how could he travel to Flanders or Italy? His reputation in Seville, as a painter, was small; for although his practice of working for the fair, had in reality increased his powers, it was little likely to add to his respectability; and it was a question, therefore, not easily solved, how he should obtain the means of effecting his design. But even in this extremity, courage did not desert him; and an expedient was found, by which he might modestly replenish his purse. He purchased a large piece of canvas; primed it himself; and dividing it into unequal parts, painted upon it, every possible variety of subject,—saints, landscapes, animals, flowers,—but particularly devotional pieces. With this treasure, he went to Cadiz, to tempt the masters of the India vessels. Among so many subjects, the taste of every one could find something to gratify it, and he returned to Seville without any of his canvas, and with a little stock of pistoles.

Murillo did not now delay a moment longer the execution of his purpose. Communicating his design only to his brother, who lived at Seville in the house of an uncle, he left his native city at the age of twenty-four, to return, and afterwards enrich it with undying memorials of that genius which is the glory of Spain, and the just pride of the city where it was chiefly exercised.

It is a long and toilsome journey from Seville to Madrid; and many must have been the anxious thoughts that filled the mind of the adventurer; but the predominating feeling would doubtless be buoyant, for youth and genius are fertile in hope. We think we see the young painter leave his native town,—long visible in the majestic tower of the cathedral, at which he often turns round to gaze. We follow his steps (for his journey was performed on foot) up the banks of the *Guadalquivir*, flowing towards his home; we see him with his scanty supplies toiling up the defiles of the *Sierra Morena*, and looking upon the other side, over the wide plain of *La Mancha*; and we see him with a quickened step, hasten towards the capital, when he first descries its towers in the midst of the desert that surrounds it.

Velasquez was, at this time, first painter to the king's bed-chamber, and highly esteemed at the court of Philip IV.; he was then past the prime of life, and almost beyond its vicissitudes; and surrounded by friends, and full of honours, he could feel no jealousy of the friendless boy who came to him for advice and protection. Murillo no sooner arrived in Madrid, than he bethought himself of waiting upon Velasquez; and he found in this good man, and excellent painter, a friend who instantly became his guide; and who never deserted him, even when the progress of the pupil seemed to point out a rival of his own immortality.

Velasquez questioned Murillo as to his family, his studies, his knowledge, his motives, and his wishes; and, like a true lover of his art, admiring the spirit and enthusiasm which were disclosed in the answers of Murillo, and approving the motive of his journey,—and, doubtless, discovering in his conversation, tokens by which a man of Velasquez's experience and knowledge, might draw a presage of his future greatness, he took the young painter under his roof as a pupil, a friend, and a countryman. Murillo did not accept the hospitality of Velasquez without immediately proving himself worthy of it. The object of his journey was uppermost in his thoughts; and Velasquez, without delay, afforded him the requisite facilities for prosecuting his design. He sent him to the different palaces, and to the convent of the Escurial, that he might see, and study, the pictures of the great masters; and directed him to select such as he might be ambitious of copying; and by this, Velasquez could not fail to obtain farther insight into the bent of his genius, and would even be able to judge better of its extent. What a moment for Murillo, when, entering the sacristy of the Escurial, he first beheld the works of Raphael, and Da Vinci, and Titian, and Paul Veronese!

The three years that followed the arrival of Murillo in Madrid, afford little incident for the biographer. During these years, he was no doubt laying the foundation of his future eminence, by practising his pencil and his eye among the excellent models to which he had access; among whom, no one was a greater favourite with Murillo than his kind friend and patron, Velasquez. It is certain, that he also highly esteemed the genius of Titian; and although he adopted no exclusive model, his admiration of that great head of the Venetian school is discernible in many of his works.

It appears, however, that Murillo did not confine himself to the study of these two masters, but that he also occupied himself with the works of Van Dyk, and of Rebera (Españoletto); for when Velasquez accompanied the king into Catalunia, Murillo, upon his return, shewed him three copies from pictures of Van Dyk, Rebera, and himself. These were presented to the king; and surprised equally the court and Velasquez, by their fidelity, and the excellence of their execution; so much so, that Murillo is said to have been advised to occupy himself henceforward with the works of only these masters.

But the time now approached, when Murillo should no longer copy the works of others; but when he should himself become a model for the imitation of succeeding ages. At the return of Velasquez from a second journey, in which he had accompanied the king to Saragossa, he was so much struck with the progress of his *protégé*, that he told him he could gain nothing more by a residence in Madrid; and advised him to travel to Rome, to which city he offered to furnish him with letters of recommendation, and other advantages; not the least of these, being the command of his purse.

The true reason of Murillo's rejection of this advice, it is impossible to ascertain; but he had resolved upon returning to his native city. It has been commonly said, that the importunities of a brother whom he highly esteemed, and certain domestic causes, recalled him: but it seems more probable, that his determination was the result of an internal conviction, that he had already accomplished the end for which he left the place of his nativity: and it is also possible, that a disinclination to be a farther debtor for the good offices of Velasquez, without which he could not have journeyed into Italy,—may have had its influence. Velasquez, although not approving the determination of his young friend, did not oppose his design; and Murillo returned to his native city.

It chanced, that at this time the Franciscan friars desired to have eleven historical pictures, to adorn the *Claustro Chico* of their convent; but, as the sum to be paid for these, arose solely from alms which a devout person had collected for the purpose, it may be supposed that the painter who might undertake to execute the order, could not expect a very liberal remuneration. Accordingly, the principal painters then in Seville, shewed no great disposition to engage in the work; and the friars, failing to secure the talents of any of those who had the reputation of being the first masters, found themselves obliged to be contented with an inferior hand, and applied to Murillo, who, being then more needy than his brethren, willingly undertook the commission, in which he no doubt perceived other advantages than the paltry remuneration proposed to him.

No sooner was this order executed, than Murillo found the reward of his perseverance, and a repayment of all his anxieties and difficulties. The utmost surprise was excited in Seville; he was universally courted; the performances of his pencil were greedily sought after; and he at once found himself the acknowledged head of the schools of Seville. This was indeed an hour of pride for the friendless artist, who, a few years before, had cast himself and his fortunes upon the wide world.

But another reward awaited Murillo,—the hand of Donna Beatrix de Cabrera y Sotomayor, a lady of Pilas, possessing many virtues, great sweetness of temper, and mistress of a considerable fortune. Her claims to beauty have been doubted; for no picture of her is known to be extant: the story, however, which is related respecting the manner in which he won her, is rather at variance with this supposition. It is said that Murillo, having occasion to visit Pilas, on account of some property which had descended to him in right of his mother, saw the Donna Beatrix; and struck with the sweetness of her countenance, and her other graces, became enamoured of her. Her station in life, however, was higher than his own; and despairing of a successful issue, he was trying to efface the impression she had made, when a circumstance occurred that renewed the recollection of her, by suggesting a means of advancing his suit. He accepted an order to paint the altar-piece for the church of St. Geronimo, at Pilas; and in the countenance of an angel, he painted that of his mistress. This delicate gallantry is said to have won the heart of the Donna Beatrix. The story may, or may not be true; but it is chronicled in Pilas.

From the time of Murillo's marriage, he appears to have run a constant career of glory; advancing in true excellence, and in public estimation. His style suffered some changes during this career; but always towards perfection; improving in sweetness and delicacy, and in warmth and richness of colouring. The earliest celebrated picture of Murillo, after his first change in style, was *The Conception*, for the Franciscan convent; from the archives of which, it appears that he received for it the sum of 2500 reals (25*l.* sterling); a small sum even in those days; but it is probable that Murillo might have taken into consideration, the reputed poverty of the order; and this is the more probable, since shortly after, in 1656, he painted the great picture of St. Anthony of Padua, for the baptismal altar of the cathedral of Seville, for which he received 10,000 reals (100*l.* sterling). But the most glorious epoch in the career of Murillo, was later in life: it was between 1670 and 1680, that he painted for the hospital *De la Caridad*, his Santa Isabella, the Prodigal Son, the Miracle of the Loaves and Fishes, Moses Striking the Rock, John of God, and others, that are looked upon as the most excellent of his works. The twenty-five celebrated pictures also, that adorn the Capuchin convent in Seville, were the production of his ripest genius; but they were painted antecedently to the pictures of the Caridad; and to those who are conversant with the works of Murillo, there is a still more perfect charm in the latter. The highest price that Murillo appears to have received for any picture, is 15,975 reals,—a little more than 150*l.* sterling. This he received for the Miracle of the Loaves and Fishes.

In the year 1658, eleven years after his return to Seville, Murillo projected the establishment of an academy of painting in his native city. This project was warmly opposed by many, especially by Herrera, who had newly returned from Italy, filled with high, and doubtless just notions, of the greatness of the Italian schools; and looking with suspicion upon a school, whose founder had never travelled beyond Spain. But the genius of Murillo, at length conquered the prejudices of Herrera; and the academy was opened on the 1st of January, 1660, with Murillo at its head, as first president. It may be mentioned, as an instance of the painter's modesty, that in the list of members of the institution, drawn out by himself, the name of Herrera appears at the head of the list.

There is one passage in the life of Murillo, connected, too, with some of the greatest efforts of his genius, upon which there appears to hang a mystery. I allude to that period during which he painted the twenty-five pictures that adorn the Capuchin convent. The usual version of the story is, that Murillo, finding himself in some difficulty, took refuge in the Capuchin convent; and in return for the protection afforded him by the monks, dedicated his talents to the embellishment of their church. But it is difficult to give credence to this. Murillo led a blameless life; and ever after his marriage, his pecuniary circumstances were flourishing. What, therefore, could be the necessity that obliged Murillo to take refuge in a convent, it is impossible to conjecture. At the same time, it is certain that in that convent there are twenty-five of Murillo's pictures; and in the archives of the convent, there is no record of any sum having been paid for these. It is certain, too, that the tradition is steadily maintained within the convent, that Murillo was an inmate of it during two years. The monks even relate little traits of his character and habits; and a picture of St. John, the Virgin, and Child, is shewn by them,—painted upon a table napkin; and it is certain that the picture is Murillo's. The only solution of these difficulties is, that upon the death of his wife, which took place some time previous to the year 1670, he retired for a time to the Capuchin convent; for it is impossible to believe that he was never an inmate of it. The event which really took place in the life of Herrera (*hermoso*) may perhaps have given rise to the false version of the story of Murillo. Herrera was forced to take refuge in the church of the Jesuits at Seville; and his genius has adorned its walls.

I must not omit the mention of an anecdote that is generally related of Murillo. At the time that he lived near the church of Santa Cruz, it contained, in one of its chapels, the well-known "Descent from the Cross," by Pedro Campaña, now adorning one of the altars in the cathedral. It is said that Murillo was accustomed to spend much of his time in that church, in admiration of this painting; and that one day, the Sacristan being about to close the gates, and finding Murillo there, asked him what detained him so long in that chapel; to which Murillo is said to have answered, "*Estoy esperando que estos santos varones acaben de baxar al Señor de la Cruz.*"—I am waiting until these holy men take down the Lord from the Cross;—a compliment, perhaps, scarcely merited by the picture of Campaña, and therefore probably never paid by Murillo.

The last picture that engaged the hand of Murillo, was one which he undertook for the Altar Mayor of the Capuchin convent at Cadiz. This was in the latter end of the year 1681; but he did not live to complete the work. While engaged upon this picture, he fell from the scaffold, and was so much injured, as to be obliged to return to Seville. But the shock he had received, aided by declining years, produced disease; and his illness increased until the evening of the third day of April in the following year, when he expired in the arms of his friend and disciple, Don Pedro Nuñez de Villavicencio.

From the will of Murillo, preserved in the Franciscan convent of Seville, it appears that he left little property besides that which he acquired by his marriage. This was bequeathed to his sons; for his only daughter had taken the veil early in life. In this will, there is also contained an inventory of his pictures, among which one of himself is mentioned. This picture, now in the possession of Mr. Williams, of Seville, represents Murillo about the age of thirty, nearly the time of his marriage, and conveys a very pleasing idea of the appearance and character of the painter. The proprietor, himself an excellent artist, and an intelligent man, has made a masterly drawing from the original: the drawing is in the possession of Mr. Brackenbury, his Britannic majesty's consul at Cadiz; and from that gentleman's admiration of Murillo, it may be hoped, that an engraving from it may soon enable every admirer of that illustrious man to have the gratification of possessing his likeness.

The character of Murillo, as a painter, can scarcely be separated from his character as a man: humility, kindness, benevolence, were conspicuous in him; and these are also seen in the choice of his subjects. Undoubtedly one of the greatest among the many charms of Murillo, consists in the beauty of his invention; his subjects seldom fail to interest the benevolent feelings: we have affection in all its varieties—charity under its many forms; and even in subjects purely divine, he contrives to throw over them a human interest. Never was affection more touchingly delineated, than in the picture of St. Felix, the Virgin, and Child, in the Capuchin convent of Seville; in which the virgin, after having put the infant into the arms of the holy man, that he might bless him,—stretches out her own, that he may be restored to a mother's embrace. Nor were ever love and benevolence more beautifully blended, than in the picture of "Santa Isabella, Queen of Portugal, curing the sick and wounded," wherein the old woman watches, with a mother's anxiety, the cure of her wounded son. And where shall we find charity, and its reward—the favour of Heaven—more impressively displayed, or more powerfully conceived, than in the picture of "John of God." This has always seemed to me, one of the happiest illustrations of the genius of Murillo. "John of God" is supposed to have gone, as was his usual practice during the night, to seek and succour objects of distress. The picture represents the Saint, carrying on his back a wretched being, whom he had found in his walk, and bending under the weight of his burden; but suddenly, feeling himself relieved of a part of his load, he looks round, and sees by the miraculous light that encircles his heavenly visitant, that an angel has descended, to assist him in his work of charity.

Innumerable examples might be given from the works of Murillo, of that peculiar charm which consists in investing spiritual subjects with a human interest. Murillo never painted a virgin and child without blending a mother's human love, and the pride of a mother in her human child, with the expression of divinity, and with the loftier pride of having given birth to the Son of God. Nor in any representation of scenes in the life of Christ, did Murillo ever forget to unite the human with the divine character. In the great painting, also, of "Moses striking the Rock," in the Hospital *de la Caridad*, there is a fine exemplification of the excellence of which I have been speaking. This miracle is not made a mere display of power; Murillo has introduced into it many varieties of human feeling—the anxiety of those who wait for the accomplishment of the miracle—the burning impatience, and eager importunities of thirst, and its contrasted satisfaction.

This peculiar charm of Murillo, consisting in his choice of subjects, has made him a painter for all men; for all, at least, who have human emotions to be excited, and human affections to be touched. But this is only one excellence of Murillo; and standing apart from others, it might belong to any man of benevolence and fine imagination, however indifferent a painter he might be. Murillo possesses, besides, that rare union of high qualities, some of them pre-eminently his own, which has made him one of the first of painters in the eye of the learned, and of all those who have loved and studied the divine art.

The most striking excellence in the conception of Murillo's figures is Nature, accompanied by Grace; but never, as in some of the Italian masters, grace running into affectation:—and what is there to desire more in the conception of a picture, than perfect nature and perfect grace, without any alloy of affectation? In the combination of these excellences, Titian, among all the Italian masters, most nearly resembles Murillo; but if a picture of this eminent master be placed beside a picture of Murillo, executed in his ripest years, the former appears feebler; this is probably owing to the unapproachable excellence of Murillo's colouring, which combines the brilliancy of the Flemish, with the truth of the Venetian. Looking at the greatest efforts of Murillo's pencil, there seems nothing left to desire. An invention noble and touching; a conception natural and graceful; a composition just, elegant, correct; a colouring rich and true; and over all a delicacy, a spirituality, a beauty,—arising from the blending of the whole,—that leave the mind satisfied, but which never satiate the eye.

There are few painters so difficult to copy as Murillo; although, perhaps, few masters have had more copies attributed to them. The greater number of these are said to be pictures in Murillo's early style; but the colouring may always be detected; for it is that which constitutes the chief difficulty to him who desires to copy this master. The Italian masters are, almost without exception, easier to copy than Murillo, because their colouring is more simple. Murillo's colouring, although appearing simple, is extremely artful; and this the copyist speedily discovers. Many pictures of the Italian schools convey an idea of a marbly surface; but the pictures of Murillo, executed at the epoch of his greatest excellence, convey the idea of flesh and blood. This effect cannot be produced by one colour, or one lay of colours; nor even in perfection by the glazing, of which Titian used to avail himself: the effect is produced by one colour shining through another; and by the skilful use of these, Murillo has often given to his ground, or back colour, the effect of air, in place of an opaque body; and the artist who attempts to imitate Murillo by a mixture of colours, will find it impossible to equal the effect of the original.

It is a common idea, that in Spain, the pictures of Murillo are scarce; and that the galleries, churches, and convents, have been despoiled of their greatest treasures. This idea is very erroneous. Spain has, no doubt, been robbed of some of her choicest paintings, and some have found their way into other countries as objects of traffic; but the Peninsula is still rich in the works of Murillo. In the gallery of Madrid, of which I shall presently speak, there are thirty pictures of Murillo's, two-thirds of them at least, undoubted originals. In the Cabinet of Natural History, three of the greatest productions of his pencil are found. In private collections in Madrid, particularly in those of the Duke of Medina Cœli, the Duke of Liria, Sir John Meade, and some other individuals, there may be nearly an equal number. In Seville, the twenty-five pictures painted for the Capuchin convent, are all in their places. In the hospital *de la Caridad*, there are four of Murillo's greatest productions. The collection of Mr. Williams of Seville, is distinguished by twelve Murillos; and in other private houses in Seville, perhaps as many more may be found. In the cathedral there are six or eight; and in Cadiz, in the possession of Mr. Brackenbury—in Murcia,—and particularly in Valencia, Murillos may be discovered by any lover of the fine arts, whose inquiries are directed towards that object.

The present government of Spain watches over the works of Murillo with a jealousy, that is not shewn in any thing else that concerns the prosperity or the honour of the country. By a late government order, the works of Murillo are prevented from leaving Spain; but as bribery is able to conquer many difficulties in that country, the exportation of pictures is not impossible.

CHAPTER VII.

MADRID.

The Picture Gallery; the Works of Murillo; the Annunciation; the Virgin instructed by her Mother; Landscapes; Velasquez and his Works; Meeting of Bacchanalians; the Forges of Vulcan; Españoletto, and his Works; Villavicencio; Juanes; Alonzo Cano; Cerezo; Morales; Juanes' Last Supper; the Modern Spanish School; Aparicio; the Famine in Madrid; Italian Gallery; Flemish School; the *Sala Reservada*; Statuary; Cabinet of Natural History; *Sala Reservada*; the Patrician's Dream; the *Desengaño de la Vida*; Private Collections; the Duke of Liria's Gallery; Churches and Convents; Church of San Isodro; San Salvador; Santa Maria; San Gines; Santiago; San Antonio de Florida; Convent of Las Salesas; de la Encarnation; the Franciscans; Santa Isabella; Hidden Pictures; San Pasqual; Santa Teresa; the Palace.

SINCE the erection of the splendid building dedicated to the reception of pictures, most of those which formerly adorned the palaces, have been transferred to it; and Madrid can now boast of a gallery equal in extent, and perhaps little inferior in excellence, to any of the other great galleries in Europe. To the lover of the Spanish school, the gallery of Madrid possesses attractions which no other can offer. Besides forty-two pictures of Murillo, it contains fifty-five of Velasquez, twenty-nine of Españoletto, seventeen of Juanes, six of Alonzo Cano, and many of Ribalta, Cerezo, Villavicencio, Moralez, &c.; other saloons contain between four and five hundred pictures of the Italian schools, and about three hundred of the Flemish school; and in the *Sala Reservada*, there are several *chef d'œuvres* of Titian and Rubens. At present, I return to the Spanish school, to notice first, a few of the most distinguished works of Murillo.

The first we remark is "A Holy Family," a picture taken away by the French, and afterwards restored. The invention in this picture is in the highest degree original: we have not a mere uninteresting group; but life and feeling. The infant Jesus—Jesus, but yet a human child—holds a bird in his hand, which he raises above his head, to save the little favourite from a dog that tries to seize it: Saint Joseph holds the child between his knees; and the Virgin, who is engaged in some female employment, lays aside her work, that she may admire the playfulness of her son. This picture is admirably suited for shewing Murillo's chaste and charming conception of female heads and children.

Passing over "An Infant Christ," "A John Baptist," and "The Conversion of St. Paul," all three, but especially the second, admirable pictures, the next strikingly fine work of Murillo's is "The Annunciation." This is considered, and with justice, a very finished composition. The angel Gabriel announces his heavenly message while the Virgin is reading; and in her countenance, as she turns to hear the announcement of Divine will, Murillo has happily displayed the blending of human surprise, with the sudden illumination of divinity that fills her mind.

A "Mother of Griefs," and a "Magdalen Seated in the Desert," the latter, a picture in Murillo's best style of colouring, might be next named; but I pass to "The Martyrdom of the Apostle St. Andrew," which may vie with the most celebrated pictures of this master. While the Saint is extended on the cross, the heavens open and the seraphim descend, bearing the palm branch and the crown of martyrdom. The blaze of celestial light which shines upon the martyr, and its contrast with the *chiaro scuro*, are unrivalled in their effect. In the design and conception too, there is great beauty of thought, particularly in illuminating the martyr with the same celestial light that encircles the heavenly hierarchy.

"The Adoration of the Shepherds," and the "Infant Jesus and St. John," are both worthy of an eulogium; the one for its force and harmony of colouring, the other for its charming simplicity. But one more beautiful than these is "the Virgin receiving a Lesson in Reading from her mother, Saint Anne." This possesses in a peculiar degree, Murillo's excellences of nature and grace. It is all human, as it ought to be; and the divine calling of the Virgin is only known by two heavenly cherubs hovering above, and dropping a crown of roses upon the head of the unconscious child.

Besides these more striking pictures of Murillo, there are several others of great merit. "Eliezar and Rebecca," two or three "Conceptions," heads of St. Paul and of John the Baptist, the Vision of St. Bernard, and two landscapes. The landscapes of Murillo are at least curious. His proficiency in this department was probably acquired in his early years, when, at the fair of Seville, he painted whatever his customers demanded.

"A Gipsy and a Spinster," also in the gallery, are specimens of that other class of pictures by which Murillo is known to many who have not been in Spain. These pictures being smaller, and not preserved by the jealousy of the convents, more easily find their way into other countries; accordingly, in this style, we find some of the choicest morsels of Murillo in foreign galleries; in Munich, in the Dulwich gallery, and elsewhere.

This slight enumeration affords but a very imperfect glimpse of the pleasure which the admirer of Murillo will find in the gallery of Madrid; but in other collections, and especially in Seville, I shall have occasion to return to the works of this head of the Spanish schools; and at present I must proceed to notice briefly the pictures of Velasquez, and others, in the Madrid gallery.

Velasquez, the worthy rival, and, in many points, the equal of Murillo, whose master he was, differs in many respects from his pupil. He studied in Italy; and there acquired that knowledge of the antique, which is by some esteemed above the greater simplicity and unaffected grace that distinguish the works of Murillo. In Velasquez, thought and invention are not so spiritual as in his pupil, but his composition is more learned; and in his colouring, he is not excelled even by Titian. His colours often disappear under his brush, because they become in reality the thing which he desires them to represent.

One of, but not the most extraordinary composition of Velasquez in the Madrid gallery, is "A Meeting of Bacchanalians." One in the midst of his companions, is seated across a barrel, which is his throne; he is crowned with vine-leaves, and presents a similar crown to another, who receives, with a kind of mock respect, this order of knighthood. There is extraordinary truth in this picture; in fact, the painter makes the spectator one of the party; he laughs in spite of himself, and almost feels as if he too had drained some bowls to the memory of Bacchus.

"The Infanta Margaritta-Mary of Austria," is one of the most splendid compositions of Velasquez. Velasquez is himself represented with his pallet and brushes, painting the Infanta; and to distract the attention of the infant princess from the portrait, two dwarfs, and her favourite dog, are made to enter the apartment. This picture, in composition, design, and colouring, is absolutely perfect.

Several portraits of Philip the Fourth, the friend and patron of Velasquez,—particularly one upon horseback,—and one exquisite portrait of the Duque de Olivares, his prime minister, deserve the highest eulogium: a magnificent portrait also, which has obtained the appellation of "Esop;" "a Suitor for a Place," who, in a garment of worn-out black, presents his memorial; a portrait of a "Dwarf and a Great Dog," the "Surrender of the Town of Breda," and a "Manufactory of Tapestry," in which the painter has introduced a charming female countenance, are all excellent in their kind; but the most striking of all the pictures of Velasquez in this gallery is, The Forges of Vulcan. The god of fire is at his forge, surrounded by his Cyclopes, when Apollo brings him intelligence of his wife's dishonour, and his own. The attitude and expression of Vulcan, are in Velasquez most powerful manner. He turns round as if scarcely crediting the message of infamy; but his dark countenance, which seems to grow darker as the spectator looks upon it, expresses that jealousy has taken possession of him; his hammer rests idle in his hand, and the Cyclopes, also, suspend their work to listen. The scene is the more striking from the true and brilliant colouring; the red light falling upon the group, and contrasting with the darkness of the subterranean world beyond. It is a pity that such a picture should contain any striking fault; and yet it is impossible to avoid perceiving that the Apollo is weakly conceived.

I have not even named the titles of the greater number of Velasquez pictures; but these few, although not better painted than many others, are more striking, owing to their subjects. The lover of portraits also, will find ample gratification in the many excellent works of this master, which adorn the gallery of Madrid.

Of the works of Españoletto, the Madrid gallery contains several *chef d'œuvres*. This painter was born near Valencia, in the year 1589; he was first the pupil of Ribalta, and afterwards, at Rome, of Caravaggio. The style of Españoletto is, perhaps, more than any other painter, opposed to that of Murillo. Simplicity, and the graces of nature, are no where to be found in his works, which are forcible,—often verging upon the terrible; and whose object seems to be, rather to seize the imagination than to touch the heart. But the painting of Españoletto, after he had seen the productions of Correggio, lost much of that exaggerated manner which the lessons of Caravaggio had taught him; and in his later styles, he has produced pictures which unite force with many other excellences. Among the best of this master's works in the Madrid gallery are, St. Peter the Apostle weeping for his sins; in which the design, the composition, and the colouring, are all excellent;—Jacob's Ladder, in which the author shews that he has profited by a study of the works of Correggio;—"The head of a Priest of Bacchus," full of character and vigour;—and "Saint Sebastian," in the last and best manner of the painter. Besides these pictures, there are many in the author's first exaggerated style; such as "Prometheus bound," "a Magdalen in the Desert," and "Christ in the Bosom of the Eternal;" which, if not pleasing, are at least interesting, as contrasts with the improved style of Españoletto's later compositions.

There are still other pictures in the gallery which must not be passed over; but I shall not classify them. "Children Playing at Dice," by Villavicencio, the disciple of Murillo, and in whose arms he died;—a picture full of nature and naïveté, and charmingly coloured.

"The Visitation of Saint Elizabeth," by Juanes. Juanes is, undoubtedly, one of the greatest of the Spanish painters after Murillo and Velasquez; and this, as well as others of his compositions, is entitled to rank immediately after the works of these two masters.

"Saint John the Evangelist writing the Revelations in the Isle of Patmos," by Alonzo Cano.

A "St. Francis in ecstasy," by Cerezo, who was an excellent painter; and who, in design and colouring, sometimes approached Van Dyk.

"The Virgin and the Infant Jesus." By Morales, sometimes called "The divine."

An incomparable "Head of Christ, crowned with Thorns," by Juanes.

"A Dead Christ," by Alonzo Cano.

"A St. Francis," by Ribalta.

"The Entombment of St. Etienne," by Juanes, a picture which partakes largely of the graces that distinguish the school of Raphael and his followers.

"The Supper," by Juanes. This is considered the *chef d'œuvre* of the author, and was taken by the French, and afterwards restored. Love and devotion have seldom been more beautifully painted than in this picture.

"Jesus Interrogated by the Pharisees, touching the Tribute," by Arias.

A saloon is dedicated to the modern Spanish school; containing the pictures both of the living masters, and of those who have lived within the last forty or fifty years. It is impossible to look upon these pictures without feeling more and more the excellences of those painters, who now live only in their works; for in the modern Spanish school, there is little to remind us of Murillo and Velasquez; or even of Juanes, Cano, or Morales. Difficult as it must be admitted to be, to imitate the unapproachable excellences of Murillo, it is surprising nevertheless, that the attempt to do this should scarcely ever be made. After the death of Murillo, as well as during his lifetime, there were innumerable artists, who, although conscious of the immeasurable distance at which they followed, yet, thought it wisdom patiently to seek the traces of his footsteps: and it is a merit of no ordinary kind, if a painter can earn the character of being a follower of Murillo; because this at least proves, that he is able to appreciate, even if he cannot approach, his excellences. But in looking through the gallery of the modern school, not one picture can be found, of which it may be said, "this is in the style of Murillo."

Aparicio and Lopez are the painters who at present enjoy the highest reputation; but neither of these will suffer a comparison with Bayeu, who died thirty-five years ago, or with Goya, who has long since retired from a professional life, but who still lives at Bourdeaux. As little can the pictures of Bayeu or Goya be compared with the compositions of the ancient school.

The two great pictures of Aparicio are, "The Glories of Spain," and "The Famine in Madrid,"—and both are more in the style of the modern French, than of the ancient Spanish school. The latter of these is intended to represent (as the author of it says), "The Triumph of Spanish Constancy." During the time of the French invasion, in the winter of 1811-12, the famine that raged in Madrid, almost realized what we read, of ancient Numantia; and many examples of heroic patriotism are recorded of this time. The painter has chosen the following:—an old man, extenuated, and apparently dying, is stretched upon the ground; and the dead bodies of his daughter, and his grandson are at his feet: three French soldiers passing by, touched with compassion, offer him food; but he, disdaining to accept food from the enemies of his country, covers his face with his hands, that he may not be tempted, and prefers death to what he considers dishonour.

The subject is undoubtedly fine, and the picture has many merits; but it is impossible, in looking at any picture, the moral of which is intended to convey an abhorrence of French dominion in Spain, not to feel that we cannot give our sympathy to it; and the same feeling has led me, in walking over those fields of battle that have been fields of glory for England and Spain, to ask "where are the fruits"? They are nowhere to be found: the purchase-money was the blood and treasure of England: and what did they purchase?—the deeper degradation of Spain.

That part of the gallery which is appropriated to the Italian schools, I shall pass over almost without notice; not because there is nothing in it worthy of being mentioned, but because I could hope to add nothing to what is already universally known of the character of the great Italian masters. In the Italian saloons, there are many copies, and many re-touched pictures: but there are also a considerable number of sterling compositions. Guido, Andrea del Sarto, Giordano, Guercino, Leonardo da Vinci, Bassano, Alexander Veronese, Sachi, Salvator Rosa, Tintoretto, Titian, and Raphael, all contribute of their abundance. The most remarkable of these pictures, is the portrait of *Mona Lisa*, a lady of incomparable beauty, and the wife of Francisco Giocondo, a gentleman of Florence. This picture cost 180,000 reals.

In the saloon dedicated to the Flemish, German, and French schools, there are also some fine originals; particularly, two *Claudes*; a Bacchanalian piece, of Nicholas Poussin, remarkable for the excellence of its design, and its inimitable harmony; "David and Goliah," also by N. Poussin; and "The Adoration of the Angels and the Shepherds," by Mengs.

To be admitted to the *Sala Reservada*, requires an order from the Director of the institution; but this is always politely given upon application. In passing to the Sala Reservada, the visitor is conducted through a large apartment, in which a picture of the King's landing at Cadiz occupies one of the walls. The painting contains upwards of twenty figures as large as life,—all portraits: this room is a favourite lounge of his majesty, who, it is said, contemplates with much complacency, the picture that records his restoration. In this Hall, the attention is speedily withdrawn from the picture, by two tables, that well merit admiration. At a little distance, they appear like exquisite flower-pieces, painted on glass,—but upon approaching, you discover that they are of marble; the ground black, and the flowers Mosaic. Upwards of eighty different flowers are represented: and, among the marbles of Spain and her late colonies, is found every variety of colour necessary to give perfect truth to the representation.

In the Sala Reservada are two "Sleeping Venuses," by Titian, both too good to be seen by every one; "Adam and Eve," by Rubens; and eight other pictures, by the same master. An excellent *Tintoretto*, "Andromeda and Perseus," by Titian; "The Three Graces," by Albano; and two delightful compositions of Breughel, in which trees, flowers, nymphs, and fountains, are charmingly mingled.

In the Hall of Statuary, I found tables quite equal in workmanship to those in the king's apartment, but in value, far exceeding them. One represented a landscape, another a marine view—and the effect was produced, not merely by marbles, but also by innumerable precious stones, especially emeralds and sapphires; these tables were executed by a Spanish workman, about fifty years ago. Several good statues adorn the Hall; and it seems to me, that the state of modern sculpture in Spain, is more promising than that of its painting. A "Venus," by Alvarez, and another, by Gines, are both excellent. There is also, connected with this Hall, a workshop, called the Hall of Restoration; there, many artists were employed in repairing the ravages of time. Venuses lay on the ground without arms; and Graces without noses. An Apollo was getting fitted with a new foot; and a Calliope with another knee.

There are two public days in the week, upon which all have access to the galleries; but I had permission to go at any time, and very frequently availed myself of it; most frequently upon the days that were not public. I generally saw a considerable number of artists engaged in copying; and all, in the galleries allotted to the Italian masters. Opportunity must not be confounded with encouragement. The artists of Spain have sufficient opportunities, but there is no encouragement; and both are needed, that the fine arts in a country may be flourishing. Spain, as well as Italy, produced her great painters when the art was considered necessary, and was therefore encouraged; when the adornment of the temples of religion was deemed essential; and when the different orders of friars, perceiving the effect of externals upon the minds of the people, vied with each other in multiplying these helps to devotion.

Another building, dedicated to the reception of works both of nature and of art, is the Cabinet of Natural History. The public galleries are allotted to mineralogy chiefly; in which department, the specimens are numerous, and many of them fine. I particularly remarked the very fine specimens of native gold; but above all, the extraordinary number and beauty of the precious stones, in which, I believe, the cabinet of Madrid excels every other in Europe. I noticed nearly forty emeralds upon one piece of rock, many of them of great size, and almost all of the purest quality. The specimens of crystal and of sulphur are also numerous and fine; but the native marbles are perhaps the most interesting of all. I counted no fewer than two hundred and seven different kinds. Other saloons in the building are appropriated to Conchology and Zoology, in which the most perfect department is considered to be that of the Butterflies.

But the Salas Reservadas are more interesting than the public rooms. One of the Salas is entirely filled with precious stones, and vessels made of them; it would almost fill a volume to enumerate the riches contained in this Hall. In the lower part of the building, also a Sala Reservada, is the Hall of Pictures; and here are preserved some of the choicest specimens of Murillo's pencil. I could not understand why these, and other pictures in this Hall, are not deposited in the great picture gallery; the more exquisite they are, the better reason there seems to be for increasing the facilities for seeing them,—especially as there is nothing in any of these pictures improper to meet the public eye; the only excuse for a Sala Reservada.

Among the paintings here, is that exquisite one of Murillo, "Santa Isabella Queen of Portugal, curing the sick and wounded," which I have already noticed in the memoir of Murillo. Another in this Hall, which ranks among the highest of Murillo's productions, and which is less known than some others of his works, is "the Patrician's Dream." A Roman noble asleep, is supposed to have a vision, in which a celestial message commands the building of a temple. The Patrician is seen buried in deep sleep, and an angel is near, pointing to a single column. The colouring in this picture is exquisite; and a spirit of the most perfect repose is thrown over the whole composition. In the same Hall hangs the companion to this picture, in which the Patrician is seen recounting his dream to the Pope.

A "Mary Magdalen Penitent," by Murillo, and a "St. Geronimo," by Españoletto, are also found here; but one of the most extraordinary pictures I have seen in Spain, is preserved in this Sola; it is by Antonio de

Pereda, and is called "the Desengaño de la Vida," which cannot be literally translated into English, but which means "the Discovery that Life is an Imposture." A Caballero, about thirty years of age, handsome and graceful, is represented asleep, and around him are seen all those things in which he has found enjoyment. Upon one table lie heaps of gold, books, globes, and implements of study; upon another are the wrecks of a feast; musical instruments are scattered here and there; magnificent mirrors and paintings adorn the walls; and on the floor lies a jewel-box, which has dropped from the hand that hangs over the couch where he reclines; and a miniature of a beautiful woman has fallen out of it. But in the air, opposite to the sleeper, is seen the vision of an angel, who holds a scroll, with certain words inscribed upon it, which the painter has left for the imagination to decipher, and which may be naturally interpreted, "Let all pass,—eternity lies beyond;" and the countenance of the sleeping figure shews not only that he sees a vision,—but there is something in it so placid, so resigned, that it seems to express an acquiescence in the advice of the angel,—"Yes, it is all a cheat."

I have perhaps dwelt too long upon this picture; but I was strongly impressed with its excellence, both in design and execution.

There are few private collections of great value in Madrid. Those of the Duke of Liria, and of the Duke of Medina Cœli, are the best. The former of these collections adjoins the duke's palace in the *Plaza de Liria*; and having carried an introductory letter to his Grace from the Marquesa de Montemar, the duke did me honour to accompany me round the gallery. I found three good Murillos,—"St. Roch," "Santa Teresa," and "Murillo's Son,"—the latter only in his best style; several pictures, which may or may not be Salvator Rosa's; but generally believed to be originals; two of Rubens: a "Battle of the Amazons;" and "Ruben's Wives,"—the latter in his best manner; "Adam and Eve chased out of Paradise," by Paul Veronese, in all the grace and sweetness of that esteemed master; "A Holy Family," by Gaspar Poussin; three landscapes, by Nicholas Poussin; a charming portrait of Mengs, by himself; two or three delightful gems of Berghem, full of beauty and repose; three Titians, "A Holy Family," the female head singularly beautiful; "St. John in the Wilderness," a picture of great richness and finish; and "A Boy playing with a Lion;" a "Venus," by Brencino; two Canalettos, but neither of them in his best style; "The Children of Velasquez," by Velasquez; and "A Holy Family," by Perucini, the well known *élève* of Raphael,—for which the present possessor paid 10,000 sequins.

The Duke of Liria's gallery also contains some statuary; a Venus, by Alvarez, the Spanish Canova; and the Mother of the Duke by the same sculptor. The Duke of Liria, although not himself a great connoisseur in the fine arts, is their liberal patron, which is better. The chapel in the Duke's house contains some good fresco, by Antonio Callione de Torino, a very promising Spanish painter, but who, by his bad conduct, was forced to exile himself, and who lately died in France.

The collection of ancient armour in the residence of the Duke of Medina Cœlie interesting than his pictures. It contains, among other things, the armour of Gonsalva de Cordova. The Duke of Medina Cœli possesses immense revenues; but, like the greater number of the grandees in Spain, he is encumbered with debt, being robbed by those to whom he has delegated the management of his property. It is a certain fact, that several of the Spanish nobles whose property lies in Andalusia, and other southern provinces, have never seen their own estates.

The lover of pictures will be disappointed in his search among the churches and convents of Madrid. The collegiate church of *San Isidro* contains the greatest number; but they are not of first-rate excellence; and this church, as well as all the others in Madrid, are so dark, that it is impossible to obtain a proper view of any thing which they contain. The church of San Isidro is not worthy of being the metropolitan church. The interior is in the ornate taste of the Jesuits, to whom it formerly belonged; but it has taken a higher rank since the real body of the patron saint of Madrid, and the ashes of Santa Maria de la Cabeza, have been deposited within its walls. There are, however, some pictures in this church which, with a favourable light, are worth visiting. Among the best are "the Conversion of St. Paul," and "San Francisco Xavier baptizing the Indians," by Jordan; a Christ, by Morales; another Baptism of the Indians, by Jordan; and several others of Cano, Coello, and Palomino. In one of the chapels are two urns, wherein are deposited the ashes of Velarde y Daoiz, and the other victims of the 2d of May, 1808, in memory, as it is recorded, of "the glorious insurrection of Spain."

The church of San Salvador is only interesting as containing the tomb of Calderon; that of Santa Maria is honoured by being the depository of the miraculous image of our lady of Alumeda. San Gines has a Christ by Cano, and the Annunciation by Jordan. Santiago contains two or three pictures by Jordan; and San Antonia de Florida boasts of a fresco by Goya. This limited interest is all that the churches of Madrid possess.

Among the sixty-eight convents in Madrid, few possess great interest from the treasures of art which they contain. It is in Seville, and in the other cities of the south, that the convents offer the chiefest attractions to the lovers of painting.

The greatest and the richest among the convents of Madrid, is Las Salesas. It was founded by Ferdinand the VIth., and is adorned with a profusion of the most beautiful marbles and porphyries of Cuenca and Granada. I noticed several columns of green marble, upwards of sixteen feet high, and each of one piece. Both in the church of the convent, and in its sacristy, there are some good pictures; and a fine marble monument, raised by command of Charles III. to the memory of the founder, does credit to the taste of Francisco Sabatini, who designed it, and to the powers of Francisco Gutierrez, who executed it. The morning service in the church of this convent is enchanting; the nuns, all of noble family, and well educated,— chiefly in the same convent,—seem to have made music a principal study. I have never heard an organ touched with so delicate a hand, as in the Convento de las Salesas.

The church of the Convent de la Encarnacion, also a female convent of bare-footed Augustins, contains beautiful marbles, and some pictures perhaps worth a visit, by Castillo, Bartolomé, Roman, and Greco.

The Franciscan convent is worth visiting, only on account of its great extent; it contains ten courts, and dormitories for two hundred monks. Every where the Franciscans are the most numerous. It is said of Cirillo, the chief, or general, as he is called, of the Franciscan order,—he who is now exiled from Madrid,—that he boasted of his power of putting 80,000 men under arms: a force almost equal to the king's. The head of the Franciscan order used formerly to reside in Rome, but the present head has made choice of Spain.

The convent of Santa Isabel was robbed by the French of many choice works of Españoletto; but it still possesses some pictures by Cerezo, Cœllo, and others,—these are in the church of the convent; but it is said that there are others in the interior, which it is difficult, if not impossible, to see. There cannot be a doubt, that among the many hundred convents in Spain, in the interior of many of which no man has ever been,—no one, at all events, whose object has been to search for pictures,—there are hidden, many productions of the first masters. These may have come into their possession in many ways; they may have been the individual property of distinguished persons previous to taking the veil; they may have been bequeathed to the convent by the founder; the gift of the painters themselves; or offerings of the devout: but it is certain, that pictures of value and merit are shut up in convents. I am acquainted with a gentleman at Seville, who himself purchased "Joseph's Dream," by Juanes, and a portrait by Giordano, from the abbess of the Dominican convent at Seville,—who sold them in order to purchase certain ornaments for one of the altars.

The convent of San Pasqual was, previous to the French invasion, the richest in paintings of any of the convents or monasteries in Madrid. It possessed the compositions of Van Dyk, Veronese, Titian, Da Vinci, Jordan, and many other eminent painters. The greater number of these have been removed; but there are still several left, that well repay the trouble of a visit to the church of the convent. There is the "Taking of Christ in the Garden," by Van Dyk; a "Conception," by Españoletto; "St. Francis in Prayer," by Veronese; and one or two others by Españoletto. Several more valuable than these, among the rest, "Jacob Blessing his Sons," by Guercino, have been removed from the church into the interior; but the porter informed me, that it was intended shortly to restore them again to the different chapels in the convent church. These paintings were bequeathed to this convent by its founder, the Duke de Medina y Almirante de Castilla; affording another example of the manner in which pictures may come into the possession of nuns.

There is reason to believe that in the convent of Santa Teresa also, there are paintings of value. During the time of the scarcity in Madrid, several pictures that used to adorn the church of the convent, were openly sold; and these have since been replaced by others,—several of them, works of merit, which could not have come from any other quarter than the interior of the convent. But in the church, there is yet preserved a picture of great beauty and value: this is a copy of the "Transfiguration of Raphael," by Julio Romano; one of the most successful disciples of that great master. This picture, also, was left to the convent by its founder, the Prince Astillano, under the condition that it should never be parted with.

The only other convents worth visiting, are the Las Salesas Nuevas, which contains a Crucifixion of Greco; and Las Descalzas Reales, in which will be found a good statue of the Infanta Doña Juana, daughter of Charles V., from the hand of Pompeyo Leoni.

I regret much that I was not able to see the palace with so much attention as it deserves. I delayed from time to time making any application for admission; and in the mean while, the situation of the queen bringing the court from La Granja two months sooner than usual, the palace was only to be seen at short intervals, when the king and queen left it; and as the hour of the *sortie* was uncertain, the interval between obtaining the order, and their majesties return, was very limited.

The new palace, although but a small part of the original plan, is nevertheless one of the most magnificent in Europe. It was begun in the year 1737, and was built under the direction of Don Juan Bautista Saquete, the disciple of Jubarra. It is a square, each front being 470 feet in length, and 100 feet in height; a balustrade runs round the whole, to hide the leaden roof, and the walls are relieved and adorned by innumerable columns and pilasters. The interior of the palace corresponds with its external magnificence; every thing within it, is of the most costly and most sumptuous kind, bespeaking the habitation of monarchs who once owned the riches of half the world. The paintings have been mostly removed to the gallery, but some yet remain; particularly "the Rape of Proserpine," and some others, by Reubens; "a Magdalen," and some others, by Van Dyk; several exquisite paintings, by Mengs; and among others, "The Agony in the Garden;" two Cattle pieces, by Velasquez; and several charming pictures, by Tintoretto, Carlo Maratti, and Andrea Vacaro. The ceilings also, by Bayeu, Velasquez, and Mengs, may well excite admiration. In the apartments of the Infantes likewise, I understand there are some valuable paintings; but these, I had not an opportunity of seeing. The great license that is allowed the public, has sometimes surprised me. The royal apartments are of course guarded; but any person may walk up the stairs, and along all the corridors, and even through the ante-rooms without being once questioned.

In the neighbourhood of the palace, is the royal armoury, which contains many ancient relics; among others, the arms of Ferdinand and Isabella, of Charles V., of King Chico, the last of the Moorish kings, and of several kings and warriors,—those hardly-used Americans, who took the Spaniards for gods, and found them worse savages than themselves.

CHAPTER VIII.

Literature; Difficulties to be encountered by Authors; the Book Fair; Digression respecting the Claims of Spain to Gil Blas; Public and Private Literary Societies; Libraries; Obstacles to Improvement, from the State of Society; Female Education; Education for the Liberal Professions; Course of Study for the Bar; Course of Medical Studies; Charitable Institutions; Consumption of Madrid; Prices of Provisions.

A PRIEST, with whom I was acquainted in Madrid, telling me one day, that he had thoughts of going to London or Paris, to print an English and Spanish Grammar, and a German and Spanish Grammar, which he had written; I asked him why he did not print them in Madrid, since they were intended for the use of his own countrymen,—especially as they could contain nothing political? His answer was, that nothing was so difficult as to obtain a license to publish a book, even although it contained no allusion to politics: and "the better the book," said he, "the more difficult it is to obtain a license, and the more dangerous to publish; because Government does not wish to encourage writing, or even thinking, upon any subject: and the publication of a good book sets men a-thinking."

This comprehensive reply explains, pretty nearly, the present state of literature in Spain; judging of it by the number and merit of published works:

The number of books published, from 1820 to 1823, was very considerable. The energy then communicated to letters, from the removal of almost all restriction, was extraordinary: books upon all subjects issued from the press; and the best proof, perhaps, that can be given, that many of these were books of talent, is, that most of them are now prohibited. Literature, however, then received an impetus, which still continues in some degree to affect it, notwithstanding the difficulties to be overcome: for there is a considerably greater number of books published now, than previous to the revolution; and no reasonable doubt can be entertained, that another removal of the restrictions which press upon literature, would bring into the field a large accession of native talent.

Even after a license has been obtained to publish a manuscript, its publication is still a dangerous speculation; because it frequently happens, that when the book is printed, and partly circulated, some great man, even more fastidious than the censors, discovers a dubious passage, and the book is prohibited. There are four difficulties, therefore, which an author must resolve to face, before he sits down to prepare his manuscript:—the probability that he may be refused a license; the probability that, before being licensed, his manuscript may be mutilated—a probability that, I am told, amounts almost to a certainty, unless the work be upon one of the exact sciences; the probability that, after the work be published, some caprice may forbid its sale; and the certainty, that if the work be a talented work, the author of it, whether obtaining his license or no, will be looked upon with suspicion; and, if in Government employment, will almost certainly lose his appointment.

These are sad drawbacks upon literary exertion. But there is yet another: men are afraid to read, as well as to write; and the sale of a work is therefore insecure. Book-sellers do not care to venture upon the publication without some guarantee; the consequence of which is, that almost every book published in Spain, is published by subscription, or in numbers, or both in numbers and by subscription; by either of which modes the risk is lessened. What should we say in England of bills posted about the streets, announcing a new novel to be published by subscription, and in numbers? Yet I saw an announcement of this kind, of a novel to be called El Dissimulador—the Dissembler. But the greater number of books at present published in Spain, are translations from French and English, adapted, of course, to the Spanish censorship. I noticed the following announcements, by bills posted on the walls:—"Universal History," from the French, in numbers: "the History of Spain," a new edition, in numbers: "the History of Spanish America," an original work, in numbers. This manuscript I should think must have been sadly carved. The following were announced by subscription:—"Selections from French and English Literature;" "Church History;" "Chateaubriand's Holy Land;" "the History of the Administration of Lord North," a singular enough choice; "the History of the English Regicides;" "the Works of Fenelon;" a new edition of "Gil Blas;" "Evelina;" and while I was in Madrid, proposals were circulated for publishing by subscription, and in numbers, the whole prose works of Sir Walter Scott. I heard of one voluminous, and rather important work, about to be published by a society called "the Academy of History," viz., all "the inscriptions in Greek and Latin, now extant, throughout Spain." The Arabic inscriptions are not included in the work, these being already collected and printed.

Although the Spanish government endeavours by every means to repress intelligence, and thwart the progress of knowledge, there is no lack of books in Spain, to those who will, and dare to read them. This is indeed done under the rose; but it is done. There are two libraries in Madrid, which contain the best French authors; and persons who are known to the librarian, or recommended to him, may obtain almost any prohibited book. I had personal proof of this. Sitting one morning with a lady connected with the royalist party, but a woman of very liberal views, and one of the few blue-stockings of Madrid, I was compassionating the situation of those who, like herself, were lovers of literature, but who were denied the means of gratifying their taste. The lady assured me she had no need of my compassion upon this score, for that she might have any French author she chose, and many English authors, from the library of———. And when I expressed some surprise at this, she desired me to fix upon any celebrated books that occurred to me, and they should be put into my hands in less than half an hour. I chose accordingly; and in ten minutes, I had in my hands a Paris edition of "the Social Compact," and the Basil edition of "Gibbon's Historical Work." Books, therefore, may be had; but persons are afraid to have and to read them.

A considerable number of prohibited books slip into circulation at the time of the fair. I was then in Madrid, and spent a few hours each day strolling among the booths and stalls, and talking with the vendors of goods. Every kind of article is exposed at this fair,—clothes, calicoes, jewellery, toys, hardware, china, but especially books and pictures. The books were innumerable; and their high prices seemed to be an index to a good demand; and yet I thought that, on the last day of the fair, the shelves were but little relieved of their burden: probably, however, the book merchants had other copies to replace those that were sold. The books were of all descriptions; but the most numerous class, was theological and religious; particularly the lives of saints, who have all their biographers. The next most numerous class was history; chiefly histories connected with Spain and America. Then followed Spanish plays, and Spanish novels. After these, Spanish translations from French and English works. And lastly, books in foreign languages. Among the Spanish translations from English works, I noticed many copies of Blair's Lectures, Clarissa Harlowe, and Goldsmith's Roman History. Among the books in English, I observed Bell's Surgery, the Life of Wellington, and Lady Morgan's Italy, whose English dress had blinded the eyes of the Inquisitors, who looked very scrutinizingly at the stalls. I saw several copies of Machiavelli,—a prohibited book, I believe,—and one Bible in 14 volumes, with notes by a Dominican friar, which I have no doubt are sufficiently curious.

I questioned the book-vendors, as to the demand, and in what current it ran. They informed me, that the demand for religious books was on the decline; and that the lives of saints especially, were almost unmarketable. Translation from French and English, especially the former, and even works in the French language, were asked for; the demand was also large and constant, for the Spanish dramatists and novels; especially Don Quixotte and Gil Blas, which were to be seen on every stall, in great numbers, and of various editions. I opened several copies of Gil Blas, and found the title-page invariably in these words,—"Aventuras de Gil Blas de

Santillana, robadas á España, y adoptadas en Francia por M. Le Sage; restituidas á su patria y à su lengua nativa per un Español zeloso que no sufre se burlen de su nacion." This is a point upon which the Spanish nation is very jealous; every educated person stoutly maintaining, that to Spain belongs the honour of having produced Gil Blas. It is evident, that in the dispute between France and Spain, regarding their respective claims to Gil Blas, the proofs must be drawn from the internal evidence afforded by the work itself. The only direct proofs that could be obtained, would be the production of the original manuscript. This however must lie upon the French; because if any plausible reason exist for supposing, that the Spanish manuscript got into the hands of Le Sage, the Spanish manuscript of course cannot be produced; and the French must produce their French manuscript. That this has never been done, seems to afford a primâ facie evidence in favour of the Spanish claims; especially if, as I believe to be the case, the internal evidence be also in favour of Spain. The belief that Gil Blas is a French work, and the work of Le Sage, is so universal, and I feel so perfect a conviction that this belief is erroneous, that I cannot allow this opportunity to escape, of introducing a short digression upon the subject.

The Spanish statement is this: that Don Antonio de Solis, a well-known Spanish author, wrote in 1665 a romance, entitled "Aventuras del Bachiller de Salamanca, ó Historia de Don Querubim de la Ronda;" that Solis could not publish this in Spain, owing to its containing many allusions to persons then existing; and that Hugo, Marquess of Lionne, ambassador from France at the Spanish court, who was a man of letters, purchased not only a library of Spanish poets and dramatists, but also many manuscripts, which were afterwards seen in the library of the Marquess's third son; that it is known that this son, Julio de Lionne, was intimately allied in friendship with M. Le Sage, and by him the manuscript of the Bachelor of Salamanca, "Don Querubim de la Ronda," was confided to Le Sage, who divided the work, making from it the Adventures of Gil Blas, and the Bachelor of Salamanca. These assertions afford a presumption; but no more. At the same time, it cannot escape observation, that a complete refutation of these assertions, or at least of the result drawn from them, would be, the production by the heirs of M. Le Sage, of the manuscript, either of Gil Blas, or the Bachelor of Salamanca. But there are many proofs drawn from the work itself, strongly supporting the presumption afforded by the tale told by the Spaniards. Of these I shall state a few:—1st. There are many French words and phrases, which do not correspond with the usual elegance of Le Sage's style, and which have the appearance of being literal translations of Spanish words and phrases. 2nd. There are innumerable Spanish proper names in Le Sage's work, and particularly small villages, of which no foreigner could know the names, still less their geographical position. 3rd. We find in Gil Blas a variety of particular circumstances, usages, and habits, peculiar to

Spanish provincial life, of which no stranger could have a sufficient knowledge. 4th. There are in Le Sage's work innumerable errors in names of persons and towns, seeming to prove, that errors have arisen in copying the Spanish manuscript. The proofs of each of these might extend to a chapter: none of them, taken singly, amount to much; but when considered along with the story told of the manner in which the MS. came into the possession of Le Sage, unanswered, as it is, by the production of any French manuscript; and along with the admitted fact, that several of the incidental stories introduced into Gil Blas are to be found in old Spanish romances,—a strong conviction is produced, that Gil Blas is a Spanish, and not a French work.

A strange enough answer was made by the Count de Neufchateau, member of the French academy, to the assertion that Le Sage had availed himself of the Spanish manuscript. He said, Le Sage would not have taken to himself the merit of having written Gil Blas, if the work had been composed from the manuscript of another; and the reason he gives for his confidence in Le Sage's honour is, that he did not hesitate to acknowledge his other plagiarisms. He acknowledged that he took from Spanish authors "the New Adventures of Don Quixotte," published by him in 1735; "The Devil upon Two Sticks," published in 1732; "The Adventures of Guzman de Alfarache," published in 1707; "The Life and Doings of Estavanillo Gonzalez," published in 1734; and *The Bachelor of Salamanca,"* published in 1738. What the force of this argument is, I leave the reader to judge.

But to return from this digression. Private literary associations are out of the question in Spain: several were set on foot in 1821-22; but after the return of the king, any thing of this kind was known to be so obnoxious, that these societies dissolved themselves, without waiting for any express order to that effect. Two public institutions only, connected with literature, exist at present. Like every other institution in Spain, they are *Real,* and therefore under the surveillance of government;—their names are, "The Royal Spanish Academy," and "The Royal Academy of History." The object of the first of these, is to perfect the Castilian language; and with this view they have published two excellent works, a Dictionary and a Grammar, besides a treatise on Orthography, and several smaller writings. The object of the Academy of History is to separate truth from falsehood in the history of Spain, and to collect all that may throw light upon the ancient and modern history, as well as geography, of that country. This society has published an excellent Geographical Dictionary, which has gone through several editions; and is now on the eve of publishing the collection of Inscriptions which I have already mentioned, accompanied by notes.

There is no want of public and valuable libraries in Spain, particularly in Madrid. The two principal of these, are the Royal Library, and the Royal

Library of San Isidro. The former, founded by Philip V., was enriched in the reign of Charles III. by the accession of the library of the cardinal Arquinto, purchased in Rome; and in the reign of his successor, Charles IV., by several other libraries; and now amounts to 200,000 volumes. The Royal Library also contains many valuable manuscripts, particularly Arabic; and a rich collection of coins and medals, illustrative of Spanish history. The Spanish press has produced some fine specimens of printing, which are preserved in this library, particularly Don Quixotte and Sallust, both from the press of Ibarra. Besides the library of San Isidro, which contains about 60,000 volumes, there are some excellent libraries in the possession of private persons, particularly the Duke of Osuna, the Duke of Infantado, and the Duke of Medina Cœli: the latter of these was formerly open to the public; but so great public spiritedness looking too much like liberalism, it is now closed.

I have already spoken of the obstacles thrown in the way of knowledge, by the regulations respecting the schools and academies; and the fetters thrown upon education of every kind: these chiefly affect the rising generation; but I may mention, as another cause of the backward state of literature in Spain, *the tone of Spanish society*. Every Spanish house has its *tertulia*; and every man, woman, girl, and boy, is a member of one tertulia or another. The introduction to the tertulia begins at a very early age. I have seen boys who, in any other country, would have been in a school-room, or at play, present themselves regularly at the tertulia, and throwing off the character of boys, act the part of grown-up men. This necessity of resorting every night to the tertulia, not only interferes greatly with habits of study, by employing much valuable time,—but the preparatory education for the tertulia, if I may so express myself, is of the most unimproving kind. The foundation of the tertulia is gallantry,—here it is that the Spanish woman, after having reaped a harvest of admiration on the Prado, retires to receive that nearer homage which is prized still higher; and here it is that the Spaniard makes his prelude to future conquest. Gallantry is the business of every Spaniard's life; his object in frequenting the tertulia, is to practise it; and his principal study, therefore, is that frivolous and gallant conversation that is essential in the first place to captivate the attention of the Spanish woman. The Spanish ladies, with all their agreeable wit and affability, are ignorant almost beyond belief; and in a country where, more than any other in Europe, the society is mixed,—the extreme ignorance of the female sex, and the channel into which conversation must necessarily run every evening of every day throughout the year, cannot fail to have its effect upon the mind, and to act as a drawback upon the desire of knowledge, and literary distinction.

I understand that female education begins to improve; and that besides embroidery and music, a little history and geography are now taught in the schools, but not in the convents; so that the highest classes, who are mostly educated in the convents, are worse educated than the middle classes. While in Madrid, I had the pleasure of being conducted to a girl's Lancastrian school by its directress, Donna Hurtado de Mendoza, a lady every way worthy of the trust. During the time of the constitution, there were also two Lancastrian schools for boys; but these were suppressed upon the return of the king, who was prevailed upon, however, to allow the school for girls to continue. In the Lancastrian school there are at present 163 pupils, and the system pursued is precisely similar to that followed in England; part of three days every week is dedicated to instruction in the tenets of the Roman Catholic faith.

There is one fact I had nearly forgotten to mention,—a fact somewhat opposed to the narrow policy of the government in its hostility to the progress of literary knowledge. Eight young men, of promising abilities, were lately sent by the Spanish government to different cities to study the various branches of chemistry, with a liberal allowance from the public purse; and his majesty's gilder was also dispatched to England to make inquiries as to the manner of gilding buttons, and gilding bronze, with an allowance of 18,000 reals; and with another stipulation as to a farther and much larger sum, to be put at his disposal for the purchase of secrets.

In Spain, the education for the liberal professions is tedious and strict, but not expensive. The course of study required of a barrister includes no fewer than thirteen years, besides a previous knowledge of Latin, in which the student is examined before entering any of the law universities. The branches of study which occupy these thirteen years, are, three years of philosophy, which consists of logic, physics, metaphysics, and ethics; and in the first of these years, the outlines of mathematics are taught; but this branch of study is never pursued farther: after this course of philosophy, the theory of Roman law is entered upon, which occupies two years; one year of Spanish law then follows; next, Ecclesiastical law, which occupies two years; and this is all that is required to take the degree of bachelor: but rhetoric, theology, digest of law, and medicine, are required for a higher degree. At the end of each year, examinations are gone through, before granting certificates; and the whole of the instructions are in Latin, excepting rhetoric and Spanish law. The philosophy used, is that of Guebarra. The expense of instruction varies according to the university; at Toledo it is all gratis; at Alcala it costs about 50*l.* per annum; but many are admitted into the colegios, in which case the student is put to no expense. These colegios are particular foundations, under the patronage of certain great families. The education of an attorney requires only an apprenticeship, and that the candidate should be twenty-five years of age, and have a certificate of good morals; he has also to pass one examination in law. Before any barrister, attorney, or notary, be admitted to practice, he is obliged to swear that he will defend the poor gratis. Thirty are appointed each year from each society to defend the poor in civil cases; and every one is entitled to be put upon the poor list who chooses to swear that he is not worth 4000 reals (40*l.*); and it is a curious fact, that, in criminal cases, the prisoner is entitled to make choice of any barrister in Madrid to defend him. In Spain they do not understand that celebrated legal fiction, so implicitly believed by some sound heads in England, that the judge is counsel for the prisoner. I learned that the course of justice, or in plainer terms a legal process, is very expensive in Madrid; two-third parts, at least, of every account being absorbed in court dues and stamps.

The Spanish government is not unmindful of the lives and health of its subjects; for medical is even more strict and tedious than legal education.

There are three kinds of medical professors in Spain:—physicians, medico-surgeons, and cirujanos romancistos.

The first of these, after a course of the usual regular scholastic studies, go to the University, where they study anatomy, physiology, pathology, and the different branches of medical education; in which four years are employed. They then go through the hospitals, with professors appointed for the purpose—note down the diseases and their treatment, and submit their notes for revision, to the instructors; this occupies two years: after which they undergo examinations upon the theory and practice of medicine, before being admitted to practice.

The medico-surgeons profess both physic and surgery: they go through the same studies as the physician, adding chirurgical pathology, midwifery, clinica medica, and surgical practice; and are subject to examination upon all these branches.

The third class, the *cirujanos romancistos*, are literally surgeons who have not studied Latin, and are an inferior class. They are not required to have the same classical education as the others; but must study, and pass examinations in anatomy, physiology, chirurgical pathology, operative surgery, and midwifery. Those belonging to this class of medical practitioners, are forbidden, by a royal edict, from prescribing for inward complaints.

Madrid does not want institutions for the alleviation of bodily infirmity; there being no fewer than thirteen hospitals in the capital. The principal of these are, the General Hospital, which is chiefly supported by the receipts of the bull-fights; and the *Hospicio real de San Fernando*, which is also a workhouse, and is supported by imposts upon the entry of goods into the city. There is also an Hospital for Illegitimate Children, which receives about 1200 yearly, nearly one-third of the number being foundlings, and which is supported by the lottery; an Orphan Hospital, which supports about 800 orphans; several smaller orphan hospitals; and two lying-in hospitals.

There are also in Madrid, ten different institutions for philanthropic purposes—the succour of the wretched, and the relief of the poor; among these, *El Monte de Piedad* deserves mention. It is a public establishment, which lends money upon goods, which may be reclaimed at any time during a year, or even longer, in particular cases, upon repayment of the loan *without any interest.*

Madrid, I have mentioned in the former chapter, is supposed to contain 170,000 inhabitants; but this is partly conjecture,—no census having been lately made. In the year 1790, there died in Madrid 5915 persons; and 4897 were born: and in the year 1810, 3786 persons died; and 5282 were born. The following was the consumption of Madrid, in the year 1825: 230,000 sheep; 12,500 oxen; 70,000 hogs; 2,417,357 arrobas[A] of charcoal; 13,245 arrobas of soap; 40,809 arrobas of oil; 800,000 bushels of corn; 500,000 arrobas of wine; 50,000 arrobas of snow; 30,000 arrobas of candles; and 18,000 bushels of salt: and supposing, as there is reason to believe, that since that time the population of Madrid has increased 5000, the addition of a thirty-fifth part to these sums, will give nearly the present consumption of Madrid.

[A] An arroba is 25lbs. weight.

Madrid, although, with the exception of Constantinople, the most interesting city in Europe to visit, owing to the perfect novelty of scene which it presents even to him who has travelled through every other country, would not be an agreeable permanent residence. It is not like Paris, or Rome, or Vienna; in any of which cities a stranger may, if he pleases, live nearly as he lived in his own country. In Madrid, this is impossible; the hotels are execrable; boarding houses there are none; and although a stranger may find lodgings, he will find Spanish habits in them. Of the state of society, and of the diversions, I have already given some idea. These possess much interest to a stranger, but not any permanent attraction; so that after he has remained in Madrid long enough to gratify his curiosity with the novel spectacle of a people differing from all the rest of the world, in dress, habits, amusements, modes of life, and modes of thinking, he will begin to feel some desire to know what the world beyond Spain is doing; because of this, he can know nothing within Spain. But let no traveller leave Madrid to return to England. Seville and Granada lie beyond; and when the

Castiles have lost their attraction, Andalusia and its thousand charms await him.

Before closing this chapter,—the last that has any reference to Madrid,—let me give some information respecting the price of provisions, &c.

The Spanish capital is probably the dearest capital in Europe; and this cannot excite surprise, when it is considered that Madrid is situated in the midst of a sterile country, where there is no pasture land, no rivers, scarcely any gardens, and no communication with the sea, or with any of the distant and more productive provinces. Notwithstanding these drawbacks, the markets are well supplied; and all kinds of meat, poultry, game, vegetables, and fruit, may be had of an excellent quality: fish, and milk, are the only scarce articles. In the following enumeration, the best quality of every article is understood; it is not easy to render the prices with precision, into English money, because they are generally reckoned in *quartos*; but if the reader recollects that eight quartos are nearly $2\frac{1}{4}d.$, one quarto being $^{18}/_{64}$ths of a penny, it will be no difficult calculation to bring the prices to English value.

Beef, per lb. of 14 oz. 18 quartos. Veal, per lb. 30 quartos. Mutton, per lb. 18 quartos. Pork, per lb. 20 quartos.

The price of fish cannot be stated with accuracy; it is never seen excepting in winter, and the supply is so precarious, that it is impossible to approach the truth.

Bread, of the first quality, is 14 quartos per lb.; the second quality 10.

Ordinary wine of La Mancha, 21 quartos.

A fine fowl, 6 reals (1*s*. 6*d*.). A chicken, from 7*d*. to 10*d*. A duck, from 1*s*. 8*d*. to 2*s*. 1*d*. A goose, 3*s*. 6*d*. A turkey, from 4*s*. to 10*s*., according to the season. Turkeys, in Madrid, are not sold in the markets, but are driven through the streets. I have several times bought a small turkey for 3*s*. Pigeons, 1*s*. 6*d*. or 1*s*. 8*d*. a couple.

Coffee, 1*s*. 8*d*. per lb. Chocolate, 2*s*. 6*d*. per lb. Green tea, 10*s*. Black tea, 12*s*.; but it is scarcely to be found. Sugar, 1*s*. 8*d*., equal to English sugar at 11*d*. The natives use sugar at 10*d*.; but it is dirty and bad.

Goat's milk 4*d*. a pint during summer,—half that price in winter; cow's milk is difficult to be had in summer,—in winter it is 3*d*. a pint; Flanders butter 2*s*. 6*d*. per lb.; salted butter, from the Asturias and Galicia, may also be had at 1*s*. 6*d*.; but it is not good.

Vegetables are rather dearer than in England, especially potatoes.

Fruit is always excellent and cheap. A melon, such as cannot be seen either in France or England, costs 5*d.*; these are the Valencia melons, extremely pale, and of the most exquisite flavour. The finest Muscatel grapes are 1½*d.* per lb.

I have mentioned in a former chapter, that the bread of Spain is, without exception, excellent; and it is nowhere finer than in Madrid. The finest, is called *pan de Majorca*; but this bread is made partly with milk, and is not fitted for general use; the bread used by the better classes, is the *pan Frances*, very ill named, because it is much superior to any French bread. The lower orders, and many too among the middle classes, use *pan Candeal*, in which there is no leaven, and no salt.

I must not omit the mention of fuel; this is an expensive article in winter to a stranger who is not accustomed to sit without a fire. The American minister told me, that his fuel cost him 20*s.* per day in the month of August.

There is only one thing in Madrid remarkably cheap; that is, the keep of horses. From the same authority I may state, that the keep of a horse does not exceed 20*l.* per annum. The usual food of horses is cut straw, and a little barley; and it appears that they thrive well upon this regimen: but in Spain, horses are lightly worked, no one travelling with his own horses, but invariably with mules hired for the purpose.

CHAPTER IX.

STATE OF PARTIES, AND POLITICAL PROSPECTS.

IN dedicating a chapter to the consideration of the state of parties, and the probable political prospects of Spain, I am anxious to avoid the imputation of any assumption of superior knowledge, or exclusive information. My knowledge upon these subjects has no farther claim to superiority than that which arises from its having been gathered upon the spot: this ought, no doubt, to count for something; both because a resident in a country is better situated for judging of the authenticity of information, and is able to avail himself of a greater number of sources; and because, from personal observation, many helps are obtained. During the several months that I remained in Madrid, my acquaintance lay among men of all parties. With Carlists, Royalists, and Liberals, I was upon terms of equal intimacy; and I never found, among men of any party, the least backwardness in speaking privately the sentiments of their party; or in avowing its views, and speculating upon its prospects. Many have been so candid as to avow themselves hypocrites. Military men in Madrid, and at Barcellona, sworn to support the government, have admitted to me that they were Carlists,—associated in private societies of that party which held their meetings every second night: and employées in Toledo, dependents upon the existing government, who, in that hot-bed of ultraism, found it prudent even to pretend some sympathy with the opinions of the Carlists, have told me in confidence, that they were neither Loyalists nor Carlists, but Liberals. From this it may be gathered, that a person residing in Spain, and unsuspected of any improper object, may, without much difficulty, learn the opinions and views of men of different parties. The conclusions which I may occasionally draw, many may think erroneous. I will only say, that I am unconscious of being biassed by prejudice; and whatever I set down shall be based as much as possible upon fact and observation.

I left England in the belief that there existed in Spain two great parties,—the Constitutionalists, and the adherents of the government; the latter party indeed somewhat divided,—and comprising many shades of opinion, ranging from absolutism, to a point somewhere between that and moderation. But this estimate I discovered to be very erroneous. I found three parties in Spain: the Absolutists, there denominated Carlists; the Government party, there called the moderate party; and the Liberals. The most influential of these parties is, beyond all question, the first. Reckoning the total population of Spain, this party is by far the most numerous; it comprises the great mass of the lower orders throughout Spain; and in many parts, almost the whole population,—as in Toledo, the towns and villages of the Castiles, and the provinces of Murcia and Catalunia. It comprises, with few exceptions, the 130,000 friars, and a great majority of the clergy, and it comprises a considerable proportion of the military, both officers and privates; but chiefly the former. With such components, it is evident that this party does not depend for its power, solely upon its numerical superiority. Every one knows, that there is uncounted wealth in the convents and churches of Spain. I do not speak merely of the wealth in jewels, and golden urns, and images, locked up in Toledo, and Seville, and Murcia, and the Escurial, and elsewhere,—though much of this would, without doubt, be made a ready sacrifice to the necessities of the party; but also of the more available riches, well known to be possessed by many orders of friars; among others, by the Carthusians, the Dominicans, and Hieronomites. Hundreds of the convents in Spain have no possible way of consuming their revenues—for it is a fact, that the poor orders are invariably the most numerous; and we generally find a very limited fraternity in those convents whose revenues are the largest. In the Carthusian convent, at Granada, there are only nine monks; and the land for more than half a league round, and comprising numerous country houses, and hamlets, is the property of this convent. In the Convento de los Reyes, in the neighbourhood of Valencia, there are indeed twenty-seven monks; but one of their number admitted to me, that the revenues of the convent exceeded 500,000 reals, (5000*l.* sterling): and in the neighbourhood of Murviedro, (the ancient Saguntum), there is another convent of Carthusians, which owns seven villages, and a tract of land as rich as any in Spain, nearly a league square, and which contains only seven monks.

In place of three of these examples, as many hundreds might be given. The same monk who admitted to me the amount of the revenues of the Convento de los Reyes, said, in reply to my question as to what they did with so much wealth, that "times of need might come;" and there can be little doubt that other friars might make a similar reply. Nor can it be doubted, that many of the reputed poor orders, who live upon charity, have no need of it. The prayers, blessings, and other godly offices of the Franciscans, bear the highest value in the market of superstition; and in those convents in which the visitor dare not put money into the hands of the friar, I have frequently been reminded, that a certain little golden saint, or silver virgin, accepted the *pecetas* which were laid upon their altars. This cannot be considered a digression, because it explains another source of influence, besides physical strength, possessed by the apostolicals.

It scarcely requires that I should adduce any proof of the fact stated, that the lower orders, and the friars, are attached to the party of Carlists. The present government of Spain is considered by the friars to be guided too much by moderate principles. They perceive that they lose a little ground; and, shut out as they are in a great measure, from commerce with the world, they are ignorant of the pace at which the world moves: and the secret is breaking upon them but slowly, that the strength of governments lies in free institutions. They still fancy that men are to be governed by the scourge and the cowl; and believe that another Philip II. would elevate the fortunes of Spain, and raise up all the props of the Roman Catholic faith. I have myself heard one of the monks in the Escurial say, that the king was no friend to them: and then, pointing to the urn of Philip, pass an eulogium upon *his* virtues and piety. If any other proof were needed, of the attachment of the friars to the Carlist party, the circumstance mentioned in a former chapter might be stated; that the chief of the Franciscan order was detected in a conspiracy to overturn, or at least to overawe the government. I need say nothing of the lower orders, because, with few exceptions, they and the friars are one.

I have said, that a great proportion of the regular clergy also are Carlists. I know that many are not; because many are intelligent men, who have at all events the acuteness to perceive, that a more despotic government would not secure its permanency; and whose alarm at the progress of liberalism in the world, is not so great as that of the friars. But the majority of the priesthood are ignorant; and the majority are therefore Carlists. Besides, their interest lies that way—the head of the church in Spain, the Archbishop of Toledo, is the head of the party; the Archbishop of Seville is one of its warmest partizans; and almost all the archbishops and bishops, hold similar sentiments: the curate, therefore, who envies the luxuries of a canon, must both profess his adherence to that party, and employ his influence in its favour.

To the friars, the priests, and the lower orders, I have added a part of the military, as partizans of the Carlists; I might also include a considerable number of the employées. That such is the fact, I have had many personal proofs, as well as information from the most authentic sources. The reason alleged by those in government employment, whether civil or military, for being favourably disposed towards that party which would rather see Don Carlos than Ferdinand at the head of the government, is, *the indecision of the king's character.* They say that merit is not rewarded; that services are not requited; that promotion is not upon a footing of justice; and that neither in civil nor military service, is there any dependence upon government favour, which shines or is withdrawn by caprice—which favouritism purchases, and slander destroys. All this they ascribe, and probably with justice, to the king's *want of character*: and the idea among them is very general, that under Don Carlos, a system of greater justice, and impartiality, and decision, would be pursued in every department of the state. I have sometimes wished, when I have heard these good qualities attributed to Don Carlos, that he possessed, along with them, some of those other virtues which Spain requires in a sovereign: there might, in that case, be a more speedy prospect of happiness for Spain.

Such appear to me to be the elements of the party called Carlists,—the strongest in numbers and wealth, and the weakest in intelligence.

Classing the parties according to their numerical strength, I must next mention the party called Liberals; but generally, in England, known by the name of Constitutionalists. If, by this party, be meant those who desire a return to the Constitution of 1820; or who would be satisfied to leave the settlement of the government to the wisdom of an army of refugees,— there is no such party in Spain: but if, by the liberal party, we are to understand those who perceive the vices of the present government, and who dread still more the ascendancy of the Carlists; those who view with satisfaction the progress of enlightened opinions in politics and in religion, and who desire earnestly that Spain should be gradually assimilated in her institutions, with the other civilized nations of Europe,—then the liberal party comprises the principal intelligence of the country; and subtracting from the population, the lowest orders, the employées, the friars, and the priests, it possesses a great numerical majority. In any other country than Spain, this party would wield an influence to which its numerical strength would not entitle it; but in Spain, the light of intellect spreads but a little way; for it has to struggle with the thick mists of ignorance and superstition; and when we say that the liberal party comprises nearly all the intelligence of the country, it must be remembered, that intelligence is but scantily sprinkled over the face of Spain; and that, therefore, enlightened Spain, and enlightened England, ought to convey very different ideas of numerical strength.

It is a curious fact, that the adherents of the existing government should be the fewest in number; yet, this is certainly the truth. With the exception of perhaps the majority of the employées, a part of the regular clergy, and the greater part of the army, its friends are very thinly scattered; and its influence scarcely extends beyond the sphere of its actual benefits. Its patronage has been greatly circumscribed since the lost of the Americas; its lucrative appointments are centred in a few; and above all, its power and patronage are held by so uncertain a tenure, that few, excepting those in the actual enjoyment of office, feel any assurance that their interests lie in supporting that which seems to hang together almost by a miracle.

The only security of a despotic government is strength; and this security the Spanish government wants altogether. It has no strength in the affections of the people generally; and even among the military and employées, which are its only strength, there are many disaffected. When the king returned, after the overthrow of the constitution, every measure was adopted that might give a fictitious strength to the government: a clean sweep was made of all the employées, from the highest to the lowest; and whether holding their offices for life, or at pleasure. These, under the constitution, had been selected from amongst the best educated classes; but all who had been connected with the liberal party being excluded from employment under the succeeding government, the public offices were necessarily filled up with persons of inferior station. Another stroke of policy was intended, in the *distribution* of office: in no country is there so great a division of labour in public employments as in Spain; the duties of an office formerly held by one person, were delegated to three, and the emoluments split in proportion,—by which policy, a greater number of persons were interested in upholding the government.

A third measure of policy I have mentioned in a former chapter; that of remodelling the universities, and seminaries of learning, and putting them under the superintendence of Jesuits: and a fourth, was intended to secure the fidelity and increase the numerical strength of the military. To effect the first of these objects, a new body of guards, in all nearly 20,000 men, was raised, and *officered* by children. The king said, he would not have a single officer in the guards old enough to understand the meaning of the word constitution; and even now, that several years have elapsed, the officers are, almost without exception, boys.

To protect the government by the numerical strength of military, his majesty invited the organization of a force to be called Royalist Volunteers, to come in place of the national volunteers who existed during the time of the constitution. The term volunteer was a misnomer; because government held out temptations irresistible to the lower classes,—a new suit of clothes, and pay two days in the week, besides some other little gratuities: the consequence was, that a body called Royalist Volunteers, amounting to about 160,000, was speedily embodied. Such were the measures adopted by a government that sought to base itself, not upon the affections of the people, or upon its own merits; but which trusted rather in the zeal of hirelings, the precepts of Jesuits, and the purchased bulwark of bayonets. But these acts of political sagacity have added little to the real strength of the government: the change of all men in public office, made as many enemies as friends; and the exclusion of so many educated men, created a necessity for the employment of many low and unprincipled men, who by their bad conduct, have helped to lower the government in public opinion.

The fetters put upon education offended many,—because the change from a better to a worse plan of education was soon perceived by the heads of families, in the more limited range of knowledge offered to their children; and the establishment of a volunteer force, is well known throughout Spain to have endangered, rather than strengthened the government. That force is composed for the most part of the lowest orders; and it is quite a matter of notoriety, that the great majority of these men are Carlists,—a thing proved indeed by the discovery of the conspiracy, in which they had agreed to take an active part.

With such elements as those which compose the adherents of government, and with so total an absence of that kind of support to which alone an absolute government dare trust, it seems impossible that the existing government can long maintain its authority; and the probability of its dissolution will appear the greater, by citing a few facts, proving its utter rottenness; its perfect contempt of honour and justice in its dealings with its subjects; and its constant and flagrant acts of oppression. I cannot well separate the examples, because the bad acts of the government are not simply oppression, or injustice; but compounds of oppression, injustice, and weakness. I shall take them as they present themselves to my memory.

While I was in Madrid, a grandee, a favourite at court, whose name I regret I cannot recollect, being deeply in debt, and harassed by his creditors, and unwilling, although extremely wealthy, to limit the number of his enjoyments, went to the king and laid the case before his royal master; who, sympathizing in the pecuniary distress of the noble, exercised the prerogative of a king who is above law, by immediately presenting him with a royal order, by which he was secured in the undisturbed possession of his revenues for ten years,—his creditors being interdicted during that time from making any demand upon their debtor. The grandee called his creditors together; and when they supposed they were about to be paid, he produced the royal order, against which there was no appeal. No act of oppression could be more base than this; it was a total suspension of law, exercised without reason; a royal license to commit robbery; and of the worst kind, the robbery of the poor by the rich. It is more than probable, however, that before the lapse of ten years, the signature of Ferdinand VII. will have ceased to inspire fear, or exact obedience.

The following circumstance I know to be true. The Duke of Liria (Berwick) having got into difficulties, put himself under, or was put under *secrésto* (sequestration), and was allowed 10,000*l.* per annum from his revenues. It so happened that the duke had an attack of gout, and that he was obliged in consequence to absent himself a few weeks from court. One evening, while he was sitting at home, a letter was delivered to him, sealed with the royal seal; and, upon opening the letter, he found it to be an order of the king, that he should pay 2500l. of his income yearly to his grandmother in Paris. Thus, without process, without cause, without any previous intimation made to the Duke of Berwick, without any opportunity being given to him of objecting to this inroad upon his property, he was deprived, by a dash of the king's pen, of 2500l. per annum. This was accomplished by the intrigue of the duke's grandmother. The sequel to the story, by which it will be seen that the duke regained his money, does not in any respect alter the act of tyranny that deprived him of it; but only exemplifies the indecision of the king's character. The duchess, who happened to be a spirited woman, and who knew the character of the king, immediately ordered her coach, drove to the palace, asked an audience, saw the king, and returned in less than an hour with the revocation of the order in her hand.

While at Seville, I learned some very gross instances of injustice practised by the government in its dealings with its subjects. My authority could not be more authentic, because my informant—an old and highly respectable merchant—was himself the person who had suffered. A debt of 1600l. was due to him by government, upon a contract for supplying cartridge boxes; this debt had been some years due, and he had applied for payment often, and in vain. At length, having some other business in Madrid, he resolved to attempt the recovery of the debt, by preferring his claim in the proper quarter. Day after day, he went to the minister; sometimes he was denied admittance,—sometimes he saw the minister, and was always treated by him with the utmost rudeness: this was his first transaction with government, and he had yet to learn its way of doing business. One day, when he was leaving the minister, and slowly passing towards the stair, a reverend gentleman touched his sleeve, and begged to know what was the cause of his frequent visits to the minister: the merchant told him his business. "And do you expect to receive payment of the debt?" demanded the priest. "I despair of it," replied the merchant. "Then," resumed the priest, "you would probably sacrifice a small part to obtain the rest;" and upon the merchant admitting that he would gladly do this,—"Come," said the priest, "to-morrow early, and I'll undertake that you shall have your money!" The merchant kept his appointment; the priest was waiting—the merchant never saw the minister; and in less than half an hour, the priest put into his hands an order for 1200l., upon the treasury at Seville; the remaining 400l. being the perquisite of the minister and his emissary:—yet even after this, it was necessary to sacrifice another 100l., before payment of the order could be obtained at Seville. All this is according to usual practice: no settlement of any government account can be obtained without making a large sacrifice; sometimes as much as a third, or even a half. The system of bribery is universal, from the minister to the lowest official: sometimes the individual is robbed, sometimes the treasury. If the transaction lie between the government and an individual, the minister and his go-between are the gainers, and the contractor is robbed. If the affair lie between individuals and employées—as officers of the customs—a false return of duties is made to government; the merchant and the employée pocket the difference; and the government is robbed: this is a regular part of the settlement of every custom-house transaction. At Malaga, I learnt a curious instance of this, adding another to the many proofs of a weak and disorganized government. All vessels chartered from Gibraltar for Malta, Corfu, or any foreign port in the Mediterranean, but carrying part cargo for Malaga, are obliged, while they remain at Malaga, to deposit all goods *in transitu* in the custom-house, as a preventive against smuggling. Such vessels are well known to be freighted with English goods, or with tobacco, or with other goods either prohibited, or upon which high duties are payable: in fact, the vessel is a smuggler,—and how is this matter arranged? The captain deposits a hundred bales of goods in the custom-house, being the whole of the goods entered for the foreign port; and when the vessel leaves the port, the same number of bales must be shipped,—and so they are; but during their deposit in the custom-house, they have suffered a wonderful diminution in bulk. Bales which measured a yard square, are reduced to the size of footballs; the bales, such as they are, are reshipped;—the vessel has disburdened herself of her contraband cargo, and in place of proceeding to Malta, returns to Gibraltar. I relate this, not of course as an example of government oppression or injustice, but as a proof of the lax and unhinged state of the government, and of the total want of integrity that pervades every department of the public service: and before recurring to other instances of government oppression or injustice, let me mention another incident, proving that the same system extends even to the army. A regiment of cavalry arrived at Granada sometime last spring; and the soldiers being in want of new spurs, the colonel sent for a tradesman, and told him what he wanted. The tradesman named a certain price: "No," said the colonel, "you must let me have them at half that price;" the tradesman agreed, premising only that the spurs would not last a week. This was of no importance to the colonel; the spurs were delivered, the account was made out at *the price first demanded*, and being presented to the government office, the money was paid; one half of which went to the blacksmith, and the other into the pocket of the colonel.

The following case of extreme hardship was related to me by an English merchant at Seville, a man once extremely wealthy, but who has suffered irreparable losses from the unjust acts of the government. He entered into a contract with government to supply the whole accoutrements for 12,000 cavalry. An order so extensive required great outlay, and constant attention. The accoutrements were completed; and one half, according to the contract, delivered; and when the time nearly approached for the delivery of the remaining quantity, an intimation was received, that no more could be taken, because, to please the people of Madrid, it was necessary to employ the workmen of the capital. Not only was there no indemnification made for the breach of the contract, by which goods to the value of 36,000*l.* were thrown upon the merchant's hands; but the price of the delivered goods is to this hour unpaid. Four years have now elapsed, and he has no expectation of ever receiving one farthing; the debt being too large to be adjusted by the sacrifice of a part.

While I was at Seville, considerable discontent was produced by a most unjust act of the government. All arrears of taxes due upon houses for the past thirty years, were claimed from the actual proprietor: the consequence of which was, that upon the mere shewing of the government officer, proprietors were forced to pay arrears for a period in which the house was in other hands, and even in many cases, before the actual proprietors were born!

But more flagrant, at least more violent, acts of injustice and oppression are sometimes committed. After the return of the king, between two and three hundred persons who had served in the national volunteers during the constitution, were seized in Barcellona, and shipped to Ceuta,—the Spanish Botany Bay,—where they now remain. Their crime was said to be, unadvised talk in the coffee houses; but this was never ascertained, because no form of trial was gone through; and three years have not elapsed, since a man was hanged at Barcellona, without any one knowing what crime he had committed.

The truest proofs of a good government, are just laws; and the best evidence of a well organized government, is to be found in their strict execution. Judging the Spanish government by these tests, it will appear the worst and weakest government that ever held together. Justice of no kind, has any existence; there is the most lamentable insecurity of person and property: redress is never certain, because both judgment, and execution of the laws, are left to men so inadequately paid, that they must depend for their subsistence upon bribery. Nothing is so difficult as to bring a man to trial who has any thing in his purse, except to bring him to execution; this, unless in Madrid, and in Catalunia, where the Conde de España is captain-general, is impossible; for money will always buy indemnity. Every thing in Spain connected with the following out of the laws, is in the hands of the escrivanos; these are the friends of all bad men: for whatever be the action a man may commit, or meditate, he has only to confide in the escrivano, and pay for his protection.

The following remarkable fact, I had from the lips of an eye-witness, a highly respectable American merchant, of Malaga. One day last winter, two butchers quarrelled in the market-place, and got to high words; and one of them, according to the usual practice in such cases, put his hand under his girdle, and half drew forth his knife. All the while, an escrivano, of known talent in his profession—a man who never allowed any one who confided in him, to be either tried or executed, stood close by. While the man still but half shewed his knife, as if uncertain whether to use it or no, the escrivano continued to jog him on the elbow: "*Da le*," (give it him), said the lawyer, "*aqui estoy yo*;" (don't you see that I am here, so that no harm can come to you). The butcher, however, had not been sufficiently roused, for he put up his knife; and the escrivano, turning to him with a look of contempt, said, "*Alma miserable!*" (mean-spirited creature), "and so, for the sake of 400 or 500 reals, you would not revenge yourself upon your enemy."

Before concluding these examples of a bad, weak, and tyrannical government, I cannot refrain from mentioning the case of a man, who has been in prison ever since the evacuation of Spain by the French army; and who has still many years of punishment before him.

Shortly after the Duke D'Angouleme took possession of Barcellona, the inhabitants were one morning awoke by the ringing of bells, and other tokens of rejoicing: the cause of this was soon announced to be, that the Virgin of *Monte Serrate*, an image of silver or wood,—I forget which,—had come to Barcellona, of her own free will, probably considering herself more secure there, than in the convent of *Montserrat*; and about a year afterwards, when it became evident that the French intended no outrage upon the convent, it was given out that the virgin had signified her intention to return; but it was determined, upon this occasion, that she should not be allowed to return by herself, but that she should be carried with great pomp. A Catalunian peasant, who stood in the line of procession, perhaps with better eye-sight—perhaps with less faith, than his neighbours,— unfortunately expressed aloud, the thought that passed through his mind: "She's only made of wood," said he;—and for this offence, he was arrested, tried, and condemned to ten years' imprisonment in the citadel!

These various facts will suffice, I think, as proofs of that which I intended they should illustrate: the despotism and the weakness of the Spanish government—the total want of integrity that characterizes all its dealings— and its absolute inefficiency to execute the laws, either for its own protection, or for the redress of others.

Such being the condition of the Spanish government, we are naturally led to ask ourselves, "What are its prospects?" Is it to be expected that a government, without one element either of virtue or of strength—without the physical strength that may long support a bad government—and without the moral strength of virtue, will be able long to maintain itself?

One naturally answers,—"No," the thing cannot be; the whole system requires ploughing up, and it is impossible that there should not be a change, and that speedily!! But the question is, what change? After the French revolution broke out, a change of government in Spain was generally expected throughout both France and England; but the expectations upon this subject were certainly grounded upon an erroneous notion of the state of public feeling in Spain. I have no party to serve in giving my opinion; it is formed, I think, without prejudice, upon what I have seen and heard while in the country; and I feel a confident persuasion, that the change hoped for by every friend of mankind, is still at a distance; and that the present government must yield to the *strongest* of the two parties that seek its downfal. Spain, I believe, has yet to pass through a fiery trial, before her days of freedom and happiness arrive: the change first to be expected, is one from despotism and weakness to greater despotism and greater strength: and this will be a new reign of terror. I am not stating my own opinion merely, but the opinion of the most thinking and best informed classes in Spain—liberals, as well as Carlists and royalists. With many, it is a miracle that the party of Carlists have not, long ere now, obtained the upper hand; a fact only to be accounted for, from the uncertainty that prevails as to the sentiments of the army. I recollect reading, in one of the French or English newspapers, a statement, that about the time the constitutionalists prepared to enter Spain, the minister sent for the different commanding officers of the guards stationed in Madrid, and demanded of them whether they could answer for their respective regiments; and that the reply was, they could answer for themselves only: this statement was true, but the interpretation put upon the answer was erroneous. The government had at that time greater fears of the Carlists than of the Constitutionalists; and the meaning of the officers, when they said they could answer only for themselves, was not—according to the interpretation annexed to the statement—that the troops were supposed to be of liberal sentiments, but that it was feared they might be attached to the Carlists. The conspiracy for elevating that party,—detected during the autumn,—cannot be supposed to have crushed it. I know that after that period, meetings of its partizans were regularly held; the intrigues of the clergy still continued in active operation; and subsequently to that period, the birth of a princess left the male succession open to the sons of Don Carlos.

That the probabilities of a change to greater in place of to less despotism, may be more obvious, not only the strength and influence of parties must be looked to, but also the peculiarities of Spanish character. Viewing the present state of Spain, there appears to exist a necessity for a more enlightened government; and one with difficulty persuades himself of the probability of a revolution which would pull down one despotic government to raise another more despotic in its place. But an Englishman would judge very erroneously of the prospects of Spain, who should measure Spanish feeling by his own; and considering what the people of England would do under similar circumstances, conclude that Spain will do likewise. The Spanish government will fall by its weakness, rather than by its vices; it is the prospect of a stronger, not of a more virtuous government, that incites the exertions of the Carlists. The mass of the population of Spain take little heed of the vices of the government, and are entirely indifferent about political privileges. The Basque provinces, which are the most enlightened, have little to complain of; for they enjoy a multitude of privileges and exemptions which are well defined, and jealously maintained: and as for the Spaniard of the southern provinces,— give him his shade in summer, and his sunshine in winter; his tobacco, his melon, his dates, his bread, and his wine; give him a hole to creep into, and put him within sound of a convent bell, and he asks no more: or if you rise a degree or two in society, and speak of the respectable peasant, then give to him his embroidered jacket, his tasseled hat, his guitar, and his *maja*, (sweetheart, in the dialect of Andalusia), and it is matter of indifference to him, whether Spain be ruled by a Caligula or a Titus.

The love of ease and pleasure, and the proneness to indolence that distinguish the character of the Spaniard, especially in the provinces south of Castile; and his total ignorance of the uses and nature of political freedom, will yet, for many years, prove a barrier to the progress of free institutions in the Peninsula. It is true that this contentedness with his condition,—this unripeness for political freedom,—this ignorance of the claims of his species, ought not to be alleged as any reason against the attempt to force free institutions upon him. It is that very ignorance, that unripeness, that false contentedness, that hasten the necessity for revolution; because instruction, without which no country can be rendered fit for the enjoyment of political rights, could never carry its light to the people, under a government like that of Spain.

A series of attempts to establish liberal institutions in Spain may be necessary, before it be found possible to sustain them; but I believe that every new attempt will be attended with fewer obstacles. The most unsuccessful struggle against despotism, must produce good effects: accordingly, I do not agree in opinion with those who contend, that the movements of 1812 and 1820, retrograded the cause of liberty. It is certain, indeed, that the Spanish liberals then attempted impossibilities; they based the constitution upon principles of liberty, which Spain, nursed so long in despotism, was unable to support; yet the glimpse which Spain then caught of the light of freedom,—the knowledge that was conveyed through the medium of a free press to every part of the kingdom, and especially to all ranks in the metropolis,—and the unrestrained interchange of sentiment, opened the eyes of many, and prepared all, for a future and wiser attempt. Such an attempt may yet be at some distance; a more despotic, but a more vigorous government, may be able to repress, for some years, the declaration of principles hostile to those by which it is maintained: but opinion will advance nevertheless; and the epoch will certainly arrive in the history of Spain,—as it must in all countries in which government stands still,—when men's opinions, which change, clash with institutions which change not.

The attempt upon the Spanish frontier which followed the revolution in France, would scarcely deserve notice, but for the ignorance which it shewed of the state of public feeling in Spain. I was then in Madrid; and I think I may venture to say, that this movement created less sensation in Spain than in any other country in Europe. An attempt far better organized, could not at that time have met with any success. The plans of the Carlists were then advancing; and the party was becoming every day more a subject of embarrassment and alarm to the government; but the views of that party were a sufficient security against the designs of the other, whose ascendancy would at once have annihilated the hopes of the Carlists. It was therefore sufficiently obvious, that if the aspect of things on the frontier became formidable, the interest of the Carlists would lie in strengthening the hands of government. But all the well-informed classes, of whatever party, looked upon the attempt as ill advised, and certain of failure. I conversed at that time with many persons of liberal sentiments, who, with scarcely an exception, deprecated the attempt as rash and useless; and expressed deep regret that so many unfortunate men should expose themselves to the merciless policy of the government. It was well known, that both the Basque Provinces and Catalunia,—the two points at which the entry was made,—were to be depended upon for their loyalty, or their ultraism—sentiments alike hostile to the liberals. The Basque Provinces, which enjoy peculiar privileges, were the least interested in the liberal cause; and Catalunia, one of the strong-holds of the Carlists, was governed by the *Conde de España*, whose great experience, staunch loyalty, and decided character, are always considered a guarantee for the tranquillity of Catalunia. It was never contemplated by the Spanish Government, to meet the attempt by any other weapon than force; and even if the strength of the Constitutionalists had been far more formidable, and their success far more probable, conciliatory measures would have been impossible; it is perfectly understood that any act of the government savouring of liberalism, would at once be sealing it over to the power of the Carlists.

The result was as all had anticipated: no indication of favourable feeling, on the part of the peasantry, attended the movements of the invading force; and without this, it was impossible that it could maintain itself. The events that took place upon the frontier, were probably better known in England than in Spain: at all events, it does not fall in with my object to enter into a detail of them.

CHAPTER X.

THE ESCURIAL—ST. ILDEFONSO—SEGOVIA.

Journey from Madrid; First View of the Escurial; Philip II.; Situation of the Escurial; the Church; Lucas Jordan; the Relics; the Santa Forma; the Sacristy and its Pictures; a Reverie; the Hall of Recreation; the Library; the Tomb of the Kings; the Manuscript Library; Ignorance and Idleness of the Monks, and Anecdotes; Manner of Life among the Monks; the Palace; Particulars of the Extent and Cost of the Escurial; Pedestrian Journey across the Sierra Guaderrama to St. Ildefonso; the Palace, Waters, and Garden of La Granja; Road to Segovia; its Remains, and Present Condition; Expensiveness of Royal Honours; Return to Madrid.

BEFORE leaving Castile for Andalusia, I made two excursions, to objects well deserving a visit,—the Escurial and Toledo. To the former of these, I shall dedicate the present chapter.

Having hired a mule and a guide, I left Madrid one charming morning, before day-break; and passing out of the city by the gate de San Vincente, I proceeded up the bank of the river Manzanares along a good road, bordered on both sides by poplars and willows. From this road, the palace is a striking and beautiful object; and the sun rising shortly after I had passed the gate, its blaze reflected from the innumerable windows, produced a magnificent and almost magical effect. A league from the city, the road, crossing the river, leaves the stripe of scanty herbage that borders it, and enters upon the wide arid country, that extends all the way to the foot of the Sierra Guaderrama. Travelling in any direction from Madrid, there is little to narrate; the country is wholly devoid of interest; there is scarcely any population; and no travellers are seen on the road, to relieve its monotony, or attract the attention.

During four leagues, the road continues to ascend almost imperceptibly, and then climbs the first of those ridges, that are connected with the outposts of the Sierra Guaderrama. From the top of the ridge, about four leagues and a half from Madrid, the Escurial is first seen reposing at the foot of the dark mountain that forms its back ground; and although still fourteen miles distant, it appears in all that colossal magnitude that has helped to earn for it the reputation of being the ninth wonder of the world. Between this point and the village of San Lorenzo, there is nothing to interest, excepting the constant view of the Escurial, increasing in extent, rising in elevation, and growing in magnificence, as the summit of every succeeding ridge discloses a nearer view of it. After a ride of seven hours and a half, I arrived in front of the Escurial a little after mid-day; and dismissing my mule, I immediately presented myself at the gate with my credentials. These were, a letter from the Marquesa de Valleverde, to El muy Rev. Padre Buendia; and another from the Saxon minister, to the Librarian to the Grand Duke of Hesse Darmstadt, M. Feder, who had been for several months resident in the Escurial, employed in collating some classical works. The monks being then at dinner, I declined interrupting the enjoyment of the Father Buendia, and was ushered into a small apartment in one of the angles opposite to the Sierra, where I remained about a quarter of an hour, while the monks continued their repast.

Most persons know that the Escurial was erected by that renowned monarch, Philip II.,—renowned for his vices, his bigotry, and his ambition. The reasons assigned by Philip for the erection of this building are three-fold:—as a token of gratitude to God, on account of the victory gained over the French at St. Quintin; as an act of devotion towards the holy martyr San Lorenzo; and in fulfilment of the wish expressed in the last will of Charles V., that a sepulchre should be erected wherein to deposit the bones of himself and the empress, the parents of Philip II. Another, and less ostensible reason assigned by this religious monarch, was that he might be able to retire at times from the turmoil of the court; and in the seclusion of a royal monastery, profit by the lessons of holy men, and meditate upon the instability of worldly grandeur: and Philip shewed in his practice the apparent sincerity of this motive; for he was wont often to be an inmate of the Escurial; and traits of his devotion and humility are yet related within its walls.

The situation chosen for the Escurial accords well with the gloomy character of its royal founder. There is no town or city nearer to it than Madrid, which is thirty-four miles distant; a wild and deserted country forms its horizon; and the dark defiles and the brown ridges of the *Sierra Guaderrama* are its cradle. In the building itself, Philip royally acquitted himself of his vows; for a structure so stupendous in its dimensions, or so surpassing in its internal riches, is nowhere to be found. The building was begun in the year 1563, under the direction of Juan Bautista de Toledo, and finished in 1584; Juan de Herrera presiding over the work during several years preceding its completion.

My meditations were interrupted by the welcome entrance of Father Buendia, whom I found an agreeable and rather intelligent man, although a great worshipper of the memory of Philip II. I was first conducted into the church of the monastery, which certainly exceeds in richness and magnificence any thing that I had previously imagined. It is quite impossible to enter into minute descriptions of all that composes this magnificence: the riches of Spain, and her ancient colonies, are exhausted in the materials;—marbles, porphyries, jaspers, of infinite variety, and of the most extraordinary beauty,—gold, silver, and precious stones; and the splendid effect of the whole is not lessened by a nearer inspection; there is no deception, no glitter,—all is real. The whole of the altar-piece in the Capilla Mayor, upwards of ninety feet high and fifty broad, is one mass of jasper, porphyry, marble, and bronze gilded; the eighteen pillars that adorn it, each eighteen feet high, are of deep red and green jasper, and the intervals are of porphyry and marble of the most exquisite polish, and the greatest variety of colour. It is, in fact, impossible to turn the eye in any direction in which it does not rest upon the rarest and richest treasures of nature, or the most excellent works of art; for if it be withdrawn from the magnificence below, by the splendour of the ceiling above, it discovers those admirable frescos of Lucas Jordan, which have earned for him the character of a second Angelo. It would be tedious to enlarge upon the subject of Jordan's frescos; they are too numerous indeed to be described within the limits of a chapter; but they comprise, it may be said, the whole history of the Christian Religion, beginning from the Promises, and are excelled only by the works of Angelo. The battle of St. Quintin, which ornaments the ceiling of the great stair-case, is considered to be one of the most excellent of Jordan's frescos.

Lucas Jordan was born at Naples in the year 1632. His father chanced to live near Españaletto, who was then in Italy; and Jordan, from infancy, was constantly in his neighbour's workshop. At nine years old, he is said to have made great progress; and at fourteen he ran away from his father's house, and went to Rome, where, it is said, his father following him, found him in the Vatican copying Michael Angelo's Last Judgment. At Rome he was the disciple of Pietro de Cortona; and he afterwards visited Florence, Bologna, Parma, and Venice, where he improved himself upon the style of Paul Veronese. Subsequently he went to Rome; but unable to forget Veronese, he again returned to Venice, where he remained until called to Florence, in 1657, to paint the cupola of the Capilla Corsini in the church of Carmine. He was afterwards invited to Spain by Charles II., and arrived in Madrid in 1692; and from that time until his death, his genius was employed in enriching the palaces and convents of Spain, particularly the Escurial.

Having satisfied my curiosity with the church, and the frescos, I wished Father Buendia to conduct me to the sacristy, where are to be seen those glorious creations of the pencil, which have added the charm of beauty, to the grandeur and magnificence of the Escurial. But my conductor led me first to the relicary, whose contents were perhaps more valuable in his eyes than those of the sacristy. In this relicary, there were five hundred and fifteen vases before the invasion of the French; but their number is now reduced to four hundred and twenty-two. These vases are of gold, silver, bronze gilded, and valuable wood; many of them thickly studded with precious stones: and upwards of eighty of the richest of these vases still remain. But the French, more covetous of the gold and silver than of the relics, made sad confusion of the latter; for not caring to burden themselves with bones, and wood, and dirty garments, they emptied the little gold and silver vases upon the floor,—irreligiously mingling in one heap, relics of entirely different value. The labels indicating the relics having been upon the vases, the bones, &c. were without any distinguishing mark; so that it was impossible to discriminate between an arm of St. Anthony, and the arm of St. Teresa,—or to know a bit of the true cross, from a piece of only a martyr's cross,—or a garment of the Virgin Sin Pecada, from one of only the Virgin of Rosalio: and as for the smaller relics,—parings of nails, hair, &c. many were irrecoverably lost. But with all this confusion, and all these losses, the Escurial is still rich in relics. Several pieces of the true cross yet remain; a bit of the rope that bound Christ; two thorns of the crown; a piece of the sponge that was dipped in vinegar; parts of His garments, and a fragment of the manger in which he was laid. Making every allowance for bigotry and excess of ill-directed faith, I cannot comprehend the feeling that attaches holiness to some of these relics: it is impossible to understand what kind of sacredness that is, which belongs to articles that have been the instruments of insult to the Divine Being. Besides these relics of our Saviour, there are several parts of the garments of the Virgin; there are ten entire skeletons of saints and martyrs; the body of one of the innocents, massacred by command of Herod; and upwards of a hundred heads of saints, martyrs, and holy men; besides numerous other bones still distinguishable.

But the peculiar glory of the Escurial, and its most wondrous relic, is the Santa Forma, as it is called; in reality, "the wafer," in which the Deity has been pleased to manifest himself in three streaks of blood; thus proving the doctrine of transubstantiation. This relic has been deemed worthy of a chapel and an altar to itself. These are of extraordinary beauty and richness; and adorned with the choicest workmanship: jaspers, marble, and silver are the materials; and *bas reliefs*, in white marble, relate the history of the Santa Forma; which is shortly this. It was originally in the cathedral church of Gorcum in Holland, and certain heretics (Zuinglianos) entering the church, took this consecrated host, threw it on the ground, trod upon it, and cracked it in three places. God, to shew his divine displeasure, and at the same time, as a consolation to the christians, manifested himself in three streaks of blood, which appeared at each of the cracks. One of the heretics, struck with the miracle, and repenting of his crime, lifted the Santa Forma from the ground, and deposited it, along with a record of the miracle, in a neighbouring convent of Franciscans, who kept and venerated it long; the delinquent, who abjured his heresy, and who had taken the habit, being one of their number. From this convent it was translated to Vienna, and then to Prague; and there its peregrinations terminated: for Philip II. being a better Catholic than the Emperor Rodolph, prevailed upon the latter to part with it, and deposited it in the Escurial; where it has ever since remained. It had a narrow escape from being again trodden upon, during the French invasion: upon the approach of the enemy it was hastily snatched from the sacred depositary, and unthinkingly hid in a wine butt, where it is said to have acquired some new, and less miraculous stains: and after the departure of the French, a solemn festival was proclaimed on the 14th of October, 1814; upon which occasion, his present majesty, assisted by all his court, and by half the friars of Castile, rescued the Santa Forma from its inglorious concealment, and deposited it again in the chapel which the piety of Charles II. had erected for it. The Santa Forma is not shewn to heretics; but its history is related: and it was evident, by the manner of the friar who related it to me, that he placed implicit belief in the miraculous stains.

Besides the general relicary and the peculiar chapel for the Santa Forma, there is another smaller relicary, called the Camarin, into which Father Buendia conducted me. Here I was shewn an earthen pitcher, one of those which contained the water that Jesus turned into wine; and affixed to the pitcher, there is a writing, narrating the manner in which the vessel found its way into the Escurial. I was also shewn three caps of Pope Pius V.; and a stone which was taken from his Holiness' bladder; besides several manuscripts written by the hand of St. Teresa, and St. Augustin; and the ink-horn of the former saint.

I might still have been gratified by the sight of more relics; but I was anxious to visit the sacristy, which contains relics of another kind. The sacristy itself, in its walls, roof, and floor, equals in beauty, any part of the Escurial; but the beauty of jaspers and precious stones, and the excellent workmanship of many rare and beautiful woods, are unheeded, where attractions are to be found so far excelling them. It is in the sacristy of the Escurial, where the choicest works of the most illustrious painters of the great schools are preserved; and of these we may say, what can rarely be said of any collection, that among the forty-two pictures that adorn the sacristy, there is not one that is not a *chef d'œuvre*. Among these, there are three of Raphael, one of them known all over the world by the name of La Perla; two of Leonardo da Vinci; six of Titian, and many of Tintoretto, Guido, Veronese, and other eminent masters. La Perla represents the Virgin embracing the infant Jesus, with her right arm round his body, while he rests his feet upon her knee; the Virgin's left hand lies upon the shoulder of Saint Anne, who kneels at her daughter's side; her elbow resting upon her knee, and her head supported by her hand. The child, St. John, offers fruits to the infant Christ in his little garment of camel-skin; and Jesus accepting them, turns at the same time his smiling face towards his mother, who is looking at St. John. Such is the subject of La Perla, a picture that would have placed Raphael where he now stands among the illustrious dead, even if he had never painted the Transfiguration,—any critique upon a painting of Raphael would be impertinent. While I was occupied with the treasures of the sacristy, a bell rang for prayers; and as it was contrary to the rules of the monastery to leave the door of the sacristy open, I was locked in, while Father Buendia went to his devotions. This was precisely the most agreeable thing that could have happened: a large chair, which looked as old as the days of Philip II., stood below the altar of the Santa Forma; and drawing it into the middle of the sacristy, and sitting down, I spent the next half-hour luxuriously; not as might have been imagined, in admiration of the immortal works around me; but in a waking dream, that carried me away from the Escurial, and back to the days of boyhood, when throwing aside my Horace, I used to seize an old book, which I have never seen since then, called "Swinburne's Travels," and devour the descriptions of the Escurial; its immensity, its riches, its monks, its tomb of the kings,—not its pictures, for I was then ignorant of even the name of Raphael,—but this knowledge came later, and all was blended together in this delicious reverie, which was in fact a vision of the Escurial, as imagination had pictured it in bygone days. But the great key, entering the door, annihilated twenty years, and brought me where I was, seated in the great chair in the sacristy of the Escurial; and after another glance at the pictures, I followed Father Buendia to the old church and the cloister; but in passing to these, we entered the Hall of Recreation, or as it is called, La Sala Prioral. Here the monks assemble at certain hours, to converse, and enjoy each other's society; and for this purpose, they have made choice of the most comfortable room in the monastery. Although in Spain, and only the beginning of September, a stove was lighted; benches, and even some stuffed chairs, were scattered here and there. The windows look over the garden and fish-ponds, from which, on meagre days, the worthy fathers contrive to eke out a repast; and the walls of the hall are adorned by some most choice pictures by Peregrini, Guercino, Titian, Guido; among others, a half-clothed Magdalen, by Titian,—scarcely a suitable study for these holy men; and, "Magdalen at the Feet of Jesus:" ascribed to Correggio, but which, Mengs, in his notices of the life and works of Correggio, supposes to have been left imperfect by that master, and to have been finished by another hand: but it is, at all events, a charming picture.

From the *Sala Prioral*, we went to the *Iglesia Vieja*, which is remarkable only on account of its pictures; among which, is one of Raphael: and from the Iglesia Vieja, I was next conducted through the cloisters, also adorned with pictures, to the great Library. This is a magnificent room; the ceilings in fresco, by Peregrini and Carducho, represent the progress of the sciences; the floor is of chequered grey and white marble; and the finest and rarest woods encase the windows, the doors, and the books. The library is more curious than extensive; it does not contain more than 24,000 volumes, but many of these are scarce; and among others, they shew a copy of the Apocalypse of St. John, with a commentary, and illuminated borders, and the devotional exercises of Charles V., &c. The day was almost spent before I reached the library; the light streamed but dimly through the deep windows; and the portraits of Charles, and his son,—the gloomy-minded founder of the monastery,—frowned darkly from the walls. It was too late to examine the Manuscript Library; and making an appointment with Father Buendia for the morning, I left the Escurial for the Posada, where I had ordered a bed, and a late dinner. I was offered both refreshments and a bed, in the monastery; but having a better opinion of the dinner I had ordered than of a supper in the refectory, (for it chanced to be Friday), I forced an excuse upon the reverend father.

Although it was almost night within the Escurial, I found day without. It was yet too early to expect dinner at the Posada; and therefore, skirting the small straggling village of *San Lorenzo*, I climbed up among the defiles and ridges of the sierra that forms the back-ground to the monastery and its tributary village. The sun had already set, and dusk was creeping over the distant landscape; and, excepting the vast and magnificent building below, there was scarcely a trace of human existence, for a ridge of the sierra shut out the little village of San Lorenzo: and the only sound I heard, was the bell from the monastery. To me, there is nothing poetic in a convent bell; it only reminds me of bigotry and ignorance, absurd penance, or sinful hypocrisy. It was almost dark before I reached the Posada, where I had the pleasure of passing an agreeable evening with M. Feder, whom I have spoken of already, and must always speak of, as a learned and an amiable man.

Next morning, I again claimed the good offices of Father Buendia, and was conducted by him to "the Tomb of the Kings;" perhaps the most magnificent sepulchre in the world. It is impossible to conceive any thing more gorgeous than this mausoleum: the descent is by a deep staircase, underneath the great altar of the church; the walls of the staircase being entirely of blood-jasper, of the utmost beauty and polish. The mausoleum itself is circular; the walls are of jasper, and black marble: and in rows, one over another, are ranged the coffins of the kings of Spain. They are all here, these masters of a hemisphere! a little dust in these gorgeous urns, is all that remains of the mighty kings whose deeds fill volumes—of Charles, who kept the world in a flame, and left it for a cloister,—of Philip, for whose ambition and crimes it was too narrow. Death certainly owns no other palace like this. The queens of Spain are not all here; only those who have given birth to an heir to the throne. There are eight kings, and eight queens, on opposite sides of the mausoleum; and a splendid urn stands empty and open, destined to receive the present inheritor of the throne, who, when he visits the Escurial, never fails to enter his tomb, there to receive, if not to profit by, a lesson upon the duties of kings, and the common destinies of all. A lamp, always burning, is suspended from the centre of the mausoleum, giving just sufficient light to make legible the names of its owners, inscribed in gold letters upon a bronze tablet. I did not enter the Pantheon of the Infantas, which contains no fewer than fifty-nine urns.

From the mausoleum, I was conducted to the Manuscript library, which is far more valuable than the other. Although, previous to the conflagration in 1671, it contained many more treasures than it does now, it is still one of the most valuable manuscript libraries in Europe. The number of manuscripts yet preserved there, exceeds 4000; nearly one half of the whole being Arabic, and the rest in Latin, Greek, Hebrew, and the vulgar tongues. I shall name a very few of the most remarkable. There are two copies of the Iliad, of the tenth and twelfth centuries; but these are not scarce; and indeed, a very great number of the manuscripts are copies of originals preserved in the libraries of Italy. There are many fine and ancient Bibles, particularly in Greek; and one Latin copy of the Gospels, of the eleventh century. There are two books of ancient councils, in Gothic characters, and illuminated; the one of the year 976, called the Codigo Vigilano, because written by a monk called Vigilia; the other of the year 994, written by a priest named Velasco. A very ancient Koran is also shewn; and a work of some value, written in six large volumes, as it is said by the command of Philip II., upon the Revenues and Statistics of Spain. But the most ancient manuscript is one of poetry, written in the Longobardic, and dated as far back as the ninth century. The Arabic manuscripts are also many and curious; and the manner in which these came into the hands of the Spaniards was accidental. Pedro de Lara being at sea, met some vessels carrying the equipage of the Moorish king Zidian: these vessels he fought with, and took; and found among other precious things, more than three thousand Arabic manuscripts. The Moorish king, subsequently offered sixty thousand ducats for their restitution; but the overture was rejected, and restitution was promised only on condition that the whole of the Christian captives should be released; but this demand not being complied with, the manuscripts were sent to the Escurial.

The monks of the Escurial live too much at their ease to acquire habits of study. The monks in the olden time were not altogether useless; for to their industry and perseverance we owe the preservation and multiplication of many of the most esteemed authors of antiquity: but the friars of the present day have sadly degenerated; they make no use of the treasures which their convents contain; and of this truth, the monks of the Escurial afford a lamentable example. A gentleman with whom I am acquainted, and who passed the whole of every day during three months in the library of the Escurial, assured me that all that time, not one friar ever entered to ask for, or examine a book. I am acquainted with another proof of the ignorance or idleness of the monks of the Escurial. A literary society in one of the German states, being desirous of publishing the works of the elder Pliny, and believing that some assistance might be obtained from the library of the Escurial, applied to the Spanish government upon the subject; and orders were accordingly given to the librarian of the Escurial, to search, and to report upon the works of Pliny contained in the library. An answer was given, that it contained no complete or useful work of Pliny,—but only an abbreviation. A literary gentleman, however, from the same German state, having obtained access to the library for other purposes, found two perfect copies of Pliny's Natural History. It is scarcely possible to suppose that the librarian could have been ignorant of the existence of these; and the only alternative therefore is, that he denied any knowledge of them, from the dread of receiving some command that might interfere with his love of idleness.

At present there are one hundred monks in the monastery of the Escurial; and from all that I could learn, they have no great reason to complain of their lot. The order of St. Geronimo, to which they belong, is not one of the strict orders: it allows a good table and uninterrupted rest; and prescribes few fasts, and probably no penance. Each monk has at least two apartments, and a small kitchen where a little *refresco* may be prepared at any time, without troubling the cooks below. There are many fine terraces round the building, and a tolerably shady garden, where the fathers have the benefit of air, without hard exercise; and in the fish ponds, there is an inexhaustible source of amusement, in which the king, when he visits the Escurial, condescends to join every day after dinner. I saw no monk, who did not seem contented; and although with the opportunities which they enjoy, they are both idle and ignorant, I found them tolerably well informed upon common topics, and greatly interested in the news of the day. It would seem, however, that they have not much access to know what passes in the world; for one of their number preferred a request to me, that before leaving Madrid, I would write him a letter containing the latest news from France, and from the frontier: scarcely any one but a monk dared have made such a request; but the friars are a privileged class.

The palace adjoining the monastery, is scarcely worth a visit after seeing the magnificence of the latter: any where else, it would be a splendid edifice. I merely walked through the apartments. Altogether, although the Escurial be scarcely entitled to the appellation of the ninth wonder of the world; it is confessedly the most wonderful edifice in Europe, whether in dimensions or riches. To give some better idea of these, than a general description can convey, I shall add the following short enumeration.

In the Escurial, there are fifty-one bells; forty-eight wine cellars; eighty staircases; seventy-three fountains; eight organs; twelve thousand windows and doors; and eighteen hundred and sixty rooms. There are fifteen hundred and sixty oil paintings; and the frescos, if all brought together, would form a square of eleven hundred feet. The circumference of the building, is 4800 feet—nearly three quarters of a mile.

From a book kept in the monastery, containing an account of the sums expended on the building, &c., I made the following extracts, which may be esteemed by some, as curious. The mason-work of the monastery cost 5,512,054 reals; the marbles, porphyries, and jasper employed on the church, cost 5,343,825 reals; the labour of placing each square on the floor, thirteen reals; the painting of the church, including the frescos of Jordan, 291,270 reals; the organs 295,997 reals; the workmanship of the choir (the king having presented the wood) 266,200 reals; the two hundred and sixteen volumes used in the choir, 493,284 reals; the whole of the bronze railings 556,828 reals; the wood, lead, bells and gilding of the church, 3,200,000 reals; the paintings of the library, 199,822 reals; the ornaments of the sacristy, 4,400,000 reals; the materials of the mausoleum, 1,826,031 reals. This is but a very small part of the cost of the edifice, because here are none of the gold and silver ornaments, urns, or precious stones; none of the bronze, except the railings; none of the oil paintings; nor almost any part of the workmanship. I have stated the cost in reals, as it appears in the book; but any of the sums divided by 100, will give the value in pounds sterling nearly, though not precisely.

After having seen all that merits observation in the interior of the building, I walked over the terraces and gardens, where I met many of the holy fathers taking their evening promenade, several with segars in their mouths; and then leaving the garden, I extended my walk to a country house which the present king built and adorned: there is nothing regal about the place, excepting a picture of his majesty.

My intention being to pass the Sierra Guadarrama to visit St. Ildefonso and Segovia, I inquired for a mule at the village where I slept; but the price demanded was so exorbitant—no less than six dollars each day, besides the maintenance of the guide—that I resolved to save the expense altogether, by being a pedestrian, and my own guide. This determination, I however kept to myself, because it is never prudent in Spain, to publish an intention of making a solitary journey.

Next morning, I left the Escurial at the earliest dawn; and following the only road I saw leading to the North, I soon found myself ascending among the ridges of the Sierra. The sun rose when I had walked about an hour. The morning was fresh, and even chill; but the sky was blue and cloudless, the sunshine bright, and the air bracing and elastic; the road, too, became more interesting as I ascended higher,—entering into the heart of the mountain, and abounding in those mountain views, which have so many charms beyond the dull monotony of a plain. I did not meet a single traveller during the first three hours; and I passed three crosses, one of them recording a murder committed so lately as the year 1828, upon a merchant of Segovia. About four leagues from the Escurial, I passed a small house, situated in a little hollow, at a short distance from the road; and although I should have been glad to rest awhile, and take what refreshment the house afforded, its situation was so solitary, and the scenery around so desolate, that I judged it safer to continue my journey. Shortly after passing this house, I reached the Puerto de Fuenfria, the summit of the Sierra; taking its name, "Pass of the Cold Fountain," from some icy springs that bubble near; from one of which I took a long and refreshing draught. The scenery here is of the wildest description. The mountain is full of deep cuts and ravines, most of them the courses of winter torrents; aged and stunted pines hang upon their edges, and are strewn upon the brown acclivities around; while bare, huge, misshapen rocks project over the path, and often force it to skirt the brink of giddy and undefended precipices. When the Pass lays open the view to the north of the Sierra, the prospect is fine and extensive; but anxious to reach St. Ildefonso, I scarcely paused to survey it; and in less than two hours more, I delivered my letter to Don Mateo Frates, governor of the palace.

The palace of St. Ildefonso, or as it is more commonly called in Spain, La Granja, was built by Philip V., who undoubtedly made a better choice than his predecessor, the founder of the Escurial; for if a cool breeze is any where to be found in Spain during the heat of summer, it is at St. Ildefonso that it must be sought. It is placed in a spot where the mountains fall back, leaving a recess sheltered from the hot air of the south, and from much of its sun; but exposed to whatever breeze may be wafted from the north. The immediate acclivity towards the south, is occupied by the garden, which, although somewhat formal in the immediate neighbourhood of the palace, is full of shade and coolness. Almost every one has heard of the waters of La Granja; these were politely offered to be displayed for my amusement; but artificial water-works have no great charms for me; and besides, when we see the fountains, it is not difficult to fancy the play of the waters. I have no doubt, however, that the effect is striking; and during the heats of summer, so many jets must produce an agreeable influence upon the surrounding atmosphere. The fountains and falls are innumerable; one of them, Fame seated on Pegasus, raises a jet to the height of one hundred and thirty-two feet; and in another spot, called the Plazuela de las ocho Calles, eight fountains unite, forming a beautiful and chaste temple of the Ionic order, adorned by columns of white marble. The expense of constructing the garden of La Granja has been enormous; it has generally been computed to amount to upwards of seven millions sterling.

The principal front of the palace faces the garden; it is one hundred and eighty yards long, and in every respect palace-like; but it struck me as being too large, too formal, and too fine, to be in perfect keeping with the surrounding scenery; the wild defiles of the Sierra Guadarrama required a different kind of palace. The interior is in every thing regal; and is adorned by some choice works of the first masters; though many which formerly belonged to this palace have been removed to the Madrid museum.

In speaking of St. Ildefonso, let me not omit to mention the renowned manufactory of mirrors; which are, at all events, the largest, if not the finest in the world. The mould in which the largest are made, is thirteen feet and a half one way, seven feet nine inches the other, and six inches deep. Some of the mirrors made at St. Ildefonso, have found their way into most of the royal palaces of Europe.

I supped luxuriously upon venison, and accepted a bed in the palace; but before retiring to it, I had the pleasure of partaking of a bottle of *Val de Peñas* from the king's cellar. This is a wine of which no idea can be formed, judging of it by the samples commonly found either in the public or private houses of Madrid. Like many other of the Spanish wines, it requires age to mellow it; and it has besides most commonly acquired, less or more, a peculiar flavour from the skins in which it is brought from La Mancha. The king's wine is no doubt carried in some other fashion.

Segovia is only two leagues from La Granja, and I had intended to have been there to an early breakfast; but whether it be that one sleeps sounder in a palace than elsewhere, or that Val de Peñas is of a soporific quality, it is certain, that in place of awaking as usual before day-break, half the mountain was bathed in sunbeams when I looked out of my window. I found a good breakfast of coffee and its adjuncts (a rare luxury in Spain) waiting me below; and I also found that a horse and a servant were in readiness to facilitate my transport to Segovia. I would willingly have dispensed with this kindness; for although I have no objection to a horse, guides and attendants of every kind are my abhorrence; but there was no escape,—and I left La Granja mounted and escorted.

The road betwixt La Granja and Segovia, is particularly pleasing: it lies along the ridges of the Sierra,—ascending and descending, and catching every moment charming views both of mountain scenery, and of a more cultivated and living landscape. The morning was beautiful, even for Spain, where all the mornings are beautiful; and I went no faster on my royal charger than if I had been on foot,—often pausing to admire the surrounding prospects: these did not rise into the sublime, nor could they be classed with the beautiful or the romantic; but they were varied and agreeable—soothing and exhilarating by turns: deep silent valleys, running up into the mountains, spotted with pine, and covered with the enamel of beauteous heaths; streams, glancing like liquid silver, or spreading over little hollows, gleaming like mirrors set in a rugged frame; smooth knolls, grown over with aromatic plants and flowering shrubs; and herds of gentle deer, raising their heads, advancing at a short run, and then stopping to gaze at me as I passed by. These deer, however, so beautiful to look at, are a scourge to this part of the country, which is in most parts susceptible of cultivation; and which, but for the license allowed these favourite animals, might yield an abundant produce.

The first sight of the celebrated aqueduct disappointed me; because it merges imperceptibly among the houses; but if contemplated in its individual parts, and followed throughout its range, it rises into that consequence which has been universally accorded to it. It contains no fewer than one hundred and fifty-nine arches; its length is seven hundred and fifty yards; and the height, in crossing the valley, is ninety-five feet. I will not, however, avow an enthusiasm which I did not feel. The celebrated aqueduct of Segovia failed to make so strong an impression upon me as the *Pont de Garde*, near Nismes. This I must ever look upon as one of the most majestic and striking relics of antiquity now extant.

I regret that I was tempted to avail myself of an opportunity of returning to Madrid, which left me too little time to devote to Segovia. I arrived in Segovia about mid-day, and chanced to learn that a *gallero*, on springs, would leave Segovia next morning, at four o'clock, and reach Madrid the same day. To walk once from the Escurial to Segovia, was rather desirable than otherwise, but a repetition of the walk would have been tedious; and as no other conveyance was likely to leave Segovia for some days, I agreed to be the fifth passenger, and had therefore only a few hours to devote to Segovia. But this time sufficed for the aqueduct, the cathedral, and the alcazar. The cathedral did not strike me as being particularly interesting; and with the recollection which I now have before me, of Toledo and Seville, the cathedral of Segovia seems scarcely worth a notice. The Alcazar pleased me more; but this too, after subsequently seeing the Alhambra of Granada, appears insignificant.

Segovia is a decayed city, like most of the other cities of Spain; and if considered with reference to its former opulence and consequence, its decay is the more striking. Two hundred years ago, the cloth manufactory of Segovia gave employment to 34,000 hands, and consumed nearly 25,000 quintals of wool; fifty years ago, these were reduced to a sixth part; and now, the manufactory is in a state of perfect abeyance, the trade having been chiefly transferred to the kingdom of Valencia. In this city, of twenty-five parishes, and containing twenty-one convents, the inhabitants scarcely reach ten thousand.

The Posada in Segovia, I found remarkably bad; and the posadero seemed resolved to give at least a fictitious value to his articles, by the high price which he set upon them. As I was to leave Segovia at the early hour of four, I called for la cuenta before going to bed; and to my astonishment, three dollars were demanded for my stewed rabbit, and a room so full of mosquitos that I spent half the night in planning warfare, and the other in executing slaughter. I told him no one would travel in his country, if all the innkeepers charged travellers as he did,—such charges would ruin any body. And now the secret of his exorbitant demand came out. "Oh, but," said he, "poor travellers don't ride upon the king's horses, escorted by the king's servants;" and so my royal bearer, and his royal attendant, cost me two dollars. I paid my money, and consoled myself with thinking that it was probably the last time I might bear a resemblance to majesty.

At the appointed hour I took my place in the gallero, smarting with mosquito bites, and glad to rest from the work of destruction; and after a drive along a road which I already knew, I found myself in my apartment in the Calle de la Madelina a little after dusk.

CHAPTER XI.

TOLEDO.

Journey from Madrid; Proofs of the backwardness of Spain; Appearance of the Country; Spanish Mule-driving; a Venta; First View of Toledo; Toledo Recreations and Society; Remains of Former Grandeur, and Proofs of Present Decay; Picturesque Views; the Tagus; Intricacy of Toledo; Bigotry and Priestcraft; Reasons for the Prevalence of Religious Bigotry in Toledo; Proofs of Bigotry; Aspect of the Population; the Cathedral and its Riches; Scene in the Cathedral; the Alcazar; Historical Retrospect; Praiseworthy Institutions of the Archbishop Lorenzana; the University; Toledo Sword Manufactory; the Franciscan Convent; Return to Madrid.

A FEW weeks before I visited Toledo, a public conveyance had been for the first time established between that city and the capital. This conveyance left Madrid every alternate day, and partook of the double nature of a waggon, and of a diligence: externally, it was a waggon; but seats within, and glass windows, entitled it to the rank of a diligence. I took my place in this vehicle, at four in the morning, after having stumbled over more than one person lying asleep on the pavement, in groping my way through the streets from my lodgings to the waggon office.

It is a striking commentary upon the backward state of Spain, and the general want of enterprise that distinguishes both the government and the people, that there should be no road from the capital, to the largest city lying within a hundred miles of it—the ancient metropolis of Spain; and yet such is the fact: for although the conveyance I speak of makes its way from Madrid to Toledo, a distance of nearly sixty miles, in about fifteen hours, it travels over any thing but a road, with the exception of the first ten miles from Madrid: after this, there is sometimes a visible track, and sometimes none; most commonly, we passed over wide sands; at other times over ploughed fields, or meadows; and it was not until we arrived within half a league of Toledo, that we again found a road.

The country between Madrid and Toledo, I need scarcely say, is ill peopled and ill cultivated; for it is all a part of the same arid plain that stretches on every side around the capital; and which is bounded on this side, by the Tagus. The whole of the way to Toledo, I passed through only four inconsiderable villages; and saw two others at a distance. A great part of the land is uncultivated, covered with furze and aromatic plants; but here and there some corn land is to be seen, and I noticed one or two ploughs in the fields; these were worked by two mules and one man, and seemed only to scratch the soil. The great curse of every part of Castile, is want of water; in this journey of sixty miles, I passed only two insignificant brooks,—so very insignificant, that a child might have dammed up either of them in a few minutes with stones and sand: in fact, from the Douro to the Tagus, there is not a stream ancle deep, unless when swoln by sudden floods.

I was much amused in this journey, by the manner of driving our diligence. We had seven excellent mules, which carried us the whole way; and these were managed in the true Spanish mode, which does not admit of postilions. Two men sit in front; one always keeps his place, holding the reins, and guiding the two nearest mules; the other leaps from his seat every few minutes, runs alongside the mules, applies two or three lashes to each, gets them into a gallop, and as they pass by, he lays hold of the tail of the hindermost mule, and whisks into his place, where he remains until the laziness of the mules, or a piece of level ground, again calls him into activity. The sagacity of the mules struck me as most extraordinary; after being put into a gallop, the three front mules were left entirely to themselves; and yet they unerringly discovered the best track; avoided the greatest inequalities; and made their turnings with the utmost precision.

We stopped some time before mid-day at a venta, to refresh the mules, the muleteers, and the travellers; who, besides myself, consisted of three priests and one woman, the wife of a tradesman in Toledo. This was one of those ventas of which I had often heard, but had not yet seen—where, in reply to the question, "what have you got to eat?" you are answered, "whatever you have brought with you." For my part, I had brought nothing; but the *clerigos* had provided well against the assaults of the flesh; and a cold stew of various fowls and bacon being produced by them, and heated by the mistress of the venta, we made a hearty and comfortable dinner; and then continued our journey.

Toledo is seen about a league before reaching it; and, with the exception of Granada, its situation is the most striking of any city in Spain. Its fine irregular line of buildings cover the summit and the upper part of a hill of considerable elevation; behind which, the dark romantic range of the Toledo mountains forms a majestic back-ground. Even at this distance, Toledo is evidently no city of yesterday; for besides the innumerable towers of its convents, churches, and stupendous cathedral—the metropolitan of Spain—the outline is broken by other buildings of a more grotesque, or more massive form; while here and there, the still greater irregularity of the outline points to ages too remote, to have left to modern times any other legacy than their ruins. Toledo was still illuminated by the setting sun when I caught the first view of it; but before arriving under its walls, all was dusky, excepting the summits of the mountains behind; these still wore the purple light of evening; and the meanderings of the Tagus, flowing westward, were also visible beneath those bright orange tints that are peculiar to Spanish skies.

I had no sooner secured a bed in the posada, than I went to deliver my letters; these were, one to a gentleman, an employée, holding a situation in the finance; the other to a prebendary, librarian of the cathedral. I was received with the greatest civility by both; and after taking chocolate with the former, I accompanied him to the castle, to be present at what was considered quite an event in Toledo: this chanced to be the king's birthday; and in honour of it, the band of royalist volunteers paraded the principal streets by torch light; and so monotonous a thing is life in Toledo, that this occurrence produced quite a sensation. It was scarcely possible to force one's way through the narrow streets, which were filled with a dense mass of people, almost entirely men; for the ancient Spanish customs still attach to Toledo too much, to sanction there the liberty which foreign usage has conferred upon the women in most of the other Spanish towns.

I must not omit a trifling fact, that throws some light upon the state of feeling in Toledo. I had purchased a grey hat in Paris, and had worn it constantly in Spain; and although I had heard in Madrid that the wearers of white hats were looked upon with suspicion, I had never suffered any interruption or insult in consequence, excepting now and then a scrutinizing look from some royalist volunteer or police agent. But the gentleman to whom I was recommended in Toledo, would not permit me to go into the street in a grey hat; he said he could not answer for my safety; and while I remained in Toledo, he was so kind as to equip me with a small round, high-crowned hat, almost the only kind worn by its inhabitants.

The same evening that I arrived in Toledo, I was presented at a tertulia, which is the sole recreation of the inhabitants; for there is no public diversion of any kind: formerly there was a theatre; but the canon, who was then at the head of the university, obtained a royal order to suppress it, and it has remained closed ever since. Bull-fights even are forbidden in this priest-ridden city; so that unless processions of Saints and Virgins are to be considered an amusement, the inhabitants have positively no resource but in the tertulia. Nowhere are Spanish customs seen more pure than in Toledo; and nowhere is the monotony of the tertulia more striking. The party assembled about nine,—there were fifteen persons present, about one half of them ladies. The sole amusement was talking, and some of the party playing *basto* for a very low stake; and after a glass of *agua fresca*, the party separated about eleven. In Toledo a certain circle agrees to form a tertulia: one house is selected, where it is to be held,—the most central, perhaps, or the most convenient; and the same individuals assemble at the same house, and at the same hour, every day throughout the year! This is Toledo society.

The morning after my arrival in Toledo, I rose early, anxious to see this ancient and truly Spanish city; and crossing the *Plaza Real*, which, at the early hour of six, resounded with the ringing of the blacksmith's hammers, whose shops half monopolise the square, I followed the widest street that presented itself; and after a steep descent, I found myself at the eastern extremity of the town, and on the bridge over the Tagus. It is impossible to walk a step in Toledo, or to turn the eye in any direction, without perceiving the remains of former grandeur, and the proofs of present decay: ruins are every where seen,—some, the vestiges of empires past away, and whose remains are crumbling into nothingness,—the empires of Carthage and of Rome: other vestiges,—those of an empire equally fallen, but more visible, in the greater perfection of its monuments,—the Empire of the Moors: and still another class of ruins,—those more recent emblems that record the decay of the Spanish monarchy through the lapse of a hundred and fifty years. Past magnificence and present poverty are every where written in a hundred forms, and in legible characters. But all this, although offering to the reflecting mind an impressive example of the "sic transit gloria mundi," gives to Toledo much of its peculiar interest in the eye of a stranger; and adds to the picturesque and striking character of the views presented from every quarter. Few of these are finer than the view of this remarkable city and its environs, from the bridge over the Tagus, where my morning walk conducted me.

The Alcazar, that immense pile, once the residence of Moors, and subsequently of the kings of Spain, forms one corner of the city. The irregular and picturesque line of buildings, at least one half of them convents, each with its tower, and terrace, and hanging garden, stretches along the summit of the hill, towards the West; while strewing the sides of the steep acclivity, and mingled with the convent gardens, are seen the remains of the Roman walls that once entirely inclosed the city, and that even yet, are in many places nearly perfect. Withdrawing the eye from Toledo, and looking across the bridge, an elevated rocky mount presents itself, crowned with the ruins of a Moorish castle; and leaning on the parapet, and looking towards the South, the river is seen far below, flowing in a deep rocky channel, one of its banks being the hill upon which the city stands,—and the other, the North front of the Toledo mountains. The peculiar situation of Toledo is best understood from this point. The river Tagus, coming from the westward, flows directly towards the north-east corner of the city; and in place of continuing to flow in the same direction—by which it would leave the city and its hill upon the left,—it makes a sudden turn, sweeps behind the city and its hill, and in front of the Toledo mountains,—and after describing three parts of a circle, it re-appears at the opposite corner, and continues its course towards the west. The course of the Tagus is singular; the Sierra de Albarracin, where it rises, is no more than eighty miles from the Mediterranean, in a straight line across Valencia; but the Tagus, taking an opposite direction, runs a course of nearly six hundred miles to the Atlantic,—traversing the interior of Spain, passing into Portugal, and forming the glory and the riches of its capital. It would be no difficult matter, to render the Tagus navigable from Toledo to the sea, a distance of between four and five hundred miles; the passage was attempted in the winter of 1829, by a boat from Toledo, and succeeded, the boat having arrived safely at Lisbon; but this could not have been done at any other season; because in dry weather, the water is in many places almost wholly diverted from its natural channel, for the use of the mills that have been erected upon its banks.

I endeavoured to find my way from the bridge to the posada by a different road,—but this was an attempt of some difficulty. I believe there is no town in Europe in which it is so difficult to find ones way, as in Toledo: the streets are innumerable; few of them are more than three yards wide; they are steep, tortuous and short, constantly branching off at acute angles, so that all idea of direction is soon lost; and there are no open spaces from which some prominent object may be taken as a guide. A gentleman who had resided fourteen years in Toledo, told me that he was not acquainted with half of the streets; and that it was no unusual occurrence to lose himself, in endeavouring to find near cuts from one place to another. Although I arrived at the posada two hours later than I expected, I had nothing to regret in the delay; my mistakes having carried me through parts of the town which I might not otherwise have had an opportunity of seeing.

Walking through Toledo, there is a subject of more melancholy reflection than that which arises from the vestiges of former greatness; I mean, the abundant proofs of bigotry and ignorance that are gathered at every step. There is no city of Spain so entirely given up to the domination of the priests and friars, as Toledo; because there is no other city in which these form so large a portion of the population, or where the riches of the religious bodies are so preponderating. Toledo, it is believed, once contained 200,000 inhabitants; forty or fifty years ago, it contained, according to the writers of those days, about 30,000; at this day, its inhabitants do not exceed 16 or 17,000; but throughout this progressive decay, the convents and churches, the priests and friars, have continued undiminished: the cathedral is still served by its forty canons, and fifty prebendaries, and fifty chaplains; the thirty-eight parish churches and chapels, have still their curates, and their assistants, and their many dependents; and the thirty-six convents and monasteries, have yet their compliment of friars and nuns. The revenues, indeed, of all these religious bodies, have suffered some diminution during the last fifty years; but this diminution has been nothing in comparison with the decrease in the resources of all the other classes of inhabitants. The revenues of the archbishop amounted fifty years ago, to seven millions of reals, (70,000*l.* sterling); at present they do not exceed four millions of reals, (40,000*l.* sterling): the incomes of the canons amounted, at the former period, to at least eighty thousand reals (or 800*l.* sterling); now, they scarcely reach one half of this sum: all these diminutions are the result of the fall in the price of corn, in which their revenues are computed. But the incomes of the curates of the parishes are still more reduced, many of the parishes having entirely fallen into decay: there are some, in which there are not now twenty inhabited houses; so that the curates of these, are in a state of absolute destitution. The revenues of the convents have of course suffered a diminution proportionate to that which has affected the church. But notwithstanding this decrease in the revenues of the religious bodies, these are still sufficiently great, to create an overwhelming interest in a city whose inhabitants scarcely quadruple the number of those who live by these revenues. In fact the whole city, with the exception of the government employées, lives by these revenues. Many are directly benefited by their collection, their management, and by the husbandry of the land that produces them; while their disbursement must necessarily benefit every class of men who administer either to the necessities, or the luxuries of life. But besides the effect which self-interest has in supporting the influence of priestcraft in Toledo, other reasons may be assigned for its preponderance.

The geographical position of Toledo is highly favourable to the success of this jugglery; for, with sufficient resources in the territory that lies along the Tagus, and with no passable road or navigation of any kind to other towns, the inhabitants have scarcely any intercourse with strangers,—none whatever with foreigners. The immense number of priests and friars, also, who may all be considered spies upon the lives of the inhabitants; and the great and secret influence of the archbishop, cannot fail to act as obstacles to the progress of information, both by reading and conversation: and, indeed, there is in Toledo a species of religious *espionnage*, which is, in fact, a remnant of the Inquisition: certain friars call every Monday morning, at every house, to receive the certificates of confession which have been given to the inmates, if they have confessed the day before. And I must not omit to mention, as another cause of the preponderance of priestly influence in Toledo, the greater correctness exhibited in the lives of the religious orders in this city, than in the other cities of Spain; and the larger alms given by the convents. With the exception of some whispers respecting the canons and prebendaries, who were said to be remarkable for the number of infant nephews, nieces, and cousins, whom they had humanely taken under their fatherly protection, I heard not one insinuation against any other of the religious orders.

The great respect, or rather veneration, in which the religious bodies,—especially the friars,—are held in Toledo, as well as many other proofs of the bigotry of the inhabitants, are every where visible. A Franciscan friar, or any monk belonging to one of the poor and self-denying orders, receives some obeisance from every one, as he passes along the street; even the portly canon or prebendary, who bears about with him the evidences of self-indulgence in place of self-denial, receives some token of respect: every shop is provided with a saint in a niche, to bless its gains; and upon every second or third door, a paper is seen with these words printed upon it,—*Maria Santa Purissima, sin Pecado concebida.* In the respect too which is paid by the inhabitants to religious processions, abundant proof is afforded of the superstition that still clings to the people of Toledo. I happened to be in the neighbourhood of the Carmelite convent when the procession of St. Theresa issued from it. This is the patron saint of the convent, and her image was carried through the streets, followed by a multitude of friars: it is considered a mark of devotion, to carry a lighted candle upon such occasions; and I noticed many persons bearing candles, who, by their dress and general appearance, must have belonged to the middle classes. In the open court in front of the convent, there were not less than 2,000 persons collected; and when the image was carried past, I did not see a single individual in any other position than upon his knees.

Another time, walking in the neighbourhood of the city, on the road, or rather track, across the mountains, I observed two university students, seventeen or eighteen years of age, busily employed in collecting stones, and laying them upon a cross erected by the wayside in commemoration of a murder,—and with each stone muttering a prayer. I did not, at that time, understand the meaning of this strange occupation; but I afterwards learned, that in virtue of some ancient papal authority, a certain indulgence is granted for every stone laid on the cross of a murdered man, if accompanied by a prayer.

The general aspect of the population of Toledo is intensely Spanish; there is no admixture of foreign, or even of modern innovation, to be seen. Men of all ranks wear the cloak; and the small round, high-crowned, Spanish hat, is worn not only by the peasantry, but almost universally, by persons of all classes. Among the women, no colours are to be seen; black is the universal dress; and scarcely any one enters a church unveiled. Largely as the friars enter into the street population of Madrid, they enter far more largely into that of Toledo. In Madrid they are spread over a greater surface. In Toledo, the only lounge is the Plaza Real; and there, at certain hours, particularly about two o'clock, it seems almost like a convent hall of recreation, and a sacristy of a cathedral united; for canons, and prebendaries, and curates, and twenty different orders of friars, are seen standing in groups, strolling under the piazzas, or seated upon benches, refreshing themselves with melons or grapes. There cannot be a more perfect realization of the conception of "fat, contented ignorance," than the Plaza Real of Toledo presents every day after dinner. Not many poor are to be seen among the population of Toledo; it has now dwindled down to that point, at which the wants of the church, the university, and the convents, can sustain it: beyond this number there are few; and those few are supported by church and convent alms: the only beggars I saw, were three or four women, who sat at the gate of the cathedral.

I was not long in Toledo before visiting its cathedral, which has no rival but the cathedral of Seville, in its claims to be the greatest and the most magnificent of Gothic temples. All the cathedrals I had ever before seen, shrunk into insignificance when I entered the cathedral of Toledo. The following are the dimensions of this majestic pile. The interior of the church is four hundred and eight feet long, and two hundred and six feet wide; and the height of the aisles is one hundred and sixty feet. The columns that run along the aisles are forty-five feet round: there are sixty-eight painted windows; and surrounding the choir, and the Altar Major, there are one hundred and fifty-six marble and porphyry pillars. I was not able to see the *Preciocidades* the first day I went to the cathedral: to be so specially favoured, a separate order was required; and I returned accordingly the following morning by appointment. I do not mean to enumerate the different articles that compose the riches of the cathedral of Toledo—the richest in the world—but I shall mention a very few of the most remarkable. I saw the Virgin's mantle,—one mass of precious stones, especially pearls, of which there must have been thousands, if not millions: I saw many images of pure gold, studded with precious stones: I saw the Virgin's crown, also of pure gold, but entirely covered with the largest and most brilliant jewels,—sapphires, emeralds, rubies, and diamonds; and surmounted by an emerald of most extraordinary size and beauty; the image which upon high days is arrayed in all this finery, is of silver. There is another room, called the *custodia*, in which I saw innumerable urns of pure gold, most of them studded with precious stones; and which contain relics: these I did not ask to see, but I was informed that there are few saints in the calendar, of whom this the relicary of Toledo does not contain something. The value of the gold and silver might be easily ascertained; but the value of jewels is more capricious: I was told, however, that every article is inventoried and valued, in a book kept for that purpose; and although my informant did not state to me the precise amount noted in the book, he said it exceeded forty millions of ducats (10,000,000*l.* sterling): whether the value of the relics be included in this estimate, I cannot tell. This is a melancholy waste of property; and when, in connexion with this, we view the deplorable condition of Spain, we naturally inquire whether the judicious employment of this wealth could materially better that condition. Undoubtedly it might accomplish much; and had the whole inert wealth of Spain been directed a hundred years ago into useful channels, Spain would at this day have been a more enlightened and a more flourishing country; but Spain could never have been made one continued garden, as some writers have supposed; because the wealth of the world could never charge Castilian skies with rain-clouds; force springs to bubble from sandy deserts; or clothe with soil, the rocky Sierras that half cover the Peninsula.

The wealth of the cathedral of Toledo had a narrow escape from the rapacity of the French: upon their approach, the archbishop—not the present, but the last archbishop—carried away the whole of the portable articles to Cadiz, and thus saved them: the heavier articles remained in their places; and the French when they took possession of Toledo, asked one fourth part of their value; but a much less sum was offered, and accepted, viz. 90 arrobas, or 2250 lbs. of silver—a mere trifle, scarcely equalling the value of one of the precious stones.

But the preciocidades, and marbles, and porphyries, and paintings, are not, in my eyes, the most interesting features of the cathedral of Toledo: its immensity, its grandeur, are its glories. The lofty and majestic aisles—the massive and far-stretching columns of a temple like this, seem almost to shadow forth the imperishable nature of the religion whose sanctuary they adorn and uphold. The longer we contemplate the vastness and majesty around, the mind is more and more filled with awe, and lifted from the insignificance of life to a sense of the greatness and solemn grandeur of eternity; we are filled with enthusiasm and admiration,—enthusiasm the more lofty, because it is mingled with religion; and admiration the more profound, since it is mixed with astonishment, that so frail a creature as man should be able to perpetuate his memory for ever. While I remained in Toledo, I spent a part of every day in the cathedral; and every evening, about sunset, I strolled through the aisles. These visits will not soon be forgotten, for it is but rarely that life gathers such subjects of remembrance. The last evening I remained in Toledo, I walked into the cathedral sometime after sunset,—it was the latest visit I had made to it: the interior was all wrapped in deep dusk;—the lofty aisles stretched darkly beyond, only shewn by a solitary lamp burning before the shrine of some inferior saint,—its ineffectual light dimly falling athwart the gloom; the painted windows had ceased to throw their gorgeous hues within,—but a speckled and faintly-coloured gleam fell upon the upper part of the columns. Two candles burnt before the Altar Major; and in the distance, at the farthest extremity of the church, a bright red blaze flashed across the aisle, and between the massive pillars,—throwing their broad shadows across the marble-chequered floor of the church: this was the chapel of the miraculous image, lighted up with an infinity of tapers,—and the only sound to be heard, save my own footstep, was the distant hum of prayer from the many devotees prostrated before her shrine. Here and there, as I walked through the aisles, I saw a solitary kneeler at the altar of a favourite saint; and at some of the remotest and obscurest spots, a cloaked caballero was waiting for good or for evil.

I dedicated my second morning in Toledo to the Alcazar, one of the most striking objects in the city, from almost whatever quarter it is viewed. This massive fabric was once the residence of the Moorish kings, and more lately of the Castilian sovereigns. It was in the reign of Charles V. that the present south and north fronts were erected, the former by Herrera. The whole building is now in a state of decay,—these magnificent fronts are falling into ruin; and the inside of the edifice is no longer habitable; one wing only, which is still entire, is used as a prison. When Toledo ceased to be the metropolis of Spain, the Alcazar was converted into a workhouse, and more lately it was employed as a silk manufactory. The archbishop undertook the establishment of this from humane motives, but the undertaking proved a failure; and it is probable that the Alcazar will now be delivered over to the hand of time.

Among other parts of the Alcazar, I visited the vaults, which are of immense extent, and open to the public, but are put to no use whatever: in one of the vaults, a party of gipsies had made their quarters; they had lighted a large fire, around which some lay sleeping; and one woman was employed in cooking. The grotesque and ragged figures of the gipsies, and the high vault illuminated by the red flare, reminded me of the strong lights, and picturesque groups of the Spanish painters.

Standing in front of the Alcazar, with the terrace which overlooks the city and the surrounding country—with ruins of Roman walls, and Moorish castles at my feet—and with the palace of three races of kings behind; it was impossible to avoid a retrospect of the past history of this remarkable city. More than two centuries before the birth of Christ, Toledo was added by Hannibal to the empire of the Carthagenians; and after being subsequently a part of the Roman empire, it was wrested from the dominion of Rome, by Eurico, king of the Goths, in the year 467. It continued subject to the Gothic line nearly two hundred and fifty years; when the Moors, after having subdued the greater part of Spain, and reduced most of the principal cities, invested Toledo, and captured it in 714. In the year 1085, after Toledo had remained under the sovereignty of the Moors between three and four hundred years, Alonzo VI., and Rodrigo Diaz—the Cid, expelled the Moors from its walls; and from that period, until the expulsion of the Moors from Spain, Toledo was alternately a stronghold of the Castilians, and of the Moors. And, even after the settlement of Spain, it became the head of an insurrection, which convulsed Castile during twenty-two years; whose object was, to restrict the privileges of the nobles, and, in fact, to re-model in many respects the constitution of Castile: but, in the year 1522, Toledo submitted to the crown; and since that period, its history has been only remarkable as recording in successive steps of decay, the gradual decline of the Spanish monarchy.

But, although Toledo is chiefly interesting, for its monuments of past glory and prosperity, it is not without some excellent and flourishing institutions even at this day. All of this kind that Toledo possesses, is the work of the late Archbishop Lorenzana, a man of very opposite character from the prelate who, at present wields the sceptre of the church. Lorenzana was an able man, and an excellent ecclesiastic; and gave practical evidence of his goodness in the many excellent institutions which he founded. Among these, I was particularly pleased with the lunatic asylum,—a noble edifice, and perfect in all its arrangements. The spectacles revealed in a mad-house, are never agreeable; but they are sometimes interesting, and here, there were several of this character. I was conducted to the cell of one person, whose insanity arose from erroneous views of religion. The walls were entirely covered with drawings in chalk, executed with great spirit, and representing funerals, tombs, death heads, devils, religious processions, priests, and ceremonies. Another, certainly a most interesting object, I saw in the large hall, where the inoffensive maniacs are permitted to be at large; this was a middle-aged woman, seated upon the ledge of the window, her eyes intently fixed upon the sky; she was a native of a village on the coast of Murcia, which had been destroyed by the earthquake the autumn before: she had been at a neighbouring hamlet selling dates; and on her return to her village, she had seen her home, and with it, her children, swallowed up: she had never spoken from that hour, and all day long she sat on the window ledge of this hall gazing upon the sky; and every day the strength of two persons was required to take her from the window to dinner. I shall only mention one other individual, whose case is interesting, as throwing light upon Spanish morals and justice. This was also a woman, but in her perfect senses; she had lived with her aunt, who was housekeeper to a canon in Toledo; and the canon had seduced her. Instigated by revenge, or hatred, she afterwards cut his throat during the night; and the public authorities, unwilling to expose the affair, by bringing her to trial, ascribed the act to a fit of madness, and sent her to the asylum.

The handsome edifice now occupied by the university, is another act of Lorenzana. The University of Toledo dates its origin from the time of the Moors; and was revived after their expulsion, in the year 1529. At present, it is chiefly celebrated as a law university; the number of students on its books, at the time I visited Toledo, was rather more than seven hundred;

and I was informed that nine-tenths of these were law students, and that, of the remaining tenth, only *eight* were students of the theological classes. When speaking of the education of members of the liberal professions, I detailed the course of study required of the law student in this university.

Lorenzana also established a college for girls, chiefly the children of officers and employées; here they are well educated in every useful and ornamental branch of education—and here they may remain all their lives, at the charge of government, if they neither marry, nor choose to go into a convent. By a fundamental rule laid down by the founder, a small dowry is given to every one who marries, but nothing is given to carry into a convent. Formerly, there used to be tertulias here every evening, at which the students of the university were welcome visitors; but the entrée of the colegio is now forbidden to all students, even to those who reside in Toledo with their families. When I visited this institution, there were twenty-seven young ladies: ten had been married the year before; and I understand, very few disappoint the intentions of the founder by going into convents.

From all antiquity the Spaniards have been celebrated for the manufacture of steel arms; and a "Toledo blade" long has been, and still is, an expression implying excellence. The celebrated sword manufactory, to which I walked one afternoon, lies about three quarters of a league from the city, close to the river, which is required for working the machinery. It is a building of extraordinary extent, comprising within it not only the forges, workshops, and depositories of arms; but also accommodations of every kind for those employed in the manufactory, who, in former times, were extremely numerous. I visited every part of the establishment, and saw the progress of the manufactory throughout all its stages. The flexibility and excellent temper of the blades are surprising; there are two trials which each blade must undergo before it be pronounced sound,—the trial of flexibility, and the trial of temper. In the former it is thrust against a plate on the wall, and bent into an arc, at least three parts of a circle. In the second, it is struck edgeways upon a leaden table, with the whole force which can be given by a powerful man, holding it with both hands. The blades are polished upon a wheel of walnut wood; and when finished, are certainly beautiful specimens of the art.

The manufactory once employed many hundred hands; but it has long been on the decline; and at present, only fifty workmen are required; these finish about eight thousand swords in the year. They work by piece, and make about one hundred reals per week (20s.), and some of the most industrious workmen, twenty-four reals more. Before the separation of the colonies, twenty-five more workmen were employed. They generally keep a stock three years in advance; but owing to the recent and unexpected equipment of two regiments of guards, the number of swords when I walked through the magazine, was only twenty thousand.

Returning to the city from the manufactory, I visited the Franciscan convent; once an immense pile, but now partly in ruins,—the effect of war. It is still however a fine building, and of great extent; and the alms of the devout have been so liberally bestowed, that I found them busily employed in raising a new and magnificent edifice upon the ruins of that which had been destroyed. Finding the gate of the convent open, I walked in, and ascending a stair, reached the dormitory of the monks without any one questioning me. The Franciscans do not earn their reputation for self-denying sanctity, without working for it. Judging by the cells which I saw in this convent, I may say, that if their comforts by day, are no greater than those provided for night, their lives are truly lives of penance and mortification. Near to the Franciscan convent are the remains of a Roman amphitheatre; but even these remains are fast disappearing.

I had spent five days in Toledo greatly to my satisfaction. From both of the gentlemen to whom I had carried introductions, I received constant civilities: with the one, I drank chocolate every evening, and found in his son an admirable cicerone,—in himself, an intelligent companion,—and in his wife and daughter, obliging and delightful triflers. From the other (the prebendary), I received the unusual compliment of being invited to dinner,—a dinner, as Dr. Johnson would have said, such as was fit to invite a man to eat. The chief dish was a roasted ham, which I had never before seen,—but which I beg to recommend to the attention of all who are not above the enjoyment of dining well. This is not an unusual dish in Spain, when it is intended to treat a guest well. I had afterwards, at Valencia, the pleasure of having my recollection of the prebendary's dinner agreeably refreshed.

I had now gratified my curiosity at Toledo, and proposed returning to Madrid by the same conveyance that had brought me; but I found that it was all engaged by churchmen; and that another extra conveyance was also engaged by them: a canon had died, and half the clergy of Toledo were going to Madrid to sue for his place. I obtained a seat in a *galera*, in which there were five priests, and I was much amused with the freedom and good humour with which they spoke of their pretensions and hopes; and upon this occasion, these were more than usually uncertain, because no one knew with whom the patronage lay. The appointment of canons to the cathedral of Toledo is shared between the king and the archbishop; seven months in the year belong to the king, and five to the archbishop. This was the first canon who had died during the seven months that belong to the king; but the patronage of the last appointment, about two months before, which had belonged to the archbishop, had been ceded by him to the king for some particular reason, in the understanding however that the first vacancy, during the next seven months, should be filled up by the archbishop; but the question was, whether his majesty would recollect his royal promise. For my part, I heartily wished he might; for among the five candidates who were my companions, one only seemed to stand in need of a better served table than he was accustomed to,—and he, as the muleteer told me, was a distant relation of the archbishop; but perhaps it was as likely that the archbishop might forget his relation, as that the king might forget his promise.

Either our mules were less sagacious, or our drivers less expert than those entrusted with the care of the galera that had brought me to Toledo; for, descending a steep sandbank, about two leagues from the city, the conversation of the clerigos was suddenly and disagreeably interrupted by the vehicle being thrown over. The sand, however, was so deep that no one sustained any injury; and after the little delay occasioned by putting the galera upright, the journey and the conversation were resumed together, and we reached Madrid without any farther hindrance.

END OF VOL. I.